WITHDRAWN

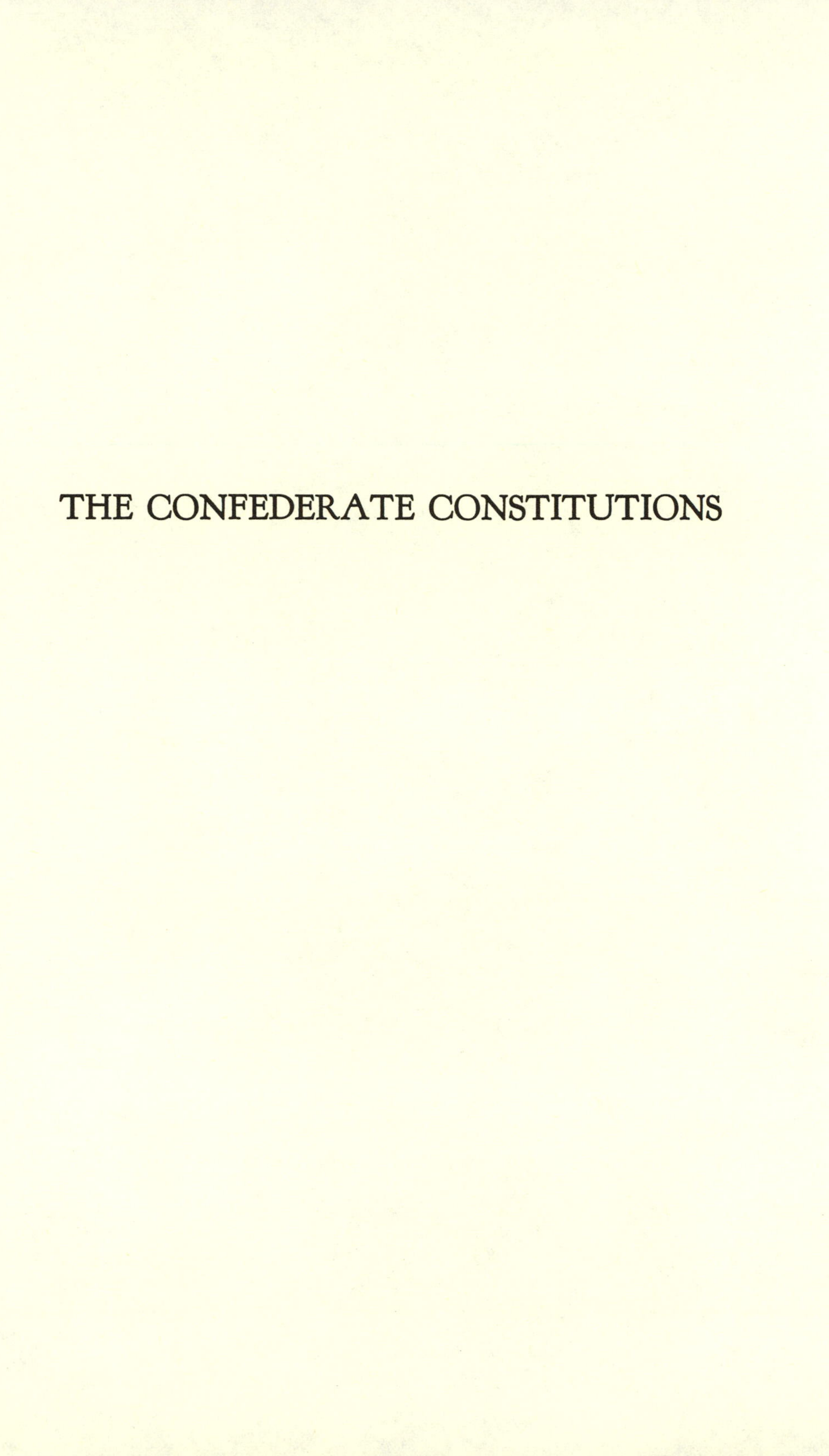

THE CONFEDERATE CONSTITUTIONS

THE CONFEDERATE CONSTITUTIONS

By

CHARLES ROBERT LEE, JR.

GREENWOOD PRESS, PUBLISHERS
WESTPORT, CONNECTICUT

Library of Congress Cataloging in Publication Data

Lee, Charles Robert.
The Confederate Constitutions.

Reprint of the ed. published by the University of North Carolina Press, Chapel Hill.
Appendices include Constitution for the Provisional Government of the Confederate States of America, and the Constitution of the United States and Constitution of the Confederate States of America.
Bibliography: p.
1. Confederate States of America--Constitutional history. I. Confederate States of America. Constitution. 1973. II. United States. Constitution. 1973. III. Title.
[KFZ9000.L4 1973] 342'.75'02 73-16628
ISBN 0-8371-7201-2

Originally published in 1963 by the University of North Carolina Press, Chapel Hill

Reprinted in 1974 by Greenwood Press
A division of Congressional Information Service, Inc.
88 Post Road West, Westport, Connecticut 06881

Library of Congress Catalog Card Number 73-16628

ISBN 0-8371-7201-2

Printed in the United States of America

10 9 8 7 6 5 4 3 2

To

A. L. L.

Preface

In contrast to the voluminous and detailed treatment of the military aspects of the Confederate States of America, the constitutional history of the nation has been virtually ignored. Confederate military activity from Fort Sumter to Appomattox may be dramatic and interesting, but the constitutional foundation of the Confederacy is only slightly less interesting, and, certainly, equal in significance. This study treats the framing and adoption of the two Confederate Constitutions by the fifty delegates of the seven seceded states of the lower South at the Montgomery Convention and the ratification of the Permanent Constitution.

Because of the similarities between the United States Constitution and the Confederate Constitution, historians have given little attention to the latter document. The similarities are striking, but the differences are more significant in that they represent the Southern dissatisfaction under the United States Constitution during the seven decades preceding the Civil War. An understanding of the similarities and differences between the two constitutions is important for the insight it gives into the greatest domestic crisis in United States history. The Confederate Constitutions not only represent the constitutional philosophy of the "Founding Fathers" of the new nation but also represent a milestone in United States constitutional development, and many of their provisions stand as a legacy in governmental reform.

In the preparation of this work, collections of the following libraries and archives were used: the National Archives, the Library of Congress, the Maryland Historical Society Library, the Confederate Museum, the University of North Carolina Library, Duke University Library, the University of South Carolina Library, the University of Georgia Library, the University of Florida Library, the Alabama State Department of Archives and History, the Mississippi State Department of Archives and History, the Louisiana State University Library, the Arkansas Department of Archives and History, the Tennessee State Library and Archives Division, the University of Kentucky Library, and the Indiana University Library. I am grateful to the librarians, the directors, and their assistants of the above named institutions for their many considerations.

This study originated in a seminar and was developed into a doctoral dissertation under the direction of Professor Fletcher M. Green of the University of North Carolina. From inception to conclusion, he gave unsparingly of his time, offered valuable suggestions, and greatly contributed to the merit, but not the responsibility, of this work. I am also indebted to Professors Frank W. Klingberg and Cornelius O. Cathey of the University of North Carolina, and Dean Frank H. Heck of Centre College of Kentucky, who read the dissertation and offered constructive criticism. I wish to acknowledge my indebtedness to the Ford Foundation for a grant under its program for assisting American university presses in the publication of works in the humanities and the social sciences. I also wish to express my appreciation of the financial assistance given me by Centre College of Kentucky during the summer of 1962. And finally, without the patience and encouragement of my wife, the completion of this work would have been impossible.

Contents

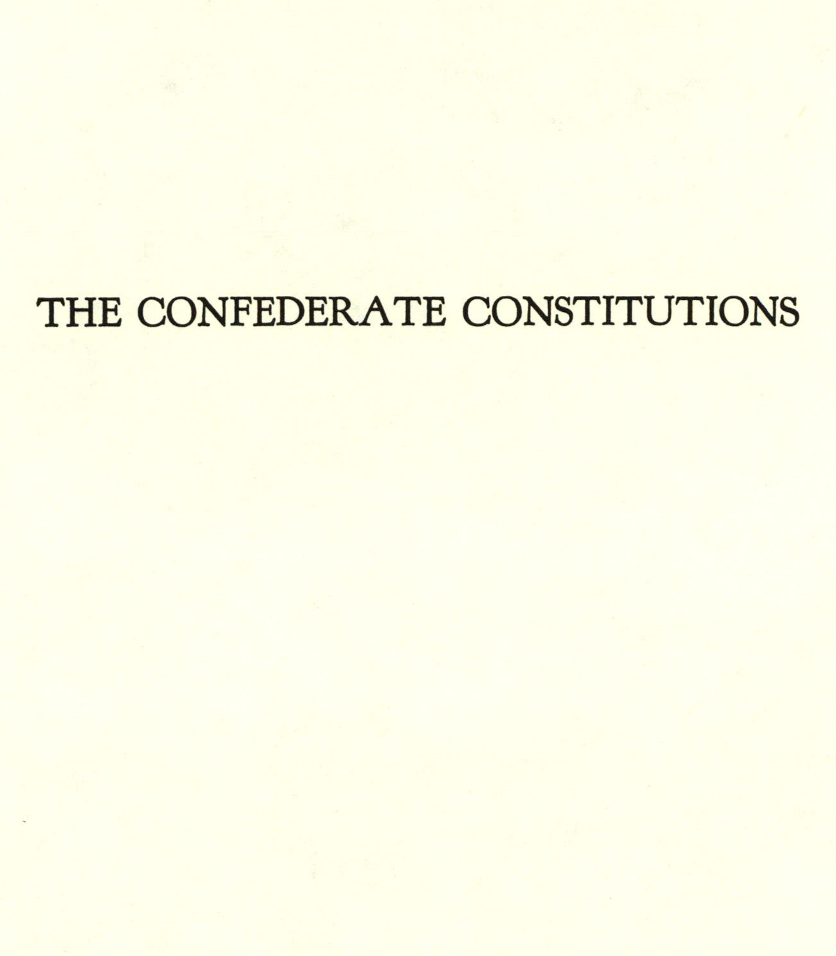

THE CONFEDERATE CONSTITUTIONS

CHAPTER I

The Calling of the Montgomery Convention

The people of South Carolina have invited the people of Alabama to meet them in Convention . . . this Convention accepted that invitation; and adopting the suggestion of the Commissioner from South Carolina, we invited . . . the other Southern States, to meet us . . . in this city, on the 4th of February, 1861. . . .

William Lowndes Yancey

Ninety days after Abraham Lincoln was elected President of the United States, delegates from six seceded states of the lower South met at Montgomery, Alabama, to establish a Southern Confederacy. Between November 6, 1860, and February 4, 1861, South Carolina seceded and presented a general secession program, inter-state commissioners were dispatched to the fifteen slave states, the rest of the lower South seceded, and Alabama issued an invitation for a meeting at Montgomery. During these tense and fateful days, the Montgomery Convention developed from a plan into a reality.

Most historians today accept the statement that "Abraham Lincoln's election to the presidency in 1860 . . . precipitated the secession movement."[1] Southern reaction to the November returns was immediate and, in many instances, personal. The feelings of a large part of the Southern people were succinctly expressed by an editorial in the New Orleans *Crescent*. It said, in part: "There is a universal feeling that an insult has been deliberately tendered our people, which is responded to . . . [by] a settled determination that the South should never be oppressed under Lincoln's administration."[2]

1. Ellis Merton Coulter, *The Confederate States of America, 1861-1865* (Baton Rouge: Louisiana State University Press, 1950), p. 1.

2. Dwight Lowell Dumond, ed., *Southern Editorials on Secession* (New York: The Century Company, 1931), pp. xvi-xvii.

Extremists viewed the election as the culmination of Northern cupidity and ambition. The mild-looking South Carolina radical Robert Barnwell Rhett said of secession and the election: "It has been a matter which has been gathering head for thirty years. The election of Lincoln and Hamlin was the last straw on the back of the camel."[3] This last straw was the first time in American history that a president had been elected who represented a sectional party with a sectional program. Following Lincoln's election,[4] the threat of secession was translated into a reality.

The climate of opinion in South Carolina, a few days after the presidential election, was expressed by the Charleston *Mercury*: "Yesterday, November 7th, will long be a memorable day in Charleston. The tea has been thrown overboard. . . ."[5] Within a few days the South Carolina General Assembly passed an act which called for the meeting of a convention at Columbia, at noon, on December 17, 1860. By providing for the assembly of the first secession convention, South Carolina had decided to lead the way.

South Carolina's decision was predicated upon the efficacy of separate state action. Cooperative state action, as a method of rectifying Southern grievances, had failed for thirty years. There was support for the cooperationist approach during the Nullification Controversy, the Bluffton Movement of 1844, the Crisis of 1850, and the tense days following the John Brown raid. Reaction to each of these events was unsatisfactory to the radicals. Indeed, R. B. Rhett, the "Father of Secession," had advocated separate state action as early as 1844.[6] Cooperationists, like Christopher Gustavus Memminger, moved more slowly toward the radical position.

3. *The American Cyclopedia and Register of Important Events* (New York: D. Appleton and Company, 1869), I, 122.

4. For two provocative views of this election, see Arthur Charles Cole, "Lincoln's Election an Immediate Menace to Slavery in the States?" *The American Historical Review,* XXXVI (July, 1931), 740-67, and Joseph Gregoire de Roulhac Hamilton, same title, *The American Historical Review,* XXXVII (July, 1932), 700-11.

5. Charleston *Mercury,* November 8, 1860. R. B. Rhett, Jr. became editor in 1857; and, by 1858, the Rhetts owned controlling interest.

6. Laura Amanda White, *Robert Barnwell Rhett: Father of Secession* (New York: The Century Company, 1931), p. 98.

Memminger was appointed Commissioner to Virginia by Governor William Henry Gist in December, 1859. His mission was to bring about, in his own words, "a meeting of a Southern Convention."[7] Because Memminger believed the Union could not be preserved, he wanted the Old Dominion to take the lead. It became evident by January that Virginia was pursuing a waiting game, so Memminger returned to Charleston. If his mission to Virginia inclined him toward separate state action,[8] the results of the November election pulled him over completely.

On October 5, Governor Gist wrote a confidential letter to the governors of some of the other Southern states. Should Lincoln be elected in November, he desired a state other than South Carolina to take the lead. If not this, he hoped other states would "at least move simultaneously with her . . . ,"[9] otherwise South Carolina would secede alone. The replies from Louisiana and Georgia were not encouraging. Mississippi, Alabama, and Florida replied favorably; however, they would not be first.

The failure of Memminger's mission to Virginia and Gist's inability to achieve the desired results from his confidential letter were significant. These failures provided fuel for the radicals of the Rhett school, and serious food for thought for the cooperationists or moderate secessionists of the Memminger school. South Carolina's attempt to secure the cooperation of her fellow Southern states in a resistance movement through a Southern Convention had failed again. Virginia's refusal of a conference exploded the desire of the cooperationists who looked to the border states for leadership; the replies to Gist's letter clearly showed that no state in the lower South would lead. The lesson was clear to a majority of the South Carolina leadership; moderate secessionists and immediate secessionists alike must unite and lead their state out of the Union. By adopting separate state action,

7. Christopher Gustavus Memminger to William Porcher Miles, January 3, 1860, in William Porcher Miles Papers, Southern Historical Collection, University of North Carolina.

8. Ollinger Crenshaw, "Christopher G. Memminger's Mission to Virginia, 1860," *The Journal of Southern History,* VIII (August, 1942), 334-49. Crenshaw holds that Memminger was a secessionist at least by January, 1860.

9. John George Nicholay and John Hay, eds., *Abraham Lincoln: A History,* 10 volumes (New York: The Century Company, 1890), II, 306.

South Carolina hoped to encourage, if not force, other Southern states to do the same.[10]

During the two weeks preceding the South Carolina Secession Convention, two important pronouncements bearing on secession were made in Washington, D.C. The first was an address by Howell Cobb, and the second was an "Address of Southern Congressmen." Howell Cobb, a Georgia politician of national stature, was selected by President James Buchanan as Secretary of the Treasury in 1857. Cobb viewed Lincoln's election as justification for immediate secession and, on December 8, 1860, he resigned from Buchanan's cabinet. Two days earlier he wrote an address entitled: "Letter of Hon. Howell Cobb to the People of Georgia, on the Present Condition of the Country," which said in part: "in conclusion [I] warn you against the dangers of delay and impress upon you the hopelessness of any remedy for these evils short of secession."[11] Cobb's address took the form of a twelve-page pamphlet, copies of which were sent to his state for local publication. He hoped that his words would move his fellow Georgians to immediate secession.

On December 13, a caucus of Southern Congressmen gathered in the rooms of Reuben Davis of Mississippi and drafted a declaration. It was signed by thirty men and telegraphed to newspapers throughout the South. Wide circulation was given to the "Address of Southern Congressmen," which stated: "The argument is exhausted. We are satisfied that the honor, safety, and independence of the southern people require the organization of a Southern Confederacy."[12] James Lawrence Pugh of Alabama, one of the authors of the address, declared that "its sole purpose was to influence the several State Conventions, then soon to assemble, in favor of immediate 'separate state secession.' "[13]

10. For an excellent study of South Carolina at this time see Charles Edward Cauthen, *South Carolina Goes to War, 1860-1865* (Chapel Hill: The University of North Carolina Press, 1950).

11. Ulrich Bonnell Phillips, ed., *The Correspondence of Robert Toombs, Alexander H. Stephens and Howell Cobb,* American Historical Association, *Annual Report, 1911* (Washington: Government Printing Office, 1913), II, 505, 516. (Hereinafter cited as Phillips, *Correspondence.*)

12. Montgomery *Weekly Mail,* December 17, 1860. Of the thirty signers, one was the future President of the Confederacy and six were members of the Montgomery Convention.

13. James Lawrence Pugh to General [Major] W. T. Walthall, May 31, 1880, in

These two pronouncements, issued by respected and influential Southerners, were received with delight in South Carolina. Being issued on the eve of the secession convention at Columbia, many delegates viewed them as timely and significant.

All but ten of the 169 delegates elected to the South Carolina Secession Convention met in the Baptist church in Columbia at noon, December 17, 1860. Also seated on the first day were a number of interested spectators from four states in the lower South. Among these were Madison Starke Perry, Governor of Florida; John Archer Elmore, Commissioner from Alabama; Charles Edward Hooker, Commissioner from Mississippi; and, Howell Cobb, an unofficial observer from Georgia. En route to Georgia from Washington, Cobb stopped in Columbia to confer with South Carolina leaders. He apparently hoped to promote "a short-lived scheme for Georgia and South Carolina to secede jointly."[14] Although Cobb returned home in a few days to help rally secession sentiment, he kept in close touch with friends in the Columbia convention.

The only significant business transacted on the first day was the decision to abandon Columbia because of the smallpox epidemic then spreading throughout the capital. The convention promptly reassembled the following day at Institute Hall in Charleston. The membership was roughly divided into two camps, the radicals or immediate secessionists and the cooperationists or moderate secessionists. The former group counted among its leaders such men as R. B. Rhett, William Porcher Miles, and Lawrence Massillon Keitt; the latter group could point to such men as C. G. Memminger, Robert Woodward Barnwell, and James Chesnut, Jr.[15] Concerning the membership as a whole, it "was primarily a wealthy, middle aged, slaveholding, native-born group of planters."[16]

Dunbar Rowland, ed., *Jefferson Davis, Constitutionalist: His Letters, Papers and Speeches* (Jackson: Department of Archives and History, 1923), VIII, 461.

14. Horace Montgomery, *Howell Cobb's Confederate Career* (Tuscaloosa: Confederate Publishing Company, Inc., 1959), p. 20.

15. All six men were later delegates to the Montgomery Convention.

16. Ralph Ancil Wooster, "The Secession Conventions of the Lower South: A Study of their Membership" (Unpublished doctoral dissertation, University of Texas, 1954), p. 33. For additional statistics see pp. 24 ff. in this excellent study.

After moving to Charleston, the delegates wasted no time in getting down to work. Rhett, Chesnut, and two other delegates were appointed immediately "to draft an Ordinance proper to be adopted by the Convention."[17] On December 20, the South Carolina Ordinance of Secession was reported and adopted 169-0. This document states in part: "The union now subsisting between South Carolina and the other States, under the name of 'The United States of America,' is hereby dissolved."[18] Thus, the first Southern state had declared itself "an independent Commonwealth."[19]

Shortly after secession became a reality, two significant reports came before the convention. The first was called "Declaration of the Immediate Causes of Secession," and was written by Memminger, Barnwell, and several others. The second report was entitled "Address to the Slaveholding States," and was prepared by a committee headed by Rhett. The Ordinance of Secession was evidence of the unity of the moderates and the extremists faced with the necessity of secession. Memminger's "Declaration" and Rhett's "Address" represented the differing philosophies of the two factions. Memminger expressed the moderate view by emphasizing the more immediate causes of secession such as the election of a sectional president with a sectional program dangerous to the South. Rhett's report detailing the extremist view pictured Lincoln's election as only the last straw. He described a struggle for Southern rights dating back to the founding of the Union. Secession, to Rhett, was the last act in a long struggle for self-determination, and the first important step pursuant to the establishment of a new nation.

On the same day that Major Robert Anderson established his headquarters on Fort Sumter in Charleston harbor, R. B. Rhett introduced an ordinance that proved to be the key to the calling of the Montgomery Convention. Rhett entitled his report: "An Ordinance recommending and providing for a Convention of the Slaveholding States of the United States, to form the Constitution of a Southern Confederacy."[20]

17. *Journal of the Convention of the People of South Carolina* (Columbia: R. W. Gibbes, 1862), p. 23. (Hereinafter cited as *Journal of the Convention of South Carolina.*)

18. *Ibid.*, p. 42.

19. *Ibid.*, p. 49.

20. *Ibid.*, p. 92.

In the first of five major points, Rhett suggested that, after seceding, other states unite with South Carolina in the formation of a Southern Confederacy by holding "a Convention at Montgomery, in the State of Alabama, on the thirteenth day of February next, to agree on the terms of said Confederacy."[21] The second provision concerned the size of delegations sent to Montgomery and the method of voting. It was recommended that each state appoint as many delegates "as they have had, or may have, members in the present Congress in the United States, . . ."[22] and that the delegates, "shall vote by States."[23] The report further suggested that "the Constitution of the United States should constitute the basis of the Confederation. . . ."[24] formed by the seceded states. Concerning ratification, the fourth point recommended that after the drafting of a new constitution, it should be submitted to the state conventions or legislatures to "be ratified or rejected by said State."[25] The last provision concerned the appointment of delegates to Montgomery and commissioners to the slave states. The ordinance proposed that eight Montgomery delegates be elected by the South Carolina convention. Moreover, one commissioner should be appointed to each state that called a convention, "in order that the policy contained in the above Ordinance may be pressed on the considerations of said convention."[26] This was Rhett's definite, workable, and well-organized "South Carolina Program." It was adopted by the convention on the last day of 1860.

During the first three days of 1861, the Charleston convention selected nine men to act as inter-state commissioners. Each commissioner was given twenty-five copies of Rhett's ordinance, and the mission of encouraging immediate secession and the adoption of the "South Carolina Program." The convention dispatched these nine men to Florida, Mississippi, Alabama, Georgia, Louisiana, Texas, Arkansas, North Carolina, and Virginia.

One historian has called these inter-state commissioners the "diplomatic corps of the secession movement."[27] As previously

21. *Ibid.*
22. *Ibid.*
23. *Ibid.*
24. *Ibid.*, p. 93.
25. *Ibid.*, p. 92.
26. *Ibid.*, p. 93.
27. Dumond, *Southern Editorials*, p. xix. The two most significant studies on the inter-state commissioners are Ellen-Fairbanks Dingledine Diggs, "The

noted, South Carolina commissioned Memminger to Virginia in December 1859. Two months later the Mississippi legislature sent Peter Starke to Virginia on a similar mission. Starke's attempt to secure a Southern convention proved as abortive as that of his predecessor. During the last month of 1860, inter-state commissioners were used for the first time on a large scale. At that time, however, they sought immediate secession by separate state action.

In point of time as well as in number of commissioners appointed, Alabama and Mississippi take precedence. Governor Andrew Barry Moore of Alabama appointed sixteen commissioners in December, 1860. They were accredited to all of the slave states in the Union. A month before Moore's action received the endorsement of the Alabama Secession Convention,[28] the state's commissioners were at work in their appointed areas. John Archer Elmore, as already mentioned, was present for the opening of the South Carolina Secession Convention on December 17. Three days later, Robert Hardy Smith of Mobile, Commissioner to North Carolina, spoke before the legislature at Raleigh.[29] Smith, born in the Tar Heel state, evidences a general attempt to appoint commissioners to the state of their birth. Alabama's sixteen commissioners were, "without exception, in favor of secession . . . well educated, successful, and politically experienced."[30] Among these men were four members of the Montgomery Convention and a future member of the Confederate Cabinet.[31]

Role of the Interstate Commissioners in the Secession Conventions, 1860-1861" (Unpublished master's thesis, University of North Carolina, 1947), (Hereinafter cited as Diggs, "Interstate Commissioners."); and Armand J. Gerson, "The Inception of the Montgomery Convention," American Historical Association, *Annual Report, 1910* (Washington: Government Printing Office, 1912), pp. 181-87. (Hereinafter cited as Gerson, "Montgomery Convention.") The best state study is in Melvin Durwood Long, Jr., "Alabama in the Making of the Confederacy" (Unpublished doctoral dissertation, University of Florida, 1959). (Hereinafter cited as Long, "Alabama in the Confederacy.")

28. William Russell Smith, *The History and Debates of the Convention of the People of Alabama* (Montgomery: White, Pfister and Company, 1861), pp. 35 ff. (Hereinafter cited as Smith, *Debates.*)

29. Joseph Carlyle Sitterson, *The Secession Movement in North Carolina* (Chapel Hill: University of North Carolina Press, 1939), p. 187.

30. Long, "Alabama in the Confederacy," p. 77.

31. Secretary of War Leroy Pope Walker, Jabez Lamar Monroe Curry, Stephen Fowler Hale, John Gill Shorter, and Robert Hardy Smith.

At the request of the legislature, Mississippi's governor appointed sixteen commissioners who were accredited to fourteen slave states. This action was confirmed by the secession convention on January 19.[32] Like Commissioner Elmore of Alabama, Charles Edward Hooker of Mississippi was present at Columbia a month previous. Only one of Mississippi's sixteen commissioners, Walter Brooke, was later a member of the Montgomery Convention. In January, 1861, he described himself "as a co-operationist, which means, as I understand it, one who is in favor of united Southern Action for the purpose of demanding further guarantees from the North, or failing in that, the formation of a Southern Confederacy."[33]

Georgia and Louisiana were the other two states to appoint commissioners. Both states, like South Carolina, made their appointments after the meeting of their secession conventions. Commissioners from Georgia were accredited to Delaware, Missouri, Tennessee, Arkansas, Maryland, Virginia, North Carolina, Louisiana, and Texas.[34] The Louisiana Secession Convention authorized the selection of but one man; he was appointed Commissioner to Texas. Being the last major cotton state to secede, apparently Louisiana saw no necessity of establishing a diplomatic corps of commissioners.

Five states appointed inter-state commissioners. Alabama sent sixteen, Mississippi sixteen, Georgia ten, South Carolina nine, and Louisiana one—for a total of fifty-two commissioners. Of this number, eleven served in their state secession conventions, and six at the Montgomery Convention. Because of the traveling required, it was very difficult for a man to serve his state as a commissioner and as a delegate to one of the conventions. Commissioners travelled to all fifteen slave states bearing the same basic mission, to press for immediate secession. Perhaps their most significant contribution was in acting as a communications net-

32. *Proceedings of the Mississippi State Convention, Held January 7th to 26th A.D. 1861* (Jackson: Power and Cadwallader, 1861), p. 27. (Hereinafter cited as *Proceedings of the Mississippi Convention.*)

33. Thomas H. Woods, "A Sketch of the Mississippi Secession Convention of 1861,—Its Membership and Work," *Publications of the Mississippi Historical Society*, IV (1902), 96.

34. One Georgia Commissioner, Augustus Romaldus Wright, was a delegate to the Montgomery Convention.

work, in gathering and supplying information. This was a major factor in the expeditious secession of the lower South. Indeed, seven states had seceded by February 1, 1861.[35]

If the commissioners from Alabama and Mississippi take precedence in point of time and number, South Carolina's commissioners take precedence in point of importance. While the commissioners from Alabama and Mississippi were sent throughout the slave states and Georgia sent hers primarily to the border states and the upper South, South Carolina concentrated her activity in the lower South. The lower South was the area where immediate secession was most likely. It followed that the "South Carolina Program," calling for a Montgomery Convention, also had the greatest possibility of success in this area.

During the first week of January, 1861, the nine South Carolina commissioners met privately in Charleston. They assembled to discuss the details of their mission, and, in particular, the time and place of the meeting of the proposed Southern convention. Rhett had suggested February 13, the second Thursday of the month, in his ordinance. Possibly feeling that time was precious and that it worked in favor of those with a definite plan, the commissioners determined to set an earlier date. This informal conference ended on January 5, with all commissioners agreeing to suggest the first Monday in February as a suitable date.[36] The final determination of time and place would be made by the Alabama Secession Convention.

On the same day that the South Carolina commissioners concluded their meeting, a very important conference of Southern Senators gathered in Washington, D.C. Present were senators from the six states of the lower South and Arkansas. Two of these men, Jefferson Davis of Mississippi and Robert Toombs of Georgia, had been members of the Senate "Committee of Thirteen," the decisive group of senators seeking compromise in the Federal Congress. After meeting for eleven days, this committee reported on the last day of 1860 that they were unable to agree on any plan of adjustment. On January 5, 1861, Davis, Toombs,

35. For the results and significance of inter-state commissioner activity in the upper South and in the border states see Diggs, "Interstate Commissioners," pp. 98 ff.

36. Gerson, "Montgomery Convention," p. 184.

and ten fellow Southern Senators met, drafted, and signed a set of resolutions encouraging specific action by their respective states. This declaration began by stating that "each of the Southern States should, as soon as may be, secede from the Union."[37] It continued by suggesting that a convention to organize a Southern Confederacy should meet, "not later than the 15th of February, at the city of Montgomery, in the State of Alabama."[38] Finally, the senators wanted advice as to whether they should withdraw immediately from the Senate, or remain and block any legislation hostile to their section. One of the signers explained: "The idea of the meeting was that the States should go out at once, and provide for an early organization of a Confederate Government, not later than the 15th of February. This time is allowed to enable Louisiana and Texas to participate."[39]

Of the twelve senators who signed these resolutions, seven had also signed the "Address of Southern Congressmen" on December 13, and two were later delegates to the Montgomery Convention.[40] Significantly, the Southern Senators' Conference marked the almost complete breakdown of compromise efforts in the Federal Congress. Moreover, the senators added their voices to those of their Southern congressional colleagues in advocating immediate secession.[41] And finally, in large part, their resolutions gave added prestige to the "South Carolina Program."

37. *War of the Rebellion: A Compilation of the Official Records of the Union and Confederate Armies,* 70 volumes (Washington: Government Printing Office, 1880), I, 443. (Hereinafter cited as *War of the Rebellion.*)

38. *Ibid.*

39. *Ibid.* This signer was David Yulee of Florida.

40. The twelve senators were: Jefferson Davis and Albert Gallatin Brown of Mississippi, John Hemphill and Louis Trezevant Wigfall of Texas, John Slidell and Judah Philip Benjamin of Louisiana, Alfred Iverson and Robert Toombs of Georgia, David Levy Yulee and Stephen Russell Mallory of Florida, Clement Claiborne Clay of Alabama, and Robert Ward Johnson of Arkansas. The first seven senators named above signed the "Address of Southern Congressmen"; Hemphill and Wigfall were Texas delegates to the Montgomery Convention.

41. The outspoken, anti-Davis editor of the Richmond *Daily Examiner,* Edward Alfred Pollard, in *Life of Jefferson Davis with a Secret History of the Confederacy, Gathered "Behind the Scenes in Richmond"* (Philadelphia: National Publishing Company, 1869), pp. 62 ff, sees the Southern Senators' Conference as a dark "conspiracy . . . to assume the destinies of the South." This writer agrees with James Ford Rhodes who, in the *History of the United States from the Compromise of 1850,* 7 volumes (New York: The Macmillan Company, 1904-1906), III, 273, says that "if secrecy inheres in a conspiracy, that quality was not here preserved. . . ." Indeed, full accounts of the conference were reported in the

On the day that the South Carolina Secession Convention met at Columbia, Mississippians voted to elect delegates to their secession convention. Like the election in South Carolina, personalities played an important role in Mississippi; unlike South Carolina, however, the election in Mississippi was closely contested in many counties. The results showed a sweeping victory for the immediate secessionists, although in Mississippi there were "exceedingly few genuine state-rights men of the Rhett type."[42]

One hundred delegates met at Jackson on January 7, 1861. The membership of the Mississippi Secession Convention "was composed primarily of a young, small planter-lawyer group whose birthplace was in one of the states of the deep South."[43] Two days later the membership voted in favor of secession 84-15. On the same day, the convention passed a resolution expressing sympathy with South Carolina. On January 11, Armistead Burt, interstate "Commissioner from the Republic of South Carolina to Mississippi, addressed the Convention."[44] The following day the convention passed six resolutions which incorporated the "South Carolina Program" almost entirely.[45] Mississippi had kept the promise made to Governor Gist the previous October.

While present at the Charleston convention, Governor Perry of Florida handed a letter to the president of the convention which read in part: "Permit me to assure you, gentlemen, that gallant little Florida will be next to follow your wise and patriotic lead."[46] The Florida Secession Convention met at Tallahassee on January 3, 1861. The typical delegate "was either a farmer or a merchant by profession, aged forty-three years, born in one of the states of the deep South (most probably Georgia), a small slaveholder,"[47] and an immediate secessionist. Indeed, like the conventions at Columbia and Jackson, the Tallahassee convention

---

Charleston *Mercury*, January 7, 1861, and the Montgomery *Weekly Mail*, January 7, 1861.

42. Percy Lee Rainwater, *Mississippi, Storm Center of Secession, 1856-1861* (Baton Rouge: Otto Claitor, 1938), p. 219.

43. Wooster, "Secession Conventions," p. 73. For additional statistics on the Mississippi membership see pp. 62 ff.

44. *Proceedings of the Mississippi Convention*, p. 19.

45. *Ibid.*, pp. 132-34.

46. *Journal of the Convention of South Carolina*, p. 81.

47. Wooster, "Secession Conventions," p. 153. For additional statistics on the Florida membership see pp. 145 ff.

was dominated throughout by immediate secessionists. An attempt by Jackson Morton, a cooperationist, to stall the secession of Florida until Alabama's action was clear was quickly defeated.

On the fourth day, Edward Courtney Bullock, Commissioner from Alabama, Leonidas William Spratt, long-standing slave trade advocate and Commissioner from South Carolina, and fiery old Edmund Ruffin of Virginia were seated and subsequently addressed the convention. On the following day, an Ordinance of Secession was reported and debated,[48] and on January 10, it was passed by a vote of 62-7.[49] At the same time, the convention acknowledged the leadership of South Carolina and accepted its program.

The acute sectionalism between North and South was mirrored in miniature in the state of Alabama during the election of delegates to the state secession convention. The results of the election gave the immediate secessionists majorities in the four congressional districts of south Alabama, while the cooperationists carried the three north Alabama districts.[50] Shortly after the secession convention met at Montgomery on January 7, one of the delegates wrote his wife: "Considerable opinion herein prevails that the North Alabama delegation should secede from the Convention. I do not think they will."[51] In this heated situation, Alabama's interstate commissioners, by their written reports and occasionally in person, played a significant role. In a real sense, the commissioners quieted the cries of the cooperationists; indeed, they "reconciled, assured and encouraged the Alabama Convention's delegates that secession was a going concern and a successful course to be achieved by peaceful means."[52]

48. Three of the "Committee of Thirteen" who drafted the Ordinance were James Patton Anderson, Jackson Morton, and James B. Owens. All were later delegates to the Montgomery Convention.

49. *Journal of the Proceedings of the Convention of the People of Florida* (Tallahassee: Dyke and Carlisle, 1861), p. 28.

50. Lewy Dorman, *Party Politics in Alabama from 1850 through 1860* (Wetumpka: Alabama State Department of Archives and History, 1935), p. 168.

51. William Henry Mitchell to his wife, January 10, 1861, in William Henry Mitchell Papers, the State Department of Archives and History, Montgomery, Alabama. The typical delegate "was a middle-aged, experienced politician, born in either Georgia, Alabama or the Carolinas . . . , a small slaveholder . . . , [and] a lawyer or a farmer." Wooster, "Secession Conventions," p. 118. For additional statistics see pp. 115 ff.

52. Long, "Alabama in the Confederacy," p. 94.

With the help of the commissioners and the astute leadership of William Lowndes Yancey, the convention was carried in favor of secession on January 11, by a vote of 61-39.

The final selection of a date and place for the meeting of a convention to establish a Southern Confederacy seems to have been the result of a speech made before the Alabama convention by the Commissioner from South Carolina. Reporting on his activities in Alabama, Andrew Pickens Calhoun wrote: "I addressed the Convention, and brought before it the points that I had been instructed to present. I . . . enclose an official copy of the action of the Convention, giving an affirmative response to every request I had made as your Commissioner."[53] Alabama's affirmative response was given two days later in the Ordinance of Secession where the other slave states were invited to meet the delegates of Alabama in convention, "on the 4th day of February next, in Montgomery. . . ."[54] In addition to the invitation, the convention, on January 17, adopted a series of resolutions accepting the "South Carolina Program" in its entirety. In speaking for the adoption of these resolutions, Yancey acknowledged the lead of South Carolina and the suggestion of Commissioner Calhoun. He said:

> The people of South Carolina have invited the people of Alabama to meet them in Convention . . . this Convention accepted that invitation; and adopting the suggestion of the Commissioner from South Carolina, we invited . . . the other Southern States, to meet us in Convention in this city, on the 4th of February, 1861, for the purpose of framing Provisional and Permanent Governments, for our common future, peace and security.[55]

Critical to the success of the secession movement was the state of Georgia. The most populous state in the lower South was probably also the most powerful economically. If Georgia failed to secede, or even long delayed her action, any confederation of seceded states would be separated into two parts. The debates in this state on the question of secession were brilliant, heated, and decisive.

Before the election of delegates to the Georgia Secession Con-

53. *Journal of the Convention of South Carolina*, p. 234.
54. Smith, *Debates*, p. 77.
55. *Ibid.*, pp. 139-40.

vention, Robert Toombs and Alexander Hamilton Stephens were invited by the Georgia legislature to address them on the secession question. Robust Senator Toombs employed his great oratorical skill in favor of secession; frail ex-Congressman Stephens applied his incisive logic to a defense of the Union. Also speaking brilliantly for secession was Thomas Reade Rootes Cobb, brother of Howell Cobb.[56] Referring to the election of delegates to the secession convention, Toombs telegraphed his constituents from Washington a month later saying: "Secession by the fourth of March next should be thundered from the ballot-box by the unanimous vote of Georgia on the second day of January next."[57]

Ulrich Bonnell Phillips has described the 301 men elected to the Milledgeville convention as "without doubt the most distinguished body of men which has ever assembled in Georgia."[58] The average delegate was a middle-aged, prosperous, lawyer or farmer, and slaveholder; slightly less than fifty per cent owned twenty or more slaves.[59] With few exceptions, every important political leader in the state was present at the convention.[60] Leading the forces for immediate secession were Robert Toombs and Alfred Iverson, T. R. R. Cobb, and, behind the scenes, Howell Cobb. Herschel Vespasian Johnson, candidate for Vice President on the Douglas ticket in 1860, was the principal leader of the cooperationists. Benjamin Harvey Hill and Alexander H. Stephens gave Johnson strong and needed support. Before Lincoln's election, Hill wrote to Johnson and said: "It seems nearly all the leading men in these states [South Carolina, Alabama, and Mississippi] are for immediate-separate-secession. We must do

56. Stephens considered T. R. R. Cobb's speech the turning point in the Georgia secession movement. Alexander Hamilton Stephens, *A Constitutional View of the Late War Between the States*, 2 volumes (Philadelphia: National Publishing Company, 1868 and 1870), II, 321.

57. Phillips, *Correspondence*, 209-10. Toombs sent this telegram on December 23, 1860, when he saw that the Senate "Committee of Thirteen" would achieve nothing. Toombs also signed the resolutions of the Southern Senators' on January 5, 1861.

58. Ulrich Bonnell Phillips, *Georgia and State Rights*, American Historical Association, *Annual Report, 1901* (Washington: Government Printing Office, 1902), II, 202.

59. Wooster, "Secession Conventions," pp. 183 ff.

60. Howell Cobb and Governor Joseph E. Brown were invited to take seats at the convention.

all we can to counteract them."[61] They continued their efforts at Milledgeville.

The importance of Georgia to the secession movement is attested to by the number of influential out-of-state visitors attending the convention. Robert Barnwell Rhett and William L. Yancey were both present, urging Georgia to add her weight to the secession movement. Commissioners John Gill Shorter of Alabama, James Lawrence Orr of South Carolina, and William L. Harris of Mississippi also attended.[62] Shorter addressed the convention, and became the first Alabama commissioner to extend an official invitation for a meeting of Southern delegates in Montgomery on February 4. Orr spoke also and encouraged Georgia to accept the Alabama invitation.

The Johnson-Hill-Stephens block concentrated their efforts in a motion to substitute delay and cooperation for immediate secession. The vote was 133 for and 164 against; it failed to carry by only 16 votes. On January 19, the immediate secessionists carried Georgia out of the Union by a vote of 208-89. The convention also accepted Alabama's invitation to meet at Montgomery, as well as the substance of the "South Carolina Program."

Secession was never as popular in Louisiana as it was in the other states of the lower South. The merchants and other commercial classes of New Orleans wanted to maintain their lucrative economic position in a great port city serving the Mississippi River Valley. The sugar industry had no desire to lose the tariff which protected it from foreign competition. Nevertheless, the election of 1860 and the example of five sister states invigorated the secession-minded elements within the state.

An overwhelming majority of immediate secessionists were elected to the state secession convention which met at Baton Rouge on January 23, 1861. The average delegate was a middle-aged lawyer, farmer, or planter, and a slaveholder, with 42.4 per cent holding twenty or more slaves.[63] Attending the convention

61. Benjamin Harvey Hill to Herschel Vespasian Johnson, December 3, 1860, in Charles Colcock Jones, collector, "Autograph Letters and Portraits of the Signers of the Constitution of the Confederate States" (Augusta, Georgia, 1884) a scrapbook, Manuscript Department, Duke University.

62. Allen D. Chandler, ed., *The Confederate Records of the State of Georgia*, 6 volumes (Atlanta: Charles P. Byrd, 1909), I, 212 ff.

63. Wooster, "Secession Conventions," pp. 229 ff.

were two ex-governors, Commissioner John Laurence Manning of South Carolina and Commissioner John Anthony Winston of Alabama. The two men addressed the convention encouraging immediate secession and the acceptance of Alabama's invitation. On the fourth day of the convention, an Ordinance of Secession was reported and adopted 113-17, and the suggestions of the commissioners were accepted.[64]

The great determination of Governor Sam Houston could not save Texas for the Union. An extra-legal group of secessionists met in Austin on December 3, 1860, and issued an address calling for the election of delegates to a convention to consider secession. Popular sentiment forced Houston to call the Texas legislature into session, and this body promptly validated the action of the Austin secessionists. The state convention met at Austin on January 28. The two outspoken advocates of secession in Texas were Senators Louis Trezevant Wigfall and John Hemphill. Although both were in Washington when the Austin convention assembled, their purposes were ably served by John Gregg, William Simpson Oldham, and John Reagan.[65] James Martin Calhoun, nephew of the famous South Carolinian and Commissioner from Alabama, and John McQueen, Commissioner from South Carolina, were also present. On the first day of February, the convention adopted a secession ordinance by a vote of 166-8. Unlike her six sister states, however, Texas submitted this ordinance to a popular vote.[66] Because of this referendum, the compliance of Texas with the "South Carolina Program" was tardy.

With this action by Texas, the secession movement was complete from the Pee Dee to the Rio Grande; the first wave of secession had ended.

During the ninety days following Lincoln's election, several cities other than Montgomery were suggested as suitable sites

64. *Official Journal of the Proceedings of the Convention of the State of Louisiana* (New Orleans: J. O. Nixon, 1861), p. 17.

65. Wigfall and Hemphill signed the "Address of Southern Congressmen" and the resolutions resulting from the Southern Senators' Conference. Wigfall, Hemphill, Gregg, Oldham, and Reagan were delegates to the Montgomery Convention.

66. *Journal of the Secession Convention of Texas, 1861,* edited from the original by Ernest William Winkler (Austin: Austin Printing Company, 1912), p. 90. The result of the vote taken on February 23, 1861, was 46,129 for, and 14,697 against.

for a Southern convention. Mayor William Ezzard of Atlanta described the attractive features of his town to the Florida Secession Convention. At the Georgia convention, Herschel V. Johnson also proposed Atlanta. A group at the Alabama convention suggested Nashville, Tennessee, and a number of Mississippians advocated Lexington, Kentucky. Nashville and Lexington were not selected for the obvious reason that their states had not as yet seceded. Atlanta was considerably smaller and had less adequate facilities. New Orleans, Charleston, Savannah, and Mobile, cities whose populations exceeded that of Montgomery in 1860, were not selected because of their inconvenient locations. Why then was Montgomery chosen?

As the Montgomery *Weekly Mail* pointed out, this city was centrally located to South Carolina, Georgia, and Florida on the east, and to Mississippi, Louisiana, and Texas on the west. Moreover, the city was easily accessible "by railroad and river communication. . . ."[67] In addition to its geographic location, Rhett seems to have recommended Montgomery for political reasons. Montgomery was a city very sympathetic to immediate secession, being the home of and much under the influence of William L. Yancey.

With the selection of Montgomery by the seven seceded states of the lower South, the stage was set for a play with a cast of fifty actors.

67. Montgomery *Weekly Mail,* February 1, 1861.

CHAPTER II

The Membership of the Montgomery Convention

The delegates generally are a grave and reverend looking body of men; and no doubt contain much of the wisdom of the six seceding States.

Montgomery *Daily Post,* February 22, 1861.

As the Montgomery Convention assembled on February 4, 1861, another group of men, with a different objective, gathered at Washington, D.C. Virginia had not acted upon Commissioner Memminger's suggestion to call a conference of Southern states in late 1859. On January 19, 1861, however, the Virginia legislature did call for a peace conference to meet in the national capital on February 4. Delegates from twenty-one of the thirty-four states of the Union attended this eleventh hour conference. Ex-President John Tyler was elected chairman. He addressed the conference on the first day and said: "The voice of Virginia has invited her co-States to meet her in council. . . . Our godlike fathers created; we have to preserve."[1]

The proposals of the Washington Peace Conference were laid before the Federal Congress on February 27. By this time, however, progress at Montgomery, and the policy of the Republican majority in Congress, precluded much hope of the acceptance of these proposals. At best, the conference had delayed the secession of the upper South.

The Washington Peace Conference and the Montgomery Convention were the antithesis of each other. History has accorded the latter convention greater attention because it succeeded where its counterpart failed. Indeed, success at Montgomery ob-

1. *The American Annual Cyclopedia and Register of Important Events,* 15 volumes (New York: D. Appleton and Company, 1869), I, 563. Tyler later served in the Confederate Provisional Congress and was elected to the Confederate Congress, but he died before that body assembled.

viated success at Washington. A major feature of the success of the Montgomery Convention was the united effort of its membership.

By February 4, 1861, the seven seceded states of the lower South had elected fifty delegates to the Montgomery Convention. Following part two of the "South Carolina Program," which suggested that each delegation consist of a number equal to the state's previous representation in the Federal Congress, Georgia's ten constituted the largest delegation, and Florida's three, the smallest.[2] All members, except those from Florida, were elected by the state secession conventions with a majority vote being necessary for election. Florida's delegates were appointed by the governor because of non-decision balloting.

Concerning the general appearance of the membership of this convention, the astute British newsman William Howard Russell commented: "I could fancy that, in all but garments, they were like the men who first conceived the great rebellion which led to the independence of this wonderful country. . . ."[3] A more detailed study of the Confederate "Founding Fathers" is necessary before their activities at Montgomery can be properly appreciated.

South Carolina

The most experienced and best known member of the South Carolina delegation was Robert Barnwell Rhett. With the Adams family of Massachusetts as part of his lineage, Rhett was born in Beaufort, South Carolina, on December 21, 1800.[4] His formal education ended when he was withdrawn from Beaufort College for financial reasons. In 1819, the well-known South Carolina lawyer and Unionist, James Louis Petigru, tutored him in law and two years later he was admitted to the bar. Shortly thereafter, he entered into partnership with his kinsman, Robert Woodward Barnwell. While a member of the state legislature, he issued the "Colleton Address" in opposition to the Tariff of 1828

2. Only one state failed to follow this procedure; Texas sent seven delegates to Montgomery, having had only four in Washington.

3. William Howard Russell, *My Diary North and South* (Boston: T. O. H. P. Burnam, 1863), p. 168.

4. Laura Amanda White, *Robert Barnwell Rhett: Father of Secession* (New York: The Century Company, 1931), p. 4.

which "launched him upon his career as a crusader and revolutionist."[5] After serving briefly as a state attorney-general, he was repeatedly elected to the United States Congress between 1837 and 1849. Rhett followed John C. Calhoun into the Democratic Party in 1838 and, six years later, acted as campaign manager for his mentor who sought the presidency. Disillusioned at seeing his efforts come to nothing, Rhett, on July 31, 1844, started the "Bluffton Movement" which called for a state convention and separate state action on the tariff. Although Calhoun quickly brought him into line for the sake of party unity, Rhett was the only South Carolinian to defy the austere Calhoun without sacrificing his political career. When Rhett was elected to fill Calhoun's empty Senate seat in 1850, he assumed the leadership of South Carolina politics. Rhett had neither the tact and wisdom nor the power and influence in South Carolina and Washington to fill Calhoun's place for long. Following the Nashville Convention, where he became an avowed secessionist, and after the South Carolina convention declined to secede,[6] Rhett resigned his cherished Senate seat in 1852.

In late 1860, however, Rhett once again assumed an important position in South Carolina politics. His activities in behalf of secession and in the formulation of the "South Carolina Program" have already been noted. Although Rhett was a mild looking man of austere habit, he had a very excitable temper. The Unionist editor of the Greenville *Mountaineer* said of Rhett: "He was all passion, excitement and fire . . . ,"[7] but continued by saying: "Mr. Rhett was a brilliant writer and an eloquent speaker, and always bold, frank and manly in his writings and speeches."[8] Rhett not only played an important role in the calling of the Montgomery Convention, but he was also prominent in all debates at Montgomery and was chairman of the committee to draft the Permanent Constitution of the Confederacy.

Christopher Gustavus Memminger, an opponent of secession

5. *Ibid.*, p. 11.

6. Leading the cooperationist forces against secession was Rhett's ex-law partner, Robert W. Barnwell.

7. Benjamin Franklin Perry, *Reminiscences of Public Men* (Philadelphia: John D. Avil and Company, 1883), p. 131. (Hereinafter cited as Perry, *Reminiscences.*)

8. *Ibid.*, p. 133.

for thirty years, was born in Nayhingen, Germany, on January 9, 1803.[9] Shortly after coming to South Carolina, his mother died and he was placed in the Charleston Orphan Home. Thomas Bennett, trustee of the orphanage and later governor of the state, became the young boy's foster parent and provided for his education. Memminger, a precocious child, graduated second in his class from South Carolina College at sixteen. He returned to Charleston where he studied, and later practiced, law. If his humble origin left no bitterness, it did, in large part, account for his serious and industrious nature. His devotion to the Episcopal church and his Germanic love for the intricacies of theology were lifelong.

His attitude toward secession was first made public during the Nullification Controversy when he wrote a satirical pamphlet in biblical style, entitled *The Book of Nullification* (1830), against the leaders of the movement.[10] In 1836, he was elected to the lower house of the state legislature where he achieved a considerable reputation as chairman of the finance committee. Memminger opposed separate state action during the crisis of 1850-1852, although he was not satisfied with the compromise measures of 1850. His cooperationist predilection was evidenced again when he served as Commissioner to Virginia in 1859. Memminger's change of mind and his important activities at Columbia the following year, when he was appointed Secretary of the Treasury of South Carolina, have already been considered.

This stern, matter-of-fact, undistinguished looking Charleston lawyer was one of the principal contributors at Montgomery; he headed the committee that drafted the Provisional Constitution. R. B. Rhett, Jr. said of his father's long-time antagonist: "In Charleston he was known as an active friend of the free school system and orphan house, a moral and charitable Episcopalian, and a lawyer, industrious, shrewd, and thrifty."[11] After be-

9. Henry Dickson Capers, *The Life and Times of C. G. Memminger* (Richmond: Everett Waddey Company, 1893), p. 7. Capers was Memminger's first clerk in the Confederate Treasury Department.

10. *Ibid.*, p. 569.

11. Robert Barnwell Rhett [Jr.], "The Confederate Government at Montgomery," *Battles and Leaders of the Civil War*, 4 volumes, edited by Robert Underwood and Clarence Clough Buel (New York: The Century Company, 1878), I, 104.

coming Confederate Secretary of the Treasury, Memminger was often described in terms not nearly so charitable.[12]

One of the wealthiest planters in the delegation and probably the most widely respected was the genial aristocrat, Robert Woodward Barnwell, who was born on August 10, 1801, near Beaufort.[13] After attending private school at home, he entered Harvard College and graduated with highest honors in 1821. Five years later, he was elected to the state senate and, from 1829-1833, he served in the Federal Congress. Four months after signing the South Carolina Ordinance of Nullification in November, 1832, he retired to his plantation near Beaufort. In 1835, he returned to public life as the third President of South Carolina College, succeeding the irascible Thomas Cooper. The college historian wrote: "Though his administration was a short one [1835-1841], Barnwell's must be considered as one of the most successful in the history of that institution."[14] After a second retirement forced by ill health, he served briefly in the United States Senate. Although Barnwell was a leader of the forces opposing separate state action in 1852, he played a prominent part in the secession convention at Columbia in 1860.

Alexander H. Stephens, a Georgia delegate at Montgomery, wrote: "Barnwell is the most accomplished gentleman in the body [South Carolina delegation]. He has sane theories . . . He always has force in point in what he says—speaks with great precision and clearness as well as condensation. . . ."[15] As well as being prominent in debate, Barnwell served on the committee that drafted the Provisional Constitution.

James Chesnut, Jr., born January 18, 1815, in Camden, South

12. As a "hard money" advocate, Memminger must have found inflationary Confederate finance quite disconcerting.

13. "Robert Woodward Barnwell," in Allen Johnson and Dumas Malone, eds., *Dictionary of American Biography,* 21 volumes (New York: Charles Scribner's Sons, 1927-1937). (Hereinafter cited as *DAB.*)

14. Daniel Walker Hollis, *University of South Carolina,* 2 volumes (Columbia: University of South Carolina Press, 1951 and 1956), I, 140.

15. Alexander Hamilton Stephens to Linton Stephens, March 3, 1861, in Alexander Hamilton Stephens Papers, Brady Memorial Library of Manhattan College of the Sacred Heart, Purchase, New York. This writer used microfilm copies of the Stephens Papers (the originals are all located in the Brady Memorial Library) in the Southern Historical Collection, University of North Carolina. (Hereinafter cited as Alexander H. Stephens to Linton Stephens, March 3, 1861.)

Carolina, was the thirteenth child of a wealthy Kershaw County planter.[16] Like his father, he was educated at Princeton; and, like R. B. Rhett, he read law in Charleston under the guidance of James Louis Petigru. After being admitted to the bar in 1837, he began practice in Camden. Three years later he married the charming and witty diarist Mary Boykin Miller,[17] daughter of ex-Governor Stephen Decatur Miller. In succeeding years he acquired considerable legislative experience. Between 1840 and 1852, except for two years, he served in the lower house of the state legislature. Chesnut was a member of the state senate from 1852-1856, serving as president the last two years. In 1858, he was elected to the United States Senate where his oratorical skill placed him in the forefront of his colleagues. On November 10, 1860, he resigned his seat to participate actively in the Columbia secession convention. At Montgomery, Chesnut was a frequent and proficient debater as well as a member of Rhett's committee to draft a Permanent Constitution.

One of the two youngest delegates from South Carolina was William Porcher Miles, born at Walterboro on July 4, 1822.[18] After graduating with highest honors from the College of Charleston in 1842, he studied law but soon abandoned it for teaching. From 1843-1855, he was Assistant Professor of Mathematics at his alma mater. During the latter year his vocation was dramatically altered. For his services during a yellow fever epidemic, Norfolk, Virginia, gave him a decoration for heroism. His fellow Charlestonians responded by electing him to a two-year term as mayor.[19] In 1857, he was elected to the Federal Congress where he remained until his resignation in 1860. Miles expressed his views on the situation in 1860 in a letter to C. G. Memminger: "I have long been in favor of a Southern Confederacy as the only true and thorough means . . . for the defense and protection of the South."[20] At Columbia and at Montgomery, where he was

16. "James Chesnut, Jr.," in *DAB*.

17. Mary Boykin Chesnut, *A Diary from Dixie*, edited by Ben Ames Williams (Boston: Houghton Mifflin Company, 1949).

18. "William Porcher Miles," in *DAB*.

19. See Clarence McKittrick Smith, Jr., "William Porcher Miles, Progressive Mayor of Charleston, 1855-1857," *The Proceedings of the South Carolina Historical Association*, XII (1942), 30-40.

20. William Porcher Miles to Christopher Gustavus Memminger, January 15,

described as "one of the brainiest men of the younger statesmen of South Carolina,"[21] Miles entered into the proceedings with vigor and determination.

The youngest member of the delegation was Lawrence Massilon Keitt who was born in Orangeburg District on October 4, 1824.[22] After graduating from South Carolina College in 1843, he studied law and was admitted to the bar. In 1848, he began four years of service in the lower house of the state legislature, where he quickly acquired the reputation of a radical. Indeed, following the inconclusive Nashville Convention, Keitt recommended immediate separate state secession by his state. During his eight years (1852-1860) in the United States Congress, Keitt became known for his long and passionate speeches. Like Chesnut and Miles, Keitt resigned his seat to work for secession at Columbia. Chesnut's wife wrote in her diary of him: "Old [36 in 1861] tempestous Keitt breakfasted with us today, I wish I could remember half the brilliant things he said."[23] Although Keitt was active at Montgomery, his speech-making was somewhat curtailed; at least such is the impression given by Alexander H. Stephens who wrote: "But Keit [*sic*] speaks seldom—He said his wife told him when he left home to keep his mouth shut and his hair brushed."[24]

William Waters Boyce was a Charlestonian born on October 24, 1818.[25] After attending South Carolina College and the University of Virginia, he was admitted to the bar and practiced in Winnsboro, South Carolina. His career in politics started in the lower house of the state legislature. As a State Rights Democrat, he was elected to the Thirty-third Congress and took his seat on March 4, 1853. The day after his state seceded, Boyce resigned his seat and returned home in time to be elected to the

---

1860, in Christopher Gustavus Memminger Papers, the Southern Historical Collection, University of North Carolina. See also William Porcher Miles Papers in the same collection.

21. Thomas Cooper De Leon, *Four Years in Rebel Capitals* (Mobile: The Gossip Printing Company, 1892), p. 47.

22. "Lawrence Massilon Keitt," in *DAB*.

23. Chesnut, *A Diary from Dixie*, p. 258.

24. Alexander H. Stephens to Linton Stephens, March 3, 1861.

25. *Biographical Directory of the American Congress 1774-1949* (Washington: Government Printing Office, 1950), p. 724.

Montgomery Convention. He was not as prominent as his fellow Carolinians in the proceedings at Montgomery.

The final member of the delegation and the only jurist was Thomas Jefferson Withers who was born at Ebenezer, in York County, in 1804.[26] After attending a private academy at home, he enrolled at South Carolina College. Immediately upon graduating in 1828, he became editor of the Columbia *Telescope,* an anti-tariff sheet sponsored by the Nullifiers. When Withers completed his legal studies in 1833, he resigned from the paper and moved to Camden. The same year he married Mary Boykin Chesnut's aunt, Elizabeth Boykin. As a respected lawyer, Withers was elected a common law judge and a member of the Court of Appeals. He held the latter post for twenty years. Withers attended the conventions at Columbia and at Montgomery with his kinsman and neighbor James Chesnut, Jr. Long before 1861, the "Judge" was widely known for his quick temper and sarcastic tongue, both of which were evident at Montgomery. But as one old friend explained: "With all his temper and irritability, Judge Withers was a very kind-hearted gentleman, and most indulgent and affectionate in all the relations of life."[27]

With the possible exception of the Georgia delegation, the seven-man delegation from South Carolina was the most able one at Montgomery. With the exception of Memminger, all were native-born South Carolinians. The delegates were mature and well educated; each man had either attended or graduated from college. With the exception of Professor Miles, all were lawyers or planters and all were Democrats. The South Carolina delegation could boast more legislative experience than any delegation at Montgomery. Every man had some legislative experience on the state level. Moreover, with the exception of Florida, South Carolina had a larger proportion of Montgomery delegates attending its state secession convention than any other state. Six of the seven had served in the national legislature, five in the House of Representatives, three in the Senate, and two in both.

26. Ulysses Robert Brooks, *South Carolina Bench and Bar* (Columbia: The State Company, 1908), p. 145.

27. Perry, *Reminiscences,* p. 224.

And finally, the chairmen of the committees that drafted the two Confederate Constitutions were both from South Carolina.[28]

Mississippi

The recognized leader of the Mississippi bar in 1861 and leader of the state delegation to Montgomery was Wiley Pope Harris who was born on November 9, 1818, in Pike County, Mississippi.[29] Some years after being adopted by his uncle, whose name he took, Harris attended the University of Virginia and, finally, law school at Lexington, Kentucky. Following his graduation in 1840, he returned home to practice his profession. At the early age of twenty-nine, Harris was elected circuit judge, a post he held with great distinction for five years. After serving in the United States Congress, 1852-1855, he withdrew from public life to devote his talents to the practice of law. Harris, who returned to serve his state at the Jackson convention, was described as "a tall, slender figure, crowned by a most intellectual head . . ." and a man endowed "with all the qualities requisite in a great lawyer and a magnificent orator."[30] At Montgomery, his abilities were utilized on the committees drafting the two Confederate Constitutions.

The only other native Mississippian in the delegation was William Taylor Sullivan Barry who was born near present day Columbus on December 10, 1821.[31] After graduating from Yale College at twenty, he returned home to study, and later practice, law. Barry entered politics in 1849 and was elected to two terms in the lower house of the state legislature. Concluding a term in the United States Congress in 1855, he was reelected to the Mississippi legislature. He was promptly elected speaker and "filled the office with efficiency and credit to him [self]."[32] A skilled orator, he was elected president of the secession convention at Jackson. At Montgomery, he was active in debate and, with

28. The information in this paragraph was derived from Appendix I.

29. "Autobiography of Wiley P. Harris," in Dunbar Rowland, *Courts, Judges, and Lawyers of Mississippi, 1798-1935* (Jackson: State Department of Archives and History, 1935), p. 270.

30. Reuben Davis, *Recollections of Mississippi and Mississippians* (Boston: Houghton Mifflin and Company, 1889), p. 407.

31. "William Taylor Sullivan Barry," in *DAB*.

32. Davis, *Recollections*, p. 98.

Harris, was a member of the committee to draft the Provisional Constitution.

Walter Brooke, born in Clarke County, Virginia, on Christmas day, 1813,[33] was the only Whig in the delegation. After graduating from the University of Virginia in 1835 and being admitted to the bar, he began the practice of law in Lexington, Mississippi. Between 1848 and 1852, Brooke served one term in the lower house of the state legislature and one in the senate. After serving a one-year term in the United States Senate in 1853, he did not seek reelection. For the next seven years, Brooke practiced law. Then, in 1860, he returned to public life and became one of the few men to serve any state as inter-state commissioner, delegate to his state convention, and delegate to Montgomery. Although he was a Whig and a cooperationist in 1860, he became a Democrat and a secessionist and placed his skillful and convincing logic at the disposal of the new Confederacy.

The largest slaveholder in the delegation was Alexander Mosby Clayton, born in Campbell County on January 15, 1801.[34] Although he had little or no formal schooling, Clayton read law at Lynchburg and was admitted to the bar in 1823. A few years later he moved to Tennessee and, in 1836, President Andrew Jackson appointed him United States Judge of the Arkansas Territory. For reasons of health, Clayton moved to Marshall County, Mississippi, the following year and practiced law. From 1842-1850, Clayton was a distinguished member of the Mississippi Supreme Court. In 1850, because of his state rights stand, he failed to be reelected. After serving as Consul to Havana during the acute filibustering days of 1853, he returned to Memphis to practice law. With the coming of the secession crisis, he returned home and was a delegate to the Jackson convention where he was one of the principal authors of the secession ordinance. Clayton was a member of Rhett's constitutional committee at Montgomery.

Although Josiah A. Patterson Campbell was the youngest Mississippi delegate, he was extremely able. Born in South Caro-

33. *Biographical Directory of the American Congress,* p. 741.

34. *Biographical and Historical Memoirs of Mississippi,* 2 volumes (Chicago: The Goodspeed Publishing Company, 1891), I, 556. (Hereinafter cited as *Memoirs of Mississippi.*)

lina on March 2, 1830,[35] the son of a Princeton trained Presbyterian minister, Campbell was educated at Camden Academy in South Carolina and Davidson College in North Carolina. The family moved to Mississippi where he studied law and was admitted to the bar at the age of seventeen. Describing one event of his remarkable career, Campbell wrote: "I was elected to the legislature when twenty one years old and was speaker of the house of representatives [state] when twenty nine. . . ."[36] A contemporary described Campbell as "young, tall, erect as a soldier, with long wavy hair, graceful in every movement and handsome as a picture. . . ."[37] Although Campbell was active at Montgomery, his greatest public service followed the Civil War.

A very distinguished lawyer and the only delegate with no prior political experience was James Thomas Harrison. Related to the Harrisons of Virginia, he was born near Pendleton, South Carolina, on November 30, 1811.[38] His nearest neighbor as a boy was the master of Fort Hill, John C. Calhoun. After graduating from South Carolina College at seventeen he, like Rhett and Chesnut before him, studied law "under the direction of one of the most acute and extensively read lawyers in the United States . . . ,"[39] James Louis Petigru. After being admitted to the bar in 1832, Harrison moved to Columbus, Mississippi, where he practiced law for many years with great skill and distinction.[40] Joseph Glover Baldwin, author of *The Flush Times of Alabama and Mississippi,* referred to Harrison as "Jim T" and wrote: "So infallible was his skill in these infernal arts [law] that it was almost a tempting of Providence not to employ him."[41] Another contemporary said: "As a pleader he had no superior, and he de-

35. "Autobiography of J. A. P. Campbell" in Josiah A. Patterson Campbell Papers, the Southern Historical Collection, University of North Carolina.

36. *Ibid.* In 1914, Campbell wrote: "I am now the only survivor of the forty-nine [50] delegates whose names were subscribed to the Constitution of the Confederate States of America."

37. Rowland, *Judges and Lawyers of Mississippi,* p. 106.

38. *Memoirs of Mississippi,* I, 884.

39. Jehu Amaziah Orr, " Life of Hon. James T. Harrison," *Publications of the Mississippi Historical Society,* VIII (1904), 189. Orr was a contemporary and an admirer of Harrison.

40. Wiley Pope Harris often consulted Harrison, his cousin, on particularly difficult legal matters.

41. Joseph Glover Baldwin, *The Flush Times of Alabama and Mississippi* (New York: D. Appleton and Company, 1853), p. 62.

bated with force and energy."[42] Harrison spoke frequently, with force and conviction, during the debates at Montgomery.

The final member of the delegation was William Sidney Wilson. Wilson was born of a prominent Maryland family on November 7, 1816,[43] and in 1860 he was a bachelor-lawyer resident of Port Gibson, Mississippi. As a delegate to the Montgomery Convention, he entered the debates on several occasions; Alexander H. Stephens wrote: "Wilson has made two or three quite sensible speeches but they were too long."[44]

The seven delegates from Mississippi were natives of four different slave states. All except Clayton and Wilson, whose educational background is unknown, were college graduates. It is fair to describe the Mississippi delegation as a highly qualified group of lawyers with local legislative and judicial experience.

Florida

The only lawyer of the three-man Florida delegation was James Patton Anderson, born in Franklin County, Tennessee, on February 16, 1822.[45] After his family moved to Mississippi, young Anderson was sent to Jefferson College in Pennsylvania and graduated in 1840. He returned home, studied law, and was admitted to the bar three years later. During the last year of the Mexican War, Anderson was called to duty as a lieutenant-colonel and, in 1849, he was elected to a term in the Mississippi legislature. In 1853, the adventurous Anderson accepted an appointment as United States Marshal for the Territory of Washington. Two years later, the Democratic Party of the territory elected him to the United States Congress. At the conclusion of his term in 1857, he agreed to supervise "Casa Bianca," the Florida plantation of his deceased aunt. After serving in the Tallahassee convention in 1861, Anderson went to Montgomery, about which he wrote: "All the principal measures of that body passed or proposed during its first session . . . met my approval."[46] Ander-

42. Davis, *Recollections,* p. 98.

43. See Joseph Breckinridge Handy, *A Genealogical Compilation of the Wilson Family* (New York: Schoharie, 1897).

44. Alexander H. Stephens to Linton Stephens, March 3, 1861.

45. "Autobiography of James P. Anderson," in James Patton Anderson Papers, Southern Historical Collection, University of North Carolina.

46. *Ibid.*

son, whom Alexander H. Stephens thought "a very interesting [and] clever gentleman,"[47] was on the committee to draft the Provisional Constitution.

Jackson Morton, the oldest and most experienced Florida delegate, was born on August 10, 1794, near Fredericksburg, Virginia.[48] Five years after graduating from William and Mary College, Morton moved to Pensacola where he settled a plantation called "Mortonia," and engaged in the lumber business. In 1836 and 1837, Morton served on the Florida Legislative Council, and the following year he was president. He returned to his business interests in 1855 after serving a six-year term in the United States Senate. Although a Whig, he acted with the radicals in 1850. In 1861, however, Morton helped lead the fight to delay secession at Tallahassee. At Montgomery, he served on Rhett's committee to frame a Permanent Constitution.

The third member of the delegation was James Byron Owens who was born in South Carolina in 1816.[49] Little is known of his activities prior to 1859 except that he moved around a great deal. This tends to validate the story that he was an itinerant Baptist minister.[50] He was an eloquent and zealous orator on behalf of John Cabell Breckinridge at the Charleston Democratic Convention in 1860. The previous year he had acquired a cotton plantation in Marion County, Florida, and represented this county at Tallahassee in 1861 as a spokesman for secession. At Montgomery, he served on both the Memminger and Rhett constitutional committees.

The three Florida delegates were college graduates, all were planters, and all, save Morton, were Democrats. The legislative experience of the Florida delegation, two had experience on the national level and all three had experience on the state level, was fully utilized at Montgomery.

ALABAMA

The only member of the Alabama delegation to have political experience on the national level was Jabez Lamar Monroe Curry

47. Alexander H. Stephens to Linton Stephens, March 3, 1861.

48. *Biographical Directory of the American Congress*, p. 1340.

49. Eloise Robinson Ott to the author, May 2, 1960. Mrs. Ott is the historian of Marion County, Florida.

50. *Ibid.*

who was born in Lincoln County, Georgia, on June 5, 1825.[51] In 1839, he entered Franklin College, later the University of Georgia, with classmates Benjamin Harvey Hill and Linton Stephens. Four years later, Curry attended Harvard College with Rutherford Birchard Hayes and studied law under the renowned jurist, Joseph Story. After graduating in 1845, and for the remainder of his life, Curry had two great loves, education and politics—he had discovered Horace Mann in New England and had met Secretary of State Calhoun in Washington.[52] Upon the completion of three terms in the Alabama lower house, he was elected to two terms in the United States Congress. He served in Washington until shortly before his state seceded. After resigning his seat, he acted as inter-state commissioner to Maryland, visited his state secession convention, and was a frequent debater at the Montgomery Convention. A contemporary said of him: "Small in person, and unpretending in his manner, he has never failed to impress his audience with the strength of his logic, and the power of his eloquence."[53]

Alabama's most influential delegate was Robert Hardy Smith, born in Camden County, North Carolina, on March 21, 1813.[54] After briefly attending West Point, he studied law, was admitted to the bar, and began practice in Livingston, Alabama. In 1849, he was elected to the lower house of the state legislature and quickly rose to leadership in the Whig Party. Failing election to the state senate in 1851, he moved to a thriving law practice in Mobile, and often appeared before the bench of the Federal Supreme Court. Opposing secession until the election of Lincoln in December, 1860, he entered upon his duties as inter-state commissioner to North Carolina with the same vigor and astuteness that he later displayed at Montgomery. Alexander H. Stephens wrote: "Smith of Mobile is the man of this state in our body. . . ."[55]

Stephens also wrote: "next to him is Walker . . . [who] seems

51. "Autobiography of J. L. M. Curry," in Jabez Lamar Monroe Curry Papers, the Alabama State Department of Archives and History, Montgomery, Alabama.

52. His political career was limited to before and during the Civil War; his great activities in behalf of Southern education were post war.

53. William Garrett, *Reminiscences of Public Men in Alabama, for Thirty Years* (Atlanta: Plantation Publishing Company, 1872), p. 648.

54. "Robert Hardy Smith," in *DAB*.

55. Alexander H. Stephens to Linton Stephens, March 3, 1861.

to be quite a young man."[56] This young man was Richard Wilde Walker who was born in Huntsville, Alabama, on February 16, 1823.[57] Upon the completion of his formal education at Princeton, New Jersey, in 1841, he returned home to study and later practice law. As a resident of Florence, he was elected to the state lower house in 1851 and again in 1855. In 1859, Governor Moore appointed Walker to the Supreme Court, a post he occupied at the time of the Montgomery Convention. Like Smith, he served on both constitutional drafting committees.[58]

William Paris Chilton, one of Yancey's Montgomery law partners, was born near Elizabethtown, Kentucky, on August 10, 1810.[59] Little is known of his life before he settled in Talledega, Alabama, and practiced law. In 1839, he was elected as a Whig to the state legislature but he was unsuccessful in his try for the Federal Congress in 1843. From 1852-1856, Chilton was Chief Justice of the Alabama Supreme Court. After a three-year return to his law practice, he was elected to the state senate, and in 1861 he was elected to the Montgomery Convention. Curry wrote of his colleague: "He was a marked man, not learned in the schools, but of vigorous intellect, of logical turn, of indefatigable labor . . . and of ardent temperature of patriotism."[60]

John Gill Shorter, a Democrat and a native Georgian, was born on April 23, 1818.[61] After graduating from Franklin College in 1837, Shorter went immediately to Eufaula, Alabama, to practice law. He served one term in the state senate and part of a term in the house. Shorter quit the house seat to take an appointment to the circuit bench in 1852. Eight years later, he resigned the bench post to become commissioner to Georgia where he issued an invitation for the Montgomery meeting. This wealthy lawyer and war-time Governor of Alabama was a keen debater at the Montgomery Convention.

56. *Ibid.*

57. Thomas McAdory Owen, *History of Alabama and Dictionary of Alabama Biography*, 4 volumes (Chicago: S. J. Clarke Publishing Company, 1921), IV, 1918. (Hereinafter cited as Owen, *Dictionary of Alabama Biography.*)

58. His brother, Leroy Pope Walker, was the first Confederate Secretary of War.

59. "William Paris Chilton," in *DAB.*

60. Jabez Lamar Monroe Curry, "Reminiscences of Talledega," *The Alabama Historical Quarterly*, VIII (Winter Issue, 1946), 362.

61. "John Gill Shorter," in *DAB.*

Stephen Fowler Hale, "a Whig of the Kentucky stamp of those days . . . ,"[62] was born in Crittenden County, Kentucky, on July 31, 1816.[63] The son of a Baptist minister, he studied law at Lexington, and later moved to Eutaw, Alabama, to practice. He was elected to one term in the state legislature, and then served as a volunteer lieutenant during the War with Mexico. While practicing law following the war, he was again elected to the house in 1857. Hale was serving in this capacity when he, like Smith and Shorter, was appointed commissioner to his native state and a delegate to Montgomery.

The only physician at the Montgomery Convention was Thomas Fearn, born near Danville, Virginia, on November 15, 1789.[64] After attending Washington College, he entered and later graduated from the Old Medical College at Philadelphia. Dr. Fearn moved to Huntsville, Alabama, in 1811 and began the practice of medicine. He was state medical examiner and a member of the state legislature from 1822-1829. During the next thirty years, he continued to practice his profession, in addition to being a successful planter and banker. The elderly doctor answered the call of his state in 1861, serving at Montgomery quietly, but with distinction.[65]

The Alabama delegation also claimed the only cotton factor at the Montgomery Convention in Colin John McRae, a North Carolinian, born on October 22, 1812.[66] After a preparatory education by tutors, McRae attended a Catholic college at Biloxi, Mississippi. Settling in Mississippi with interests in commerce and politics, he was elected to the state legislature in 1838. In later years, McRae moved to Mobile and became a successful and respected cotton commission merchant. He was acting in this capacity when called to serve at Montgomery.

The final member of the delegation, David Peter Lewis, was born in Charlotte County, Virginia, in 1820.[67] He grew up in

62. Garrett, *Reminiscences,* p. 665.

63. Owen, *Dictionary of Alabama Biography,* III, 724.

64. *Ibid.,* 567.

65. Dr. Fearn's son-in-law, William T. S. Barry, was a delegate from Mississippi.

66. Owen, *Dictionary of Alabama Biography,* IV, 1139.

67. *Ibid.,* 1043.

Madison County, Alabama, and, after being admitted to the bar, began what became a successful practice in Lawrence County. The only delegate from Alabama to attend the state secession convention, Lewis bitterly opposed secession. Although he attended the Montgomery Convention, he remained a "Unionist."[68]

It is indeed surprising to find William L. Yancey absent from the nine-man Alabama delegation to the Montgomery Convention. At the state secession convention where Yancey led the immediate secessionists, a cooperationist introduced a motion that would require the convention to choose its Montgomery delegates from outside the convention and outside the state legislature.[69] The motion was defeated, but the idea was accepted by a tacit understanding.[70] Perhaps Yancey was sacrificed as an inducement to the border states, or perhaps, like many radicals in history when their ideas are near fruition, he was simply discarded by his more conservative colleagues.[71]

Walter Lynwood Fleming wrote: "A few politicians among the secessionists united with the cooperationists and, passing by the most experienced and able leaders, chose an inexperienced Whiggish delegation."[72] The Alabama delegation was Whiggish, there being four Whigs and five Democrats; however, it was not altogether inexperienced. Although only Curry had served in the United States Congress, all nine members had legislative experience on the state level, and three members had been notable jurists, not to mention the four inter-state commissioners.

GEORGIA

The large and able delegation from Georgia was headed by the famous triumvirate of Stephens, Toombs, and Cobb. Alexander Hamilton Stephens was born in what later became Taliaferro County, Georgia, on February 11, 1812.[73] After attending

68. In 1863, he left the Confederacy but returned to Huntsville after the war. He joined the Republican Party and became an unpopular governor in 1872.

69. William Russell Smith, *The History and Debates of the Convention of the People of Alabama* (Montgomery: White, Pfister and Company, 1861), p. 148.

70. Except for Chilton and Lewis, this procedure was followed.

71. Rhett met a similar fate after the establishment of the Confederacy.

72. Walter Lynwood Fleming, *Civil War and Reconstruction in Alabama* (New York: The Columbia University Press, 1905), p. 42.

73. "Alexander Hamilton Stephens," in *DAB*. "My name is Alexander for my grandfather, and Hamilton for a preacher of that name [Alexander Hamilton

an academy, he subsequently graduated first in his class from Franklin College. Finding rural teaching too exhausting, Stephens turned to law and, upon admittance to the bar in 1834, began his practice at Crawfordville. Between 1836 and 1843, save one year, he was repeatedly elected to the state legislature where he adopted the Whig philosophy. For the next sixteen years, Stephens was a distinguished member, among many such men, of the United States Congress. During this time, he opposed the annexation of Texas, the Mexican War, and the Wilmot Proviso. Along with Cobb and Toombs, he favored the compromise measures of 1850; and, in 1854, Stephens acted as the floor manager in the House of Representatives for the Kansas-Nebraska Bill. He resigned his seat in 1859 and returned to his beloved home, "Liberty Hall," and his law practice. His impressive speech for the Union, given before the state legislature in November, 1860,[74] and his cooperationist efforts at Milledgeville have already been mentioned. He signed the state secession ordinance and was sent to Montgomery where his incisive and experienced mind was applied to the drafting of a set of operational rules and the Provisional Constitution. Stephens' reputation as a formidable adversary in debate preceded him to Montgomery for a local paper called him "the 'John Randolph' of our time. . . ."[75] Curry of Alabama described him: "Tall, spare, not weighing over one hundred pounds, nearly bloodless with a feminine voice and appearance . . . he was often jocularly spoken of as 'a refugee from the graveyard.' "[76] Although Stephens was elected Vice President of the Confederacy, he never seemed to have his heart in the cause.

Probably the greatest orator in the South in 1861 was Robert Toombs. The fifth son of a rich cotton planter, he was born

---

Webster of the Washington, Georgia Academy], and not for Alexander Hamilton, the statesman . . ." (Alexander Hamilton Stephens to unidentified newspaper, March 18, 1860, in Alexander Hamilton Stephens Papers, the Southern Historical Collection, University of North Carolina).

74. His old congressional colleague, Abraham Lincoln, was impressed and wrote Stephens for a copy of the speech.

75. Montgomery *Weekly Mail,* February 22, 1861.

76. Jabez Lamar Monroe Curry, *Civil History of the Government of the Confederate States of America with Some Personal Reminiscences* (Richmond: B. F. Johnson Publishing Company, 1901), p. 56.

in the uplands of eastern Georgia, in Wilkes County, on July 2, 1810.[77] After graduating from Union College at Schenectady, New York, he returned home to practice law. In addition to a very successful practice at Washington, Georgia, Toombs invested in slaves and plantations in the southwestern part of the state. Toombs' career in politics very closely paralleled that of his friend Stephens. Both men served in their state legislature from 1837-1843 and, for years thereafter, both men served their state in Washington. Wiley Pope Harris of Mississippi wrote: "Stephens was a conservative statesman, Toombs was headstrong and progressive. Each seems to have felt that Georgia needed the other and the people of Georgia were disposed to employ both."[78] After six years in the United States Congress and after vigorously supporting the Compromise of 1850, Toombs was elected to the Senate where he mildly supported the Kansas-Nebraska Bill. By late 1860, he had become a staunch secessionist as evidenced by his eloquent speech before the Georgia legislature in November and his telegram from Washington in December. At Montgomery, his talents, especially in matters of finance, were utilized on the committee drafting the Permanent Consititution. A fellow delegate said: "In conversation Toombs was fascinating and bright, more suggestive and interesting than anyone I ever heard, except Calhoun. . . ."[79]

The third member of the triumvirate was Howell Cobb, born in Jefferson County, on September 7, 1815.[80] By virtue of his wealth, Cobb enjoyed freedom from financial worries and devoted his life to public service. After graduation from Franklin College and admittance to the bar in 1836, the legislature elected him solicitor of the western circuit for three years. Elected to the United States Congress in 1842, he was later a supporter of the Polk administration. In January, 1849, Cobb advocated unity within the Democratic Party and opposed Calhoun's call for a Southern *bloc*. The following December he was elected Speaker of the House after a long and heated fight. Cobb stood against the state rights wing of his party in 1850. With his Whig friends,

77. Ulrich Bonnell Phillips, *The Life of Robert Toombs* (New York: The MacMillan Company, 1913), p. 6.

78. Rowland, *Judges and Lawyers of Mississippi*, p. 316.

79. Curry, *Civil History*, p. 19.

80. "Howell Cobb," in *DAB*.

Toombs and Stephens, he advocated, in his words, *"the finality of the compromise."*[81] Although he won the governorship of Georgia the next year on a coalition ticket, he also gained the lasting enmity of many Southern Democrats. Cobb lost the fight for a seat in the United States Senate in 1854, but was elected to the Federal House the following year. After being instrumental in the election of James Buchanan, Cobb was made Secretary of the Treasury. He resigned his post in 1860 to work for immediate secession. Although Cobb could not match the flamboyancy of Toombs, nor the incisive mind of Stephens, he understood and practiced the art of compromise to a degree unknown to Toombs or Stephens. He played a significant role at Montgomery as the president of the convention. "This tribute," said Curry, "to high character and great excellence was paid to the most popular member of the body without a dissenting vote."[82]

Howell's brother, Thomas Reade Rootes Cobb, was born in Jefferson County, on April 10, 1823.[83] After graduating from Franklin College, he studied law and was admitted to the bar in 1842. From 1849-1857, he was reporter for the Supreme Court of Georgia and, in 1851, was selected to codify the laws of the state. Speaking for the cause of immediate secession after the election of Lincoln, he entered politics for the first time. His vast knowledge of constitutional law was most helpful as he served on the committee to draft the Permanent Constitution and as he spoke in debate at Montgomery. Cobb's correspondence with his wife during the convention stands as the most complete and enlightening single documentation of the Montgomery Convention.[84]

A much experienced Whig delegate was Eugenius Aristides Nisbet, born in Greene County, on December 7, 1803.[85] After graduating from Franklin College, he studied law at the famous

81. Howell Cobb to John [Lamar], February 23, 1853, in Charles Colcock Jones, collector, "Autograph Letters and Portraits of the Signers of the Constitution of the Confederate States" (Augusta, Georgia, 1884), a scrapbook, Manuscript Department, Duke University.

82. Curry, *Civil History*, p. 46.

83. "Thomas Reade Rootes Cobb," in *DAB*.

84. Thomas Reade Rootes Cobb Papers, Special Collections Division, University of Georgia.

85. "Eugenius Aristides Nisbet," in *DAB*.

school of Tapping Reeve and James Gould at Litchfield, Connecticut. From 1827-1835, Nisbet served in the Georgia legislature and, in 1838, was elected to the Federal Congress as a Whig. He was later one of three original justices of the Georgia Supreme Court, but he returned to his law practice in 1853. Although he was a state leader of the Know-Nothing Party in the fifties, in 1861 he headed the committee to draft an ordinance of secession at Milledgeville. At Montgomery, he served with Stephens on the committee to draft a Provisional Constitution.

One of the last Georgians to accept secession was Benjamin Harvey Hill, born in Jasper County, on September 14, 1823.[86] Following graduation from Franklin College with highest honors and passing the bar, he quickly established himself as a competent criminal lawyer. After the dissolution of the Whig Party, he cast his fortunes with the Know-Nothing Party. During the presidential campaign of 1856, political tempers ran high and Stephens challenged him to a duel, but Hill refused.[87] The following year Hill ran for governor but lost to Joseph Emerson Brown. Like Nisbet, he opposed secession but, also like Nisbet, he signed the secession ordinance. At Montgomery, his full energies were devoted to the good of the Confederacy.

Martin Jenkins Crawford, like Hill, was born in Jasper County, on March 17, 1820.[88] After one term at Mercer College, he left college to read law and was admitted to the bar before he was twenty. He served one term in the state legislature, and later was elected a superior court judge. Crawford, a tall, slim, gifted orator, resigned his seat in the United States Congress in 1861 when his state seceded and appointed him to Montgomery.

Augustus Romaldus Wright was born in Columbia County on June 16, 1813.[89] He entered Franklin College with Alexander H. Stephens but withdrew before graduation. After attending law school at Litchfield, Connecticut, and being admitted to the

86. Haywood Jefferson Pearce, *Benjamin H. Hill, Secession and Reconstruction* (Chicago: The University of Chicago Press, 1928), p. 1.

87. "Hill declined, saying privately that he had a family to support and a soul to save, while Stephens had neither." ("Alexander Hamilton Stephens," in *DAB*.)

88. "Martin Jenkins Crawford," in *DAB*.

89. Bernard Suttler, "Augustus Romaldus Wright," William J. Northern, ed., *Men of Mark in Georgia,* 6 volumes (Atlanta: A. B. Caldwell, 1907-1912), III, 336.

bar at home, he made two unsuccessful races for the Federal Congress. In 1842, Wright was elected circuit judge and held the office for seven years. Finally winning a seat in the Federal House in 1859, he resigned the next year to act as inter-state commissioner to Maryland and later delegate to Montgomery.

Augustus Holmes Kenan was born in Baldwin County in 1805 and received his formal education at Orange-on-the-Hudson.[90] He was admitted to the bar in 1825 and began a practice in Milledgeville that lasted for forty years. After serving four terms in the state legislature, he attended the state secession convention as an ardent cooperationist. Although he signed the secession ordinance and then threw away the pen with which he signed it, he was an ardent Confederate at Montgomery.

The final member of the delegation, Francis Stebbins Bartow, was born in Savannah on September 6, 1816.[91] After graduating from Franklin College and being admitted to the bar, he practiced law in Savannah for many years. Like Hill and Nisbet, Bartow joined the Know-Nothing Party in the fifties. He won one term in the state lower house but failed in his try for Congress. Unlike his two friends, he favored immediate secession at Milledgeville. Although quiet and reserved, his colleagues at Montgomery came to know him as a warm and able person.

In size, prominence, and contribution to the Montgomery convention, the Georgia delegation stood first. No other delegation had three such able men as Stephens, Vice President of the Confederacy; Toombs, Secretary of State; and the elder Cobb, President of the Montgomery Convention. The entire delegation was Georgia born and college educated. These Georgians were a middle aged, prosperous, and highly experienced group of lawyers. Four delegates had judicial experience, eight of the ten had legislative experience on the state level, and six had legislative experience on the federal level. Only in the Georgia and Louisiana delegations did the Whigs outnumber the Democrats.

Louisiana

At the head of the Louisiana delegation was nationally prominent Charles Magill Conrad, born in Winchester County, Virginia,

90. R. J. Massey, "Augustus Holmes Kenan," in *ibid.*, 555.
91. A. B. Caldwell, "Francis Stebbins Bartow," in *ibid.*, 115.

on December 24, 1804.[92] After studying at the only English school in New Orleans, he read law and began to practice in 1828. The Jackson bank controversy converted Conrad to a Whig and, as such, he was elected to the state legislature. In 1842, he was appointed to the United States Senate but failed to be reelected the next year. Conrad served in the state constitutional convention in 1844 and, in 1848, was elected to Congress. Eight months after taking his seat he resigned to become President Millard Fillmore's Secretary of War. In 1853, he retired to a thriving law practice at home. Small in stature, but intense and tenacious in all endeavors, Conrad spoke often during the debates at Montgomery.

The largest slaveholder at Montgomery was Duncan Farrar Kenner, born in New Orleans on February 11, 1813.[93] After graduating from Miami University at Oxford, Ohio, he enjoyed four years of travel and study in Europe. Upon his return home, he studied law, was engaged in commercial activity,[94] and settled down to the responsibilities and remunerations of his sugar plantation at "Ashland." His successful endeavors gave him the leisure to serve several terms in the state legislature as well as in the state constitutional conventions of 1844 and 1852. Kenner's abilities impressed Stephens at Montgomery for he wrote: "Kenner is a very superior man in any body. . . . He always had point and sense in what he says—as well as method and system in saying it."[95] Kenner aided in the drafting of the Provisional Constitution.

John Perkins, Jr., the only Democrat in the delegation, was born on July 1, 1819, in Natchez, Mississippi.[96] After graduating from Yale College, he received a law degree from Harvard and established a practice in New Orleans in 1843. Four years later, he abandoned his practice because of ill health and helped re-

92. "Charles Magill Conrad," in *DAB*.

93. "Duncan Farrar Kenner," in *DAB*.

94. Ulrich Bonnell Phillips in *American Negro Slavery* (New York: D. Appleton and Company, 1918), p. 246, says that Kenner was a slave trader, with headquarters in New Orleans, who became a respectable sugar planter, and one of the largest slaveholders in the South.

95. Alexander H. Stephens to Linton Stephens, March 3, 1861.

96. Robert Dabney Calhoun, "The John Perkins Family of Northeast Louisiana," *The Louisiana Historical Quarterly*, XIX (January, 1936), 76.

organize the Louisiana Historical Society. With an appointment as district judge, Perkins returned to Madison Parish in 1851 and, the following year, was elected to the Thirty-third Congress. In 1857, Perkins took over the management of his father's cotton plantations which included some 17,500 acres, 250 slaves, and were valued at over $600,000.[97] At the secession convention in Baton Rouge, he was temporary chairman and head of the committee that drafted the secession ordinance. The editor of *De Bow's Review* described Perkins, who served with Kenner on the Provisional Constitution drafting committee, as "a man of the highest personal character and of strong intellect."[98]

Alexander DeClouet was born in St. Martin Parish on June 9, 1812.[99] He studied law briefly after receiving his formal education at Bardstown, Kentucky, and Georgetown College in Washington, D.C., but he soon found agricultural pursuits more to his liking. DeClouet became a very prosperous sugar planter. During the late thirties, he was elected several times to the state legislature and, in 1849, was an unsuccessful Whig candidate for governor. In 1861, DeClouet left his lovely plantation near Bayou Vermillion to attend the state secession convention and the convention at Montgomery.

Edward Sparrow, a very wealthy cotton planter, born in Dublin, Ireland, December 29, 1810, was educated at Kenyon College, Ohio, and came to Louisiana in 1831.[100] After practicing law and serving in various judicial capacities and after being elected brigadier general of militia during the Mexican War, Sparrow moved to Carroll Parish and acquired "Arlington" plantation. He served a term in the state legislature, was a member of the Baton Rouge convention, and worked with DeClouet at Montgomery on the Permanent Constitution. A contemporary wrote: "General Sparrow was one of the lights of the Louisiana Bar . . . [and enjoyed an] enviable reputation . . . throughout his career."[101]

97. *Ibid.*, 74.

98. James Dunwoody Brownson De Bow to William Porcher Miles, February 15, 1861, in William Porcher Miles Papers.

99. *Biographical and Historical Memoirs of Louisiana*, 2 volumes (Chicago: The Goodspeed Publishing Company, 1891), II, 475.

100. Robert Dabney Calhoun, "A History of Concordia Parish," *Louisiana Historical Quarterly*, XV (July, 1932), 447.

101. *Ibid.*, p. 448.

The last member of the delegation was Henry Marshall who was born in South Carolina in 1807.[102] He was a member of the Baton Rouge convention. While at the Montgomery Convention, Stephens wrote: "From La we have Marshall a plain sensible well educated [Union College of New York] planter."[103]

Of the six delegates from Louisiana, only two were native born. With the exception of Conrad, all of the delegates were college educated. This extremely wealthy planter delegation numbered only one Democrat. All had local legislative experience, and two had experience on the national level.

Texas

Louis Trezevant Wigfall was born near Edgefield, South Carolina, on April 21, 1816; he attended and graduated from South Carolina College, was admitted to the bar, and settled in Marshall, Texas, in 1848.[104] As a member of the Texas lower house in 1850, Wigfall favored secession and, three years later, led the state rights Democrats in his state senate. In 1859, he was elected to the United States Senate over the strong opposition of Governor Houston. He signed both the "Address of Southern Congressmen" and the resolutions of the Southern Senators' Conference. By virtue of his temperament, ability, and persuasion, Wigfall would have led the Texas delegation at Montgomery; however, he left Washington too late to participate.

Leadership of the delegation fell to John Hemphill, born in South Carolina on December 18, 1803.[105] After graduating from Jefferson College in only two years, he returned home and practiced law in Sumter from 1831 to 1838. Hemphill moved to Washington, Texas, in the latter year and, in 1840, was elected a district judge. From 1841-1858, he acted as Chief Justice of the Texas Supreme Court and resigned to go to the Federal Senate. At Montgomery, the "John Marshall of Texas" was "quiet modest and unobstrusive, but firm and unyielding, when convinced of the correctness of his conclusion."[106]

102. See Appendix I; little information is available on Marshall.

103. Alexander H. Stephens to Linton Stephens, March 3, 1861.

104. "Louis Trezevant Wigfall," in *DAB*.

105. William Hemphill to Robert Hemphill, April 30, 1895, in Hemphill Papers, Southern Historical Collection, University of North Carolina.

106. The Richmond *Enquirer*, January 6, 1862.

Born in Sevier County, Tennessee, on October 8, 1818, John Henninger Reagan pursued many vocations including overseer, surveyor, and soldier.[107] After settling in Texas, he was elected to the legislature in 1847. The next year he was admitted to the bar and, in 1852, was elected to a six-year term as district judge. Reagan maintained a seat in the United States Congress from 1857 until he resigned to attend his state secession convention and subsequently, the Montgomery Convention.[108] President Davis appointed him Postmaster General of the Confederacy.

The only Whig in the Texas delegation was William Beck Ochiltree, born in Cumberland County, North Carolina, on October 18, 1811.[109] Lacking any formal education, he first practiced law in Alabama,[110] but soon he moved to Texas. In 1842, he was appointed district judge and, three years later, joined the Cabinet of the Republic of Texas as Secretary of the Treasury and later Attorney General. After serving in the constitutional convention of 1845, Ochiltree was elected to the legislature. This long-time state Whig leader and distinguished jurist was elected to the Austin secession convention. Stephens considered Ochiltree one of the most competent members of the Texas delegation at Montgomery.[111]

Another Tennessean in the Texas delegation was Williamson Simpson Oldham, born in Franklin County, on June 19, 1813.[112] After being admitted to the bar in 1836, he moved to Fayetteville, Arkansas, and established a successful practice. Oldham served in the legislature, one term as speaker, and, in 1844, was elected to the Supreme Court. Because of illness, he moved to Austin and became one of the editors of the Texas *State Gazette*. Oldham supported secession at the Austin Convention in 1861 and ably represented his state at Montgomery.

The youngest delegate and the only Alabamian in the Texas

107. "John Henninger Reagan," in *DAB*.

108. John Henninger Reagan, *Memoirs, with Special Reference to Secession and the Civil War,* edited by Walter Flavius McCaleb (New York: The Neale Publishing Company, 1906), p. 109.

109. James Daniel Lynch, *The Bench and Bar of Texas* (St. Louis: Nixon-Jones Printing Company, 1885), p. 81.

110. Robert H. Smith and Ochiltree were law partners for a brief time.

111. Alexander H. Stephens to Linton Stephens, March 3, 1861.

112. "Williamson Simpson Oldham," in *DAB*.

group was John Gregg, born on September 28, 1828.[113] After graduating from La Grange College in Alabama, he practiced law for several years in Tuscambia before moving to Freestone County, Texas. In 1855, he was elected district judge and, in 1861, served in the Austin Convention. Gregg was present at Montgomery, but he took little part in the proceedings.

Thomas Neville Waul, born in South Carolina on January 5, 1815, was compelled to leave South Carolina College before graduation because of limited means.[114] Seeking his fortune in the West, he was admitted to the Mississippi bar in 1835, and later he was elected a circuit judge. After practicing law with considerable success in Mississippi and later in Louisiana, he moved to Texas where he was elected to the Montgomery Convention. Waul, along with Gregg, participated infrequently in the convention debates.

Texas, like Florida, had no native born delegates. Although only four of the Texans had attended college, all were lawyers and all except Ochiltree were Democrats. The seven delegates had a variety of political experience. Five had judicial experience, five had legislative experience on the state level, and three had legislative experience on the national level. The Texans made the least contribution at Montgomery since the Texas delegation was absent during the writing of and the debates on the Provisional Constitution and since it was not officially seated until nine days prior to the adoption of the Permanent Constitution.

The Confederate "Founding Fathers" were a group of Southern-born, middle-aged, well-educated, slaveholding lawyers and planters who were prosperous and highly experienced in public service.[115] These fifty men, with the exception of Memminger and Sparrow, were born in slave states, thirty-three being natives of the lower South. A majority of the membership at Mongomery was born in the two states of South Carolina and Georgia, with Florida and Texas having no native-born delegates. The youngest member was Josiah A. Patterson Campbell of Mississippi (31),

113. "John Gregg," in *DAB*.

114. Lynch, *Bench and Bar of Texas*, p. 404.

115. In conjunction with the following paragraphs, see Appendix I, and, in particular, "Statistical Table on the Montgomery Convention."

and the oldest was Dr. Thomas Fearn of Alabama (72). The Mississippi delegation had the youngest average age (44.1), and South Carolina had the oldest (50.6). The average age of the Montgomery Convention was 47.1 years.

The educational background of the members is most impressive. All of the delegates from South Carolina, Florida, and Georgia were college trained. Forty-two members (85.7 per cent) of the convention were college trained.[116]

The overwhelming majority of the "Founding Fathers" were lawyers or planters. Forty-two members (84 per cent) of the convention were trained in the law; and every member of the Mississippi, Georgia, and Texas delegations was a trained lawyer. Of the total membership, thirty-three (66 per cent) followed agricultural pursuits as planters; only the Florida delegation consisted of all planters. And, of the forty-two trained lawyers at Montgomery, twenty-seven were also planters. Thus, a majority of the authors of the two Confederate Constitutions were lawyer-planters.

All of the members listed in the census of 1860, except Harris of Mississippi, were slaveholders. Kenner of Louisiana, who owned 473 slaves, was the largest slaveholder. Of the 33 planters, 21 owned 20 or more slaves, and 14 owned 50 or more slaves.

The membership had functioned in a wide variety of executive, judicial, and legislative capacities. One member (Miles) had been a mayor, one (Howell Cobb) had been a governor, two (Conrad and Howell Cobb) had served in Federal Cabinets, and one (Ochiltree) had served in two positions in the Cabinet of the Republic of Texas. Sixteen members of the convention had occupied judicial positions. Nine had been circuit or district judges, one had been a federal judge, four had been state associate justices, and two had been chief justices of their respective state supreme courts. The membership was, however, most widely experienced in the legislative branch of government. Every member of the delegations from South Carolina, Florida, Alabama, and Louisiana had served in state legislatures. The entire mem-

116. College graduates—37; attended college but did not graduate—5; did not attend—7; unknown—1. Since the college training of one member is unknown, 49 was used as 100 per cent in this calculation.

bership of the convention, save five, had done service in state legislatures. Almost half (23) of the membership had served in the United States Congress; eighteen delegates served in the House of Representatives, nine in the United States Senate, and four in both.

Although the founding of a new Confederacy was a radical act, the convention that performed this act was not radical in nature. The members of the Montgomery Convention were representatives of the slaveholding realty interests and the political leadership of the South. The major motivation or objective of the membership was not to derive economic gain from the two constitutions that they were to write. It is more realistic to hold that the principal objective was to establish a government that would preserve and perpetuate the political, social, and economic conditions which represented the Southern way of life in 1861.

Additional information on the nature of the convention is indicated by the political affiliations of the members. Thirty-two members or about three-fifths of the membership were Democrats, and seventeen or about two-fifths were Whigs. Twice as many Democrats favored secession as opposed it while the reverse is true for the Whigs. The Whigs were thus more moderate. Of the total membership, approximately two-fifths had been cooperationists or unionists. This group joined with the immediate secessionists and directed the establishment of the Confederacy. From Montgomery, Stephens wrote: "There is more conservatism . . . than I expected to see, and this increases my hopes."[117] The men responsible for the election of the Montgomery membership surely felt that a conservative convention could better handle the situation than one oriented to the lead of Rhett-Yancey radicals. Would not such a convention better perpetuate the Southern way of life; would not such a convention be more attractive and encouraging to the border states and to Europe?

Certainly the two most significant features of the membership of the Montgomery Convention were the high degree of political experience and moderate character of the delegates. After making an extensive study of the Confederate Congress from 1861-

117. Alexander H. Stephens to Linton Stephens, March 3, 1861.

1865, one historian stated: "As a whole, the Provisional Congress [Montgomery membership] represented a higher type of leadership than either of the subsequent [Confederate] congresses."[118] Like the Philadelphia "Founding Fathers," the Montgomery "Founding Fathers" were more interested in framing a practical document than in political experimentation.

118. Wilfred Buck Yearns, Jr., *The Confederate Congress* (Athens: The University of Georgia Press, 1960), p. 9.

CHAPTER III

The Organization of the Montgomery Convention

It is now a fixed and irrevocable fact. The separation is perfect, complete, and perpetual.

Howell Cobb

Delegates from six seceded states began to arrive in Montgomery during the first days of February, 1861. The small inland city that greeted them was located in the heart of a belt of rolling and wooded prairies that stretched from the Savannah River to the Mississippi River. Named after General Richard Montgomery who died in the attack on Quebec in 1775, the city was situated on the eastern bank of the Alabama River about three hundred miles from the Gulf of Mexico. Montgomery was perched upon high bluffs that dropped sharply down to the river on the city side. Like most Southern inland cities in 1861, Montgomery had one wide central avenue. Main Street ran from the river bluffs to the state Capitol, which was situated on a high hill a mile away. One visitor, who felt that the city gave a very pleasant picture to the newly arrived, wrote: "Streets, various in length, uncertain in direction . . . , ran into Main street at many points; and most of them were closely built with pretty houses, all of them surrounded by gardens and many by handsome grounds."[1]

Overlooking the city at the head of Main Street was the impressive Capitol building which had been completed only ten years earlier. With a high central cupola and tall Corinthian columns as a facing, the Capitol was one of the finest examples of neo-classic architecture in the South. The southern wing of the building was the chamber of the Alabama House of Repre-

1. Thomas Cooper DeLeon, *Four Years in Rebel Capitals* (Mobile: The Gossip Printing Company, 1892), p. 24.

sentatives. Occupying this chamber when the delegates arrived was the legislature of the Republic of Alabama. Across the hall in the northern wing was the Senate chamber. Above the neatly placed desks was a curving balcony for spectators. In the chamber below, paintings, donated by various people in Montgomery, adorned the walls. Among these were portraits of John C. Calhoun, Andrew Jackson, Henry Clay, Francis Marion, William L. Yancey, and three of George Washington including a Gilbert Stuart painting which hung on the wall behind the rostrum. The Senate chamber was unoccupied and in readiness for the meeting of the Montgomery Convention on the first Monday in February.

Alexander H. Stephens wrote to his brother from Montgomery on February 4 saying: "I arrived here yesterday. . . . We first went to the Exchange Hotel—there it was said rooms had been provided for the Georgia delegation. . . ."[2] In 1861, Montgomery could boast of only two large hotels. The Exchange Hotel and Montgomery Hall were located between the river and the Capitol. The Exchange was much the more pretentious and comfortable of the two, having accommodations for over three hundred guests. Most of the delegates stayed there, although some stayed at Montgomery Hall and others, like Stephens, were fortunate enough to secure quarters in private residences.

Accommodations of all kinds became increasingly crowded as more and more people arrived in Montgomery. In addition to the Montgomery delegates and the members of the Alabama legislature, numerous people who usually congregate at the seat of government began to arrive. One observer wrote: "Montgomery seemed Washington over again, but on a smaller scale, and with the avidity and agility in pursuit of the spoils somewhat enhanced by the freshness of the scent."[3] The spoilsmen provided color to an already highly charged atmosphere. As the day for the opening of the Montgomery Convention approached, the city was buzzing with excitement, anticipation, and confidence.

February 4, 1861, was a clear and sunny day; the air was crisp

2. Alexander Hamilton Stephens to Linton Stephens, February 4, 1861, in Alexander Hamilton Stephens Papers (microfilm), Southern Historical Collection, University of North Carolina. (Hereinafter cited as Alexander H. Stephens to Linton Stephens.)

3. DeLeon, *Four Years in Rebel Capitals*, p. 48.

and invigorating. Small groups of delegates began drifting into the Senate chamber shortly after ten o'clock in the morning. Many of the members renewed acquaintances with old friends.

Promptly at noon, Judge Chilton of Alabama called the convention to order and moved that Robert W. Barnwell be appointed to preside temporarily. After taking the chair behind the rostrum and tendering his thanks to the members, Barnwell called upon the Reverend Dr. Basil Manly of Montgomery to give the invocation. Dr. Manly concluded by saying: "Thus, has been inaugurated this important movement. May the Father of Lights guide the Whole."[4] Immediately thereafter, a motion was passed calling upon the members to present their credentials. Thirty-seven delegates from South Carolina, Mississippi, Florida, Alabama, Georgia, and Louisiana came forward, presented their credentials, and signed the roll.[5] Thirteen delegates, including the entire Texas delegation, had not yet arrived.[6]

Robert Barnwell Rhett rose and moved that the membership elect a permanent convention president; he placed in nomination the name of Howell Cobb of Georgia. The motion prevailed by acclamation. Cobb was best qualified of his colleagues to preside over the proceedings of the convention that came to be known as the Provisional Congress.[7] He brought to the post considerable national prestige, having served in the United States House of Representatives for thirteen years, and as Speaker of that body from 1849-1851. Moreover, he had served as United States Secretary of the Treasury from 1857-1860. Cobb's reputation rested primarily upon his special talents as a negotiator.[8] In the difficult days ahead, his convention colleagues expected him to preside

4. William Stanley Hoole, "The Diary of Dr. Basil Manly, 1858-1867," *The Alabama Review,* IV (April, 1951), 146.

5. *Journal of the Congress of the Confederate States of America, 1861-1865,* 7 volumes (Washington: Government Printing Offive, 1904-1905), I, 17. (Hereinafter cited as *Confederate Journal.*)

6. Morton of Florida arrived on February 6, Conrad of Louisiana on the 7th, Fearn and Lewis of Alabama and Clayton of Mississippi on the 8th, and Campbell of Mississippi on the 12th. The Texas delegation was not officially seated until March 2.

7. After the adoption of the Provisional Constitution, the Montgomery Convention became the Provisional Congress. Cobb presided over the five sessions of this Congress, two in Montgomery and three in Richmond.

8. Horace Montgomery, *Howell Cobb's Confederate Career* (Tuscaloosa: Confederate Publishing Company, Inc., 1959), p. 24.

firmly but justly over the deliberations. Many also looked to him to help overcome the opposition to secession in the upper South. Cobb also had friends among Northern Democrats and there was a chance that they would aid him in avoiding a conflict with the incoming Lincoln administration.

Cobb's pleasant disposition and determined character were apparent to the delegates as he stood behind the speaker's rostrum to tender his appreciation. After a few introductory remarks, Cobb said: "It is now a fixed and an irrevocable fact. The separation is perfect, complete, and perpetual. . . . The great duty is now imposed upon us of providing for these States a government for their security and protection. . . ." He concluded confidently by saying: "With a consciousness of the justice of our cause, and with confidence in the guidance and blessing of a kind Providence, we will this day inaugurate for the South a new era of peace, security and prosperity."[9]

Following President Cobb's remarks, Judge Chilton placed in nomination for secretary the name of Johnson Jones Hooper. Hooper was elected Secretary of the Convention by acclamation. As senior editor of the Montgomery *Mail* and strong advocate of a Southern Confederacy, Hooper was well suited for the position. He was, however, better known to the delegates as the author of the humorous and satirical book *Some Adventures of Captain Simon Suggs,* published in 1846.[10] Hooper soon found his duties too time consuming and sold his interests in the newspaper. He had the very important responsibility of keeping the journals of the convention proceedings.[11]

The final business of the first day was initiated by Stephens of Georgia. Upon his motion, the President appointed a committee of five to report a set of rules for the government of the convention. Cobb appointed Stephens as chairman, Keitt, Curry, Harri-

9. *Confederate Journal,* I, 16.

10. See William Stanley Hoole, *Alias Simon Suggs, The Life and Times of Johnson Jones Hooper* (University, Alabama: University of Alabama Press, 1952).

11. When the Permanent Congress was established in Richmond on February 18, 1862, Howell Cobb commissioned Hooper to prepare the journals for publication. Hooper died in June and the uncompleted journals were sent to Athens for further work. To avoid capture, the journals were moved from place to place during the next three years and, in 1865, were turned over to the Union Army in Athens. In 1904, the United States Government published the journals which were in the possession of the War Department.

son, and Perkins.[12] Later that evening, the committee, except Curry who was ill, met in Stephens' parlor to formulate rules. Before the committee convened, however, Stephens had drafted a tentative set of rules. They were selected from the rules of the Federal House of Representatives, the Federal Senate, Jefferson's Manual, and included a few original to Stephens. These rules, wrote Stephens, "with one or two slight variations were adopted by this committee."[13] Shortly after noon of the second day, Stephens reported the work of his committee to the convention. After a brief debate, Stephens' twenty-nine rules were adopted. Voting in the convention was to be by states, one vote to each state, with a majority of the states represented being necessary to pass all motions. Any number of members from a majority of the states was to constitute a quorum to transact business; and, the record of yeas and nays would be recorded in the Journal upon the demand of one state, or of one-fifth of the members.[14]

The most important debates of the second day concerned the authority and the procedure of the convention. One delegate described the situation when he wrote: "The first question, which necessarily arrested the attention of the convention was what powers should it exercise, in view of the authority conferred and the condition and wants of the constituency represented."[15] This issue was detailed in general terms in the instructions that the delegates brought with them to Montgomery. These instructions had been framed by the various state secession conventions and, without exception, followed the "South Carolina Program." For example, the Alabama Secession Convention followed Rhett's suggestions when it instructed its delegation to "frame a provisional government upon the principles of the Constitution of the United States, and also to prepare . . . a plan for . . . a permanent government . . . which shall be submitted to the conventions of the seceding States for adoption or rejection."[16]

12. *Confederate Journal,* I, 16.
13. Alexander H. Stephens to Linton Stephens, February 5, 1861.
14. *Confederate Journal,* I, 17.
15. Robert Hardy Smith, *An Address to the Citizens of Alabama on the Constitution and Laws of the Confederate States of America* (Mobile: Mobile Daily Register Print, 1861), p. 4. (Hereinafter cited as Smith, *An Address.*)
16. *Confederate Journal,* I, 17.

Although favorable to a Southern Confederacy, some Southerners opposed the establishment of a provisional government. Until a majority of the slave states seceded, they felt that the formation of a definite political system, even temporarily, would jeopardize the movement for Southern independence. The idea of imposing a government upon states that had no part in its creation was distasteful to them. With adequate state governments, the thing to do was wait until more slave states acted and then form a government. This idealistic position ignored the exigency of time, a factor critical to the success of the new Confederacy.

The primary reason for establishing a provisional government was imposed by the uncertainty of coming events. Southerners did not know what would follow the inauguration of a new administration at Washington. Indeed, the extremists would have preferred to form a permanent government to avoid any possibility of reconstruction. All shades of opinion in the lower South realized, however, the importance of the upper South and the border states. Deference to the uncommitted slave states was reflected in a letter written by one of the Montgomery delegates on the eve of the convention. He said: "The idea seems to prevail . . . that we shall only organize a temporary government and put it in motion, leaving to the full complement of Southern States that shall finally come in, to determine in *full council* the final form and boundaries of a Southern Confederacy."[17] Although the general plan of instituting a provisional government and later a permanent government was thoughtfully considered and included in the instructions of the several states, the specific details had to be worked out in the Montgomery Convention.

Memminger initiated the debates on the morning of February 5. He proposed "that a committee be appointed to report a plan of a provisional government . . . upon the basis of the Constitution of the United States."[18] Following this proposal, three plans were presented to the convention. T. R. R. Cobb of

17. Robert Hardy Smith to Helen Smith, January 31, 1861, Charles Colcock Jones, collector, "Autograph Letters and Portraits of the Signers of the Constitution of the Confederate States" (Augusta, Georgia, 1884), a scrapbook, Manuscript Department, Duke University.

18. *Confederate Journal,* I, 19.

Georgia suggested: "That the committee thus appointed be instructed in framing the provisional government to provide—For a single executive head, . . . For a vice-president, . . . [and] For the continuance of this Congress as the legislative branch of this provisional government, so long as may be necessary, not exceeding twelve months."[19] Boyce of South Carolina would have prevented the convention from acting in a legislative capacity. He proposed that the convention draw up a constitution based on the United States Constitution, elect a president and vice president, and, finally, appoint a senate and a house of representatives to execute the government, and then adjourn. Hale of Alabama proposed that the convention write a constitution, elect a provisional president and vice president, and then act as a Congress until such time as regular elections could be held.

The principal difference among the three plans concerned whether or not the Montgomery Convention should exercise the functions of a legislature. Some of the delegates were uncertain; others felt that their instructions allowed them to establish only the executive branch of a provisional government. A local paper stated its opinion: "To leave the Provisional Government without a legislative branch would be to make of it practically a dictatorship. . . ."[20] During the debates, Kenner of Louisiana introduced a resolution that specifically called upon the convention to accept the legislative function as "a part of the duties incumbent upon the members of this Congress."[21] A majority of the delegates agreed with Kenner, Cobb, and Hale.

When the debates ended, the convention had determined its procedure and the extent of its authority by default. The Cobb, Boyce, and Hale resolutions were not brought to a vote. Memminger's original motion was adopted; and the Provisional Constitution embodied the essence of the Cobb and Hale plans. Thus, the convention decided to exercise the functions of a legislature.

The Montgomery Convention determined upon a procedure

19. *Ibid.*, p. 20.
20. Montgomery *Weekly Advertiser*, February 13, 1861.
21. *Confederate Journal*, I, 20.

that would embody three separate and distinct functions of government. First, the delegates acted as a convention or constituent assembly by drafting a Provisional Constitution and, shortly thereafter, a Permanent Constitution. There was much historical precedent for this action; indeed, between 1776 and 1860, every state in the Union had held similar conventions. Second, they acted as an electoral college by choosing a provisional president and vice president. And, finally, they functioned as a legislature in their capacity as the Provisional Congress. Other conventions in United States history, like the Continental Congress and several state constitutional conventions, had performed these three functions of government. The Montgomery Convention, unlike the Continental Congress, drafted a Provisional Constitution which was not submitted to the states. Although some state conventions submitted their work for approval and some did not, none concerned themselves with two fundamental documents at the same session. Thus, other conventions in the past had performed these three functions of government; however, the procedure at Montgomery was unique.

Shortly after the debates got under way, Perkins of Louisiana moved that the convention go into secret session. Thereafter, the convention began each day in open session but all of its important work was done in secret session. Such action was most unsatisfactory to many of the news correspondents who charged the convention with conspiracy and deceit. But most Southern newspapers understood the reasons for such measures. The Montgomery *Weekly Mail* said: "Madam Gossip will have a fine field of speculation in the absence of authentic information . . . ," but continued by saying that it would "cheerfully admit the wisdom of a policy which proposes to withhold from our enemies too intimate an acquaintance with the preliminary affairs of a (and it may be antagonistic) government."[22] Smith of Alabama expressed the sentiment of the delegates when he wrote: "Calm, unbiassed deliberations . . . as well as freedom from all motive or hope of individual eclat were promoted by closed doors . . . it was of the highest importance that our actions should not be an-

22. Montgomery *Weekly Mail*, February 8, 1861.

ticipated and misrepresented through the appliances of news mongers and sensation telegrams."[23]

With the determination of the authority and procedure of the delegates and the passage of Memminger's motion, the primary organization of the convention was completed. The next step was to draft a Provisional Constitution and to elect a president and a vice president.

23. Smith, *An Address,* p. 7.

CHAPTER IV

The Provisional Constitution and the Election of a President

> *We have changed the constituent parts, but not the system of our government. The Constitution formed by our fathers is that of these Confederate States, in their exposition of it, and in the judicial construction it has received, we have a light which reveals its true meaning.*
>
> Jefferson Davis

Memminger's resolution of February 5 provided for a committee of thirteen members, with a chairman appointed by the convention, to draft the Provisional Constitution. His resolution was modified, however, so as to provide for a committee of twelve, with each state appointing two members and the selection of a chairman devolving on the committee itself. The final action of the convention on its second day was the appointment of the First Committee of Twelve; the members were Memminger and Barnwell of South Carolina, Barry and Harris of Mississippi, Anderson and Owens of Florida, Walker and Smith of Alabama, Stephens and Nisbet of Georgia, and Perkins and Kenner of Louisiana.[1]

The members of this committee were mature and experienced; they ably represented their colleagues in the drafting of the Provisional Constitution. Eleven of the members were college graduates, and the other member, Smith, had attended college. Ten were trained lawyers, two were planters, and eight men combined the pursuits of law and plantation life. The committee, like the convention, was moderate in nature, numbering seven Democrats and five Whigs among its members. And finally, all of the

1. *Journal of the Congress of the Confederate States of America, 1861-1865,* 7 volumes (Washington: Government Printing Office, 1904-1905), I, 22. (Hereinafter cited as *Confederate Journal.*)

members had previously had state legislative experience, seven had served in the United States Congress, and four had served in judicial capacities.

The committee chose Memminger of South Carolina to be its chairman. Mindful of the value of preparation and the exigency of the situation, Memminger had arrived at Montgomery with a draft for a Provisional Constitution.[2] Although this draft was probably destroyed during the Civil War,[3] Memminger published a pamphlet prior to the Montgomery Convention which sheds light on the situation. This pamphlet was entitled *Plan of a Provisional Government for the Southern Confederacy* and contained some interesting and very practical ideas.[4] Memminger's plan called for the establishment of a Provisional Government "upon the basis of the Constitution of the late United States. . . ."[5] Some parts of the plan and certain provisions of the draft of the Provisional Constitution are very similar. With few changes, the wording of the preamble of the two documents is the same. The section that gave Congress the power to lay duties and imposts solely for the purpose of raising revenue for the government later found its way into the draft of the Provisional Constitution. Moreover, the provisions of the plan that dealt with the executive and the judiciary are very much like the draft.

There were two important parts of the plan that were not used later. The legislative department was to consist of a Senate and a House of Representatives, an idea that was included in the Boyce resolutions but was rejected. Under Memminger's plan, however, the Southern senators and representatives who were in the United States Congress at the time of secession would have constituted the Provisional Congress. The second provision concerned the election, by the convention, of a "General-in-Chief of the Army,

2. Jabez Lamar Monroe Curry, *Civil History of the Government of the Confederate States of America With Some Personal Reminiscences* (Richmond: B. F. Johnson Publishing Company, 1901), p. 48. (Hereinafter cited as Curry, *Civil History.*)

3. Memminger's chief clerk and biographer, Henry Dickson Capers, was unable to find this draft; and, this writer, after an extensive search, was unable to find any trace of this document.

4. *Plan of a Provisional Government for the Southern Confederacy* (Charleston: Evans and Cogswell, 1861). Although this plan was published anonymously in Charleston, this writer believes that it was written by Memminger.

5. *Ibid.*, p. 3.

with the rank of Lieutenant-General. . . ."[6] The selection of such a person before the war, not near the end, might have made a considerable difference.

Although the First Committee of Twelve undoubtedly used Memminger's draft, its principal guide was the Constitution of the United States. The reasons for using the constitution of their forefathers are quite clear. The Montgomery delegates were not dissatisfied with the United States Constitution; indeed, they held it dear. The South had always been proud of its part in the Philadelphia Convention. Curry of Alabama wrote that "the states withdrew not from the Constitution, but from the wicked and injurious perversion of the Compact."[7] Stephens echoed the sentiments of his colleagues when he said that the "leading object was to sustain, uphold, and perpetuate the fundamental principles of the Constitution of the United States."[8] The Montgomery Convention intended to retain the old instrument of government, making such changes as history and experience directed to be urgent and necessary. Also, the delegates felt that a new constitution, based on the Federal Constitution but including new guarantees and protections, would act as a powerful incentive to the uncommitted slave states to join the Confederacy.

Since the activity of the convention would be sharply curtailed until the First Committee of Twelve made its report, Memminger's committee worked long hours and was given every consideration by the convention. In writing his brother on February 6, Stephens said: "I had dinner at 6—and then met a committee [drafting the Provisional Constitution] which did not adjourn until after 12 o'clock—The same committee meets at 10 o'clock this morning at the capital—Last night they met in my parlor."[9] The committee did meet in the Senate chamber at ten o'clock on the morning of February 6; however, it was granted leave to

6. *Ibid.*, p. 5.

7. Curry, *Civil History*, p. 50.

8. Alexander Hamilton Stephens, *A Constitutional View of the Late War Between the States*, 2 volumes (Philadelphia: National Publishing Company, 1868 and 1870), I, 339.

9. Alexander Hamilton Stephens to Linton Stephens, February 6, 1861, in Alexander Hamilton Stephens Papers (microfilm), the Southern Historical Collection, University of North Carolina. (Hereinafter cited as Alexander H. Stephens to Linton Stephens.)

continue its work during the session. After again working late into the night, the convention recessed the next morning to give the committee additional time to perfect its report. During a secret session on the afternoon of the seventh, Memminger presented the draft of the Provisional Constitution to the convention, and it was spread upon the journal.[10] On a resolution by Stephens, consideration was postponed until the proposed constitution could be printed and distributed to the convention members.[11] It had taken only two days to prepare the draft of the Provisional Constitution.

The debates on the draft of the Provisional Constitution took place, in secret session, on the afternoon and evening of February 8, 1861. The length of time given to debate is an indication of the relatively few objections that were raised to the committee report. Although haste was necessary and harmony was desired, it was inevitable that some disagreement would arise in the convention. The preamble and provisions of a draft concerning the presidential veto, the tariff, the importation of Negro slaves, and state debts aroused important discussion.

The short debates on the preamble concerned its phraseology; specifically, some mention of the Deity was desired. Although the United States Constitution did not contain such a phrase, every one of the thirty-three state constitutions in 1860, except those of Kentucky and Michigan, recognized the presence of the Deity.[12] At the very time that this subject was being discussed in the convention, a Montgomery newspaper published an editorial entitled "No God in the Constitution." After describing the over-

10. Memminger's biographer wrote: "There is, and for some time has been, a tradition ascribing the authorship of the provisional Constitution of the Confederacy to Mr. Memminger. I can find no records among the papers of Mr. Memminger that would justify me in claiming for him the authorship of this Constitution. . . . It has been stated, however, in an editorial sketch of Mr. Memminger, I find in the *Charleston Courier* of March 8th, 1888, that as chairman of the special committee appointed to draft a constitution for the provisional government of the Confederacy, he submitted the same in his own handwriting." Capers does remark on Memminger's modesty as possibly explaining his failure to claim the credit. Henry Dickson Capers, *The Life and Times of C. G. Memminger* (Richmond: Everett Waddey Company, 1893), p. 304.

11. *Confederate Journal*, I, 30.

12. Franklin Benjamin Hough, *American Constitutions: Comprising the Constitutions of Each State in the Union and of the United States*, 2 volumes (Albany: Weed, Parsons and Company, 1872), I, 439 and 668.

sight of the Philadelphia "Founding Fathers" and discussing the long time need of a statement expressing the peoples' dependence on God, the editorial concluded by saying: "Let our rulers and representatives who are about to frame a new Constitution of the Confederacy bear these facts in mind. . . . Then shall we be 'that happy people whose God is Jehovah.' "[13] Harrison of Louisiana moved for the inclusion of the phrase, "Invoking the favor of Almighty God."[14] Since there was no one like Benjamin Franklin at Montgomery to oppose the acceptance of any foreign intervention, this invocation became part of the constitution.

Later the same afternoon, Robert H. Smith of Alabama introduced an item veto provision. The general executive veto was first adopted in South Carolina in 1776, but it was discarded two years later. Massachusetts was the first state to include this provision in its constitution of 1780; Georgia adopted this idea in 1789.[15] Distrust of the governor's prerogative had so diminished by 1860 that most of the state constitutions had the executive veto provision. The delegates to the Philadelphia Convention adopted a similar provision which allowed the executive to veto legislation. This veto could, however, be overridden by a vote of two-thirds of the Congress. Smith's item veto resolution at Montgomery read: "The President may veto any appropriation or appropriations and approve any other appropriation or appropriations in the same bill."[16] The past experience of many of the delegates, particularly those who had served in Washington, guided their acceptance of this provision. All too often the President had been required to sign an appropriation bill to continue the operation of the government while, at the same time, he had to give his sanction to unacceptable measures attached to the bill. Also, this first expression of the item veto was adopted to promote greater harmony between the executive and legislative branches of government. The item veto was included in the Provisional Constitution to protect the budget estimates of the

13. Montgomery *Weekly Mail*, February 8, 1861.

14. *Confederate Journal*, I, 33.

15. Frank Williams Prescott, "A Footnote on Georgia's Constitutional History: The Item Veto of the Governors," *The Georgia Historical Quarterly*, XLII (March, 1958), 1.

16. *Confederate Journal*, I, 34.

President.[17] Smith's amendment represents the most significant addition to the draft of the Provisional Constitution. It was later included in the Permanent Constitution; and, after the Civil War, in many state constitutions.

The last deletion made in the committee draft before the convention adjourned for the evening meal concerned the powers of Congress. The provision subjected to debate gave to Congress the power to "lay and collect taxes, duties, imposts and excises for revenue necessary to pay the debts and carry on the government of the Confederacy. . . ."[18] Congress was not allowed, however, to lay taxes or excises for the purpose of promoting one branch of industry rather than another; nor was it allowed to enact a tariff for revenue on imports higher than fifteen per cent. This latter part of the provision was stricken from the draft upon motion of Kenner. Very little debate preceded the passage of this motion made by a Louisiana sugar planter. There was a tacit understanding that the tariff and related issues would be deferred until consideration of the Permanent Constitution.

Shortly after the opening of the evening secret session, the subject of the importation of Negro slaves was presented. The First Committee of Twelve had drafted a section which stated: "The importation of African negroes from any foreign country other than the slave holding States of the United States, is hereby forbidden; and Congress is required to pass such laws as shall effectively prevent the same."[19] The objections to this provision came from South Carolina, the only state in the South where there was strong support for the revival of the foreign slave trade. The leader and strong advocate of this movement for the past ten years had been Leonidas W. Spratt.[20] He had served in the state legislature, the Columbia convention, and as Commissioner to Florida. Rhett and Chesnut, the two Carolinians who raised objections to the provision in the committee draft, were not adherents to the factious activities of Spratt. Rhett wanted to include a statement that said: "The importation of African negroes

17. The executive budget provision will be treated in connection with the Permanent Constitution in Chapter V.

18. *Confederate Journal,* I, 35. 19. *Ibid.*

20. Harold Seessel Schultz, "Movement to Revive the Foreign Slave Trade 1853-1861" (Unpublished master's thesis, Duke University, 1940), p. 1.

and slaves from Africa may be prohibited by Congress."[21] Chesnut wanted to give Congress the power to prohibit such importations. Both men simply did not want the foreign slave trade so positively closed. If, at a later date, it seemed advisable to reopen this trade, they thought, it could be done without resorting to the amendment process.

Most of the secession conventions had declared themselves opposed to the revival of the foreign slave trade. The delegates at Montgomery did not accept the particularistic views of Rhett and Chesnut in this matter. The committee in writing the provision and the convention in adopting it, undoubtedly had one eye on the uncommitted slave states and the other on Europe.

One section of Article III of the committee draft called for the continuation of the system of district and circuit courts in the several states. Richard W. Walker, who was an Associate Justice of the Alabama Supreme Court, made a motion to streamline this section. The convention adopted the change that combined the two courts in favor of one district for each state. By this substitution, Walker hoped to establish a more efficient judicial system, as well as one that was less costly.

Near the end of the evening's debates, Harris of Mississippi introduced a motion concerning state debts. He proposed to have stricken from the draft the section that stated: "All sums of money expended by any State before the adoption of this constitution, in asserting and maintaining its separation from the late United States, are charged upon this confederacy, and shall be paid from its treasury."[22] This motion was agreed to by the convention. The retention of this section would have appealed to the seceded states and would have acted as an incentive to the uncommitted slave states. The experienced delegates, however, were well aware of the financial problems that plagued newly established governments. Such a provision was not practicable at that time.

Close to midnight on February 8, the debates were finally concluded. The Provisional Constitution, as amended, was read a third time and was unanimously adopted.[23] After only four

21. *Confederate Journal,* I, 36.
22. *Ibid.,* p. 38.
23. *Ibid.,* p. 39.

days, the Provisional Constitution had been drafted by the First Committee of Twelve, debated, and adopted.

Before the meeting of the Montgomery Convention, there was wide speculation as to what would be the name of the new Confederacy.[24] The day after the adoption of the Provisional Constitution, James T. Harrison of Mississippi wrote to his wife and said: "The new Government or Confederacy, as we call it, is named the Confederate States of America. We omitted the word 'United' in the old name and substituted 'Confederate,' so as still to be known abroad as American citizens and the word Confederate truly expresses our present conditions."[25] Some of the delegates were not content with the adopted name. T. R. R. Cobb wrote: "By the way I tried to get the name 'The Republic of Washington' but failed. The name . . . does not give satisfaction and I have no doubt that it will be changed for the permanent constitution."[26]

The Preamble is especially significant for an appreciation of the Provisional Constitution and, indeed, for an understanding of the constitutional philosophy of the Montgomery membership.

> We, the Deputies of the Sovereign and Independent States of South Carolina, Georgia, Florida, Alabama, Mississippi, and Louisiana, invoking the favor of almighty God, do hereby, in behalf of these States, ordain and establish this Constitution for the Provisional Government of the same: to continue one year from the inauguration of the President, or until a permanent Constitution or Confederation between the said States shall be put in operation, whichsoever shall first occur.[27]

The Provisional Constitution stands as a general answer to the enigmatic question concerning the nature of the Union. The Preamble gives a specific answer to the long standing debate as

24. Some of the suggested names were "The Gulf States Confederacy," "Columbia," "Washingtonia," and "The Southern United States."

25. James Thomas Harrison to [his wife], February 9, 1861, in Charles Colcock Jones, "Autograph Letters and Portraits of the Signers of the Constitution of the Confederate States" (Augusta, Georgia, 1884), a scrapbook, Manuscript Department, Duke University. (Hereinafter cited as Jones, "Letters and Portraits of the Signers.")

26. Thomas Reade Rootes Cobb to [his wife], February 12, 1861, in Thomas Reade Rootes Cobb Papers, Special Collections Division, University of Georgia. The Cobb letters quoted henceforth will all be to his wife. (Hereinafter cited as T. R. R. Cobb to his wife.)

27. *Confederate Journal,* I, 899.

to whether the United States was a confederation of sovereign states or a sovereign union of people. The Montgomery delegates viewed the United States as a union of sovereign and independent states joined together by a compact or treaty called the Constitution of the United States. They made this state sovereignty concept explicit in the Preamble and made it the theme of the Provisional Constitution. The phraseology of the Confederate Preamble was changed, wrote Curry of Alabama, so as "to assert the derivative character of the Federal Government and to exclude the conclusion which Webster and others had sought to draw from the phrase, 'We the people of the United States.' "[28] To insure an understanding of the derivative character of the Confederate Government, such words as "delegated," "expressly granted," and "expressly delegated" were used in the constitution.

The second part of the Preamble shows that T. R. R. Cobb's suggestion as to the duration of the Provisional Government was accepted. Both the Provisional Government and the Provisional Constitution expired upon the inauguration of Jefferson Davis as permanent President of the Confederacy on February 18, 1862.

The legislative power of the Provisional Government was vested in a unicameral Congress. Moreover, upon the adoption of the constitution, the Montgomery Convention became the Provisional Congress. Harris of Mississippi and Walker of Alabama had opposed this plan during the debates. William S. Wilson wrote to a friend: "Our delegation [Mississippi] opposed this scheme thinking that . . . we were virtually instructed to ask [for] a Constitution giving the legislative power to a Senate and House as in the old Constitution. . . . The majority however finally determined that the exigency required more prompt and decisive action."[29] The necessity of proceeding immediately led to a provision whereby the Congress would also exercise executive powers until the inauguration of the Provisional President. Moreover, all bills and resolutions passed by the Congress would become law without presidential approval, during the interim.[30] Thus, the Montgomery Convention was given both legislative

28. Jabez Lamar Monroe Curry, *The Southern States of the American Union* (Richmond: B. F. Johnson Publishing Company, 1895), p. 195.

29. William Sidney Wilson to H. G. Eliett, February 9, 1861, in Jones, "Letters and Portraits of the Signers."

and executive powers with which to give life and direction to the new government.

The president and vice president of the new government were to be elected by the Congress, each state casting one vote with a majority of the whole being necessary for election. These executive officers were to hold their positions for one year, or until the Provisional Government was superceded by a Permanent Government, whichever occurred first. The president would receive a compensation of $25,000 per year.[31]

One feature of the executive article refers to a constitutional problem that is evident in the United States Constitution today. How to determine the inability of the President and who is to make this determination are questions unanswered by the United States Constitution.[32] The Montgomery delegates were aware of this issue in 1861; indeed, they offered a solution. Part of the second article stated: "In case of removal of the President from office, or of his death, resignation, or inability to discharge the powers and duties of the said office, (which inability shall be determined by a vote of two-thirds of the Congress), the same shall devolve on the Vice-President. . . ."[33] Giving Congress the power to determine presidential inability is debatable, but at least the delegates adopted a solution.

Although the Provisional Constitution, like the Federal Constitution, provided that the judicial power of the government would be vested in a Supreme Court and inferior courts, the third article of the two documents differed in several respects. The Confederate Constitution stated: "Each state shall constitute a District, in which there shall be a court called a District Court. . . ."[34] This restriction of each state to a single judicial district is unusual since, under the United States Constitution, each state had no less than two districts. On May 21, 1861, Congress was empowered, by the adoption of the only amendment to either of the Confederate Constitutions, to increase the

30. *Confederate Journal,* I, 901. 31. *Ibid.,* p. 904.

32. An excellent survey of this problem with some interesting solutions is found in *Presidential Inability* (Washington: Government Printing Office, 1956). See also Ruth Caridad Silva, *Presidential Succession* (Ann Arbor: University of Michigan Press, 1951).

33. *Confederate Journal,* I, 904. 34. *Ibid.,* p. 905.

number of districts in each state.[35] The two documents differed also in that the Montgomery delegates accepted Walker's motion to abolish the costly dual system of district and circuit courts in favor of the simpler system of district courts.

The judicial article of the Provisional Constitution provided further that "the Supreme Court shall be constituted of all District Judges, a majority of whom shall be a quorum. . . ."[36] This was a temporary arrangement and, of course, differed radically from the United States Supreme Court. Nevertheless, the idea of organizing the highest court in the land with the judges of the next lower court is unusual. This is especially true since the concept "had been tried out in many Southern States and had been abandoned everywhere except in South Carolina, where the plan had been successfully questioned,"[37] that is, altered. Article III was drastically modified in the Permanent Constitution.

The state rights philosophy, that particularistic argument committed to the defense of the rights of the individual states as opposed to the expansion of national power, and the past experience of the delegates combined to direct the inclusion of a strong fugitive slave provision in the constitution. Indeed, with the exceptions of the Rhett and Chesnut motions, the slavery issue was not discussed. There was a general understanding that debate on this vital subject would be delayed until the Permanent Constitution was drafted.

The amendment provision of the constitution was additional testimony of the transitory nature of the document. Article V stated: "The Congress, by a vote of two-thirds, may, at any time, alter or amend this Constitution."[38] This provision was used only once when the Congress was given the authority to enlarge the number of judicial districts. With this simplified amending process, the Congress acquired yet another source of power and authority. The Montgomery Convention adopted a constitution that gave it legislative and executive power; and, by Article V,

35. *Ibid.*, p. 909.
36. *Ibid.*, p. 906.

37. William Morrison Robinson, Jr., *Justice in Grey* (Cambridge: Harvard University Press, 1941), p. 421. This is the definitive study of the Confederate judicial system.

38. *Confederate Journal*, I, 908.

the convention was authorized to continue in its capacity as a constituent assembly.

The final article of the Provisional Constitution gave the Congress the power to admit other states.[39] It was under this provision that Texas was admitted to the Confederacy on March 2, 1861, as well as the other states that ultimately made up the Confederate States of America.

A significant omission from the Provisional Constitution concerned the prohibition against congressmen holding any other office under the Confederate government. Such a prohibition was a feature of the United States Constitution. Alexander H. Stephens was responsible for the exclusion of this provision from the committee draft. He explained his reasons for doing so in a letter to his brother, in which he wrote: "All I wanted was that the President should not be forbidden to go to the House of Congress in the selection of his cabinet. I think it would be better still to require him to do it—but that is not so important. . . ."[40] During the debates on the constitution, Withers of South Carolina sponsored a motion which sought to include a prohibitory statement. Had this motion passed, the executive branch of the Provisional Government would have been deprived of some of the South's outstanding leaders. Following Stephens' suggestion, the Congress was able to elect him Vice President of the Confederacy. Moreover, Davis could select Congressmen Memminger, Toombs, and Reagan to be members of his cabinet.

Stephens best captured the spirit and objective of the Provisional Constitution when he wrote: "It is the constitution of the United States with such changes and modifications as are necessary to meet the exigencies of the times. . . ."[41] In the Preamble and in such provisions as the item veto, the clause on presidential inability, and the abolition of the old circuit court system, the constitution showed the results of considerable thought and insight into the problems of a new Confederacy. The constitution also showed signs of its hasty origin. This is particularly true in light of the important provisions that are not

39. *Ibid.*, p. 901.
40. Alexander H. Stephens to Linton Stephens, February 17, 1861.
41. *Ibid.*

included in the framework of government. Evidence of haste is also seen in such provisions as those defining the Supreme Court and the amending process. One of the two most significant general features of the Provisional Constitution is that it was written under the pressure of time and as a temporary document. The best example is the failure of the constitution to include a provision to provide for ratification. The second general feature of significance is the tacit understanding among the members that such important issues as slavery, internal improvements, and the tariff would be deferred until the Permanent Constitution was drafted.

After the adoption of the Provisional Constitution on the evening of February 8, Miles of South Carolina "moved that the Congress proceed to the election of a President immediately."[42] This motion was defeated and the election was postponed until open session the following morning. Speculation as to who would, or should, be the first President of the Confederacy was much in evidence in the local papers before the election. The person most often mentioned before the meeting of the convention was William L. Yancey. Other men who were prominently mentioned for the top executive post or for positions in the cabinet were Cobb, Stephens, and Toombs of Georgia, and Rhett of South Carolina. Although Jefferson Davis was referred to as being acceptable as president, every poll that was published highly recommended him for the position of Secretary of War.[43]

The letters of several of the Montgomery delegates reflect the climate of opinion within the convention before the election. On February 3, T. R. R. Cobb wrote: "As to the Provisional President of the Confederacy the strongest current is for Jeff Davis. Howell [Cobb] and Mr. Toombs are both spoken of and there seems to be a good deal of difficulty in settling down on any person."[44] Three days later he wrote: "There is but little speculation as to the probable President. Jeff Davis is most prominent, Howell next. Toombs, Stephens, Yancey and even Joe Brown [Governor of

42. *Confederate Journal,* I, 39.

43. Montgomery *Weekly Mail,* January 31, February 9, 1861; Montgomery *Daily Post,* February 18, 1861.

44. T. R. R. Cobb to his wife, February 3, 1861.

Georgia] are talked about."[45] And on the day preceding the election, Cobb wrote: "Stephens is *looming up* for President since Howell's name has been almost withdrawn. I still think Davis has the best chance."[46] Although not mentioned by the younger Cobb, R. B. Rhett was also under consideration. Thus, on the evening before the election, Davis, Howell Cobb, Toombs, Stephens, Rhett, Yancey, and Joe Brown had their supporters within the convention.

Some of the extreme secessionists in the Alabama delegation favored Yancey, but the delegation as a whole did not support him. This group came to the convention promised to the support of Robert Toombs of Georgia, but changed its mind. In late January, 1861, Francis Meriwether Gilmer, inter-state Commissioner from Alabama, met with Virginia leaders in Richmond. Gilmer found that Senators James Murray Mason and Robert M. T. Hunter were much alarmed at the possibility that Yancey might be elected President of the Confederacy.[47] The Virginians were quite receptive, however, to the name of Jefferson Davis. Believing that "upon the cooperation of Virginia depended the cooperation of the border States,"[48] Gilmer reported the Virginia preference to Governor Moore in Montgomery. Governor Moore conferred with the Alabama delegation, and they "upon receipt of this information from Virginia, changed their purpose and supported Mr. Davis."[49]

Before leaving for Montgomery, Alexander M. Clayton wrote to Davis to ascertain whether or not he would accept the presidency. Davis replied that he preferred the position of Commander-in-Chief of the Army, "but that he would give himself to the cause in any capacity whatever."[50] Had Davis let it be

45. *Ibid.*, February 6, 1861. 46. *Ibid.*, February 8, 1861.

47. Mason was later Confederate envoy to England and a participant in the celebrated "Trent Affair." Hunter, a good friend of Davis, was the second Confederate Secretary of State.

48. Francis Meriwether Gilmer, "Memoir Concerning the Organization of the Confederate Government," *Jefferson Davis Constitutionalist: His Letters, Papers and Speeches,* 10 volumes, edited by Dunbar Rowland (Jackson: Mississippi Department of Archives and History, 1923), VIII, 463.

49. *Ibid.*

50. Alexander Mosby Clayton to Memphis *Appeal,* June 21, 1870, quoted in Jefferson Davis, *The Rise and Fall of the Confederate Government,* 2 volumes (New York: Thomas Yoseloff, 1958), I, 237.

known that he would accept only the top army position, the Mississippi delegation would probably have supported a Georgian. As it was, the delegation was firm in its support for Davis.

The Louisiana delegation, on the evening of February 8, was still undecided. Duncan F. Kenner wrote: "The name of Mr. Rhett, of South Carolina, was probably most frequently mentioned than any other person, next to Mr. Davis."[51] Several of the Louisiana delegates looked to Howell Cobb of Georgia.

A majority of the three-man Florida delegation favored Davis. While a member of President Pierce's Cabinet, Davis had aided Anderson in securing a political appointment; moreover, Anderson admired Davis for his knowledge of military affairs. Jackson Morton had served with Davis in the United States Senate and had supported his stand in 1850. Owens, who had family ties in South Carolina, leaned toward R. B. Rhett, or a person of his choice.

South Carolina and Georgia, the two most influential delegations at Montgomery, were split in their choice of a president for the new Confederacy. William Porcher Miles received a letter from a fellow South Carolinian two days before the election. It said: "I think there can be no doubt that the popular expectation is that Cobb will be President and Davis Lieut. General. People would be equally satisfied with Davis as President but one of the two they do expect."[52] This opinion is seconded with an amendment by Chesnut's wife, who wrote in her diary: "Everybody wanted Mr. Davis to be either General-in-Chief or President. Keitt and Boyce and a party preferred Howell Cobb for President, and the fire-eaters *per se* wanted Barnwell Rhett."[53] Rhett wanted very much to be president; indeed, he felt that he had earned a right to the office. He did not press his candidacy upon his colleagues and the delegation did not unite behind him. Seeing that his chances were hopeless, Rhett supported Howell Cobb. He was joined in this opinion by Keitt, Boyce, and Miles,

51. *Ibid.*, pp. 238-39.

52. William Henry Trescott to William Porcher Miles, February 6, 1861, in William Porcher Miles Papers, Southern Historical Collection, University of North Carolina.

53. Mary Boykin Chesnut, *A Diary from Dixie*, edited by Ben Ames Williams (Boston: Houghton Mifflin Company, 1949), p. 5.

but this was not a majority of the eight-man South Carolina delegation. On the day of the election, Robert W. Barnwell wrote: "I desire that Jeff Davis should be President rather [than] Cobb. I think that Davis will be elected though without much zeal."[54] Chesnut also favored Davis, but Memminger and Withers were undecided. Thus, in the South Carolina delegation, four supported Cobb, two supported Davis, and two were undecided.

With three men of presidential caliber, the Georgia delegation at Montgomery, like South Carolina, was split as to their choice. Stephens, Toombs, and Cobb had worked together for compromise in 1850 and, during succeeding years, the two former men had remained very close friends. Then, in 1860, because of the presidential election of that year and because of Stephens' opposition to secession, the two old Whigs had a parting of the ways. Cobb was very wary of Stephens because of the position he took on secession. The relationship between the three men was somewhat uncertain during the first days at Montgomery although all three certainly felt that they were qualified for the presidency.

On the day before the convention assembled, Howell Cobb wrote to his wife: "From all I hear there is a general disposition to make me president of the convention. It is thought that my taking that position will exclude me from the Presidency of the Confederacy and some of my friends doubted on that account the policy of my taking it. In this I differed from them and have determined to follow my own judgement."[55] Three days later he wrote: "Little or nothing is said about President of the Confederacy, and yet we shall elect one in a day or two, perhaps before you get this letter. So far from making an effort to obtain this position, I have frankly said to my friends that I greatly prefer not to be put there. . . . I rather think Jeff. Davis will be the man, though I have not heard any one say that he is for him." Referring to the absence of any electioneering in the convention,

54. Robert Woodward Barnwell to James Lawrence Orr, February 9, 1861, in James Lawrence Orr Papers, Southern Historical Collection, University of North Carolina.

55. Howell Cobb to his wife, February 3, 1861, in Ulrich Bonnell Phillips, ed., *The Correspondence of Robert Toombs, Alexander H. Stephens and Howell Cobb*, American Historical Association, *Annual Report, 1911* (Washington: Government Printing Office, 1913), II, 536.

Cobb concluded his letter by saying: "The truth is—and it is credible to our public men here—there is no effort to put forward any man, but all seem to desire in everything to do what is best to be done to advance and prosper the cause of our independence."[56] Although Cobb's letters to his wife veiled his ambition, they did affirm his unwillingness to seek actively the presidency.

On the night that the Provisional Constitution was adopted and an election ordered for the next day, what T. R. R. Cobb called "a counting of noses" took place.[57] It was found that Alabama, Mississippi, and Florida supported Jefferson Davis. The Louisiana delegation, although still undecided, leaned toward Howell Cobb. South Carolina was split between Davis and Cobb with Memminger and Withers undecided. And the Georgia delegation evidenced its confusion by showing support for Cobb, Toombs, and Stephens. Thus, three states favored Davis and he had strength in Louisiana and South Carolina; Cobb probably had one state and had support in two others; and Stephens and Toombs had support in only their own delegation. Although Davis was close, none of the four men had a majority vote of the six states. At this critical point in the convention, "Howell immediately announced his wish that Davis should be unanimously elected."[58] With this information, the delegations, except that of Georgia, met in secret caucus to determine their position for the election the next day at noon. The Georgia delegation decided to meet the next morning.

In giving his support to Davis, Cobb, of course, had made a key move. He undoubtedly realized that to win the election he would have to wage a contest. As President of the Congress, Cobb perhaps realized more than most the necessity of a quick and uncontested election. Moreover, it was very important that the Congress present to the uncommitted slave states in particular, but to the North and to Europe as well, a picture of unanimity in the election of their leader.

The indecision within the influential Georgia delegation was significant and was best accounted for by the personalities in-

56. *Ibid.*, p. 537.
57. T. R. R. Cobb to his wife, February 11, 1861.
58. *Ibid.*

volved. By election eve, the Cobb brothers and Stephens were most unfriendly toward each other; Stephens and Toombs, however, had renewed their warm and close relationship. One can imagine how the third side of the triangle was drawn by an incident described by Stephens in a letter to his brother. Stephens wrote: "He [Toombs] never lets Cobb pass without giving him a lick. The other night in high glee he told Cobb . . . that he had done more for secession than any other man. He depressed the currency. . . . He left Washington without a dollar in the Treasury—He did not even leave Old Buck [Buchanan] even two quarters to put on his eyes when he died."[59] Cobb had been very close to President Buchanan and did not appreciate Toombs' humor.

The Georgia caucus met at ten o'clock on the morning of February 9. Stephens moved to give Toombs a complimentary vote from the delegation. T. R. R. Cobb explained that a majority of the states had conferred and agreed on Davis and that Stephens' proposal would place Toombs and the delegation in a delicate position.[60] Toombs was apparently surprised by Cobb's statement, and Judge Crawford was sent out to canvass the other delegations. Crawford found Cobb's explanation to be correct. Toombs thereupon returned Stephens' compliment by suggesting his friend for Vice President. There being a majority for this action, the delegation left for the Senate chamber.

Before Congress assembled, both South Carolina and Georgia had decided in favor of Davis, thus giving the Mississippian the unanimous support of the six states. The best explanation of the final selection of Davis seems to be as follows. Since Rhett and Yancey had not been supported by their own states, and in as much as their election would have been most objectionable to the upper South, both men were soon discounted as possible candidates. Although Governor Brown of Georgia was mentioned, he was never seriously considered for the presidency. Stephens had scattered individual support; however, the renewal of his *entiente cordial* with Toombs, coupled with his strong Union leanings, disqualified his candidacy. From first to last, the three

59. Alexander H. Stephens to Linton Stephens, February 11, 1861.
60. T. R. R. Cobb to his wife, February 11, 1861.

men most seriously considered were Davis, Cobb, and Toombs. Neither Toombs nor Cobb could have won the election without a struggle. As Cobb stated, there was no electioneering, management, or intriguing by any of the candidates; indeed, there could be none if unanimity was to be maintained. The extreme and vocal position Toombs took on secession, his frequent drinking to excess,[61] the fact that his own delegation was split, and that another very capable man, Jefferson Davis, was available, probably best accounts for his failure to become President. There were Democrats at the convention who remembered Cobb's defection in 1850. This, plus the split in his delegation, his failure to make a contest and his strong desire for unanimity, and the feeling among many delegates that his election to the Presidency of Congress was honor enough, probably explains Cobb's defeat. The simple conclusion is that Davis had substantial support from the outset, and that his absence from Montgomery aided his election. Moreover, his national reputation and his acceptability by the upper South were important factors leading to his election as President of the Confederacy.

When the Congress assembled, and after Howell Cobb administered the constitutional oath to the Congress, swearing support to the newly adopted Provisional Constitution, the membership proceeded to the election. Jefferson Davis received six votes and was "duly declared unanimously elected President of the Provisional Government."[62]

Immediately after Davis was elected, Alexander Hamilton Stephens received six votes and was "duly declared unanimously elected Vice-President of the Provisional Government."[63] Some of the delegates were bitter at Stephens' election. T. R. R. Cobb

61. In a confidential letter, Stephens wrote to his brother the following words: "I concur with you as to Mr. Toombs' superior qualifications for the Presidency. . . . And I have but little doubt that he would have been elected but for one thing. . . . He was in the habit of getting tight every day at dinner. One day in particular, about two days before the election, he got quite tight at dinner and went to a party in town *tighter* than I ever saw him—too tight for his character and reputation by far. I think that evening's exhibition settled the Presidency where it fell." Alexander H. Stephens to Linton Stephens, February 23, 1861. Toombs' drinking was probably not decisive; and it is interesting to note that after the Civil War, Stephens attributed his friend's failure to be elected solely to the split in the Georgia delegation (Stephens, *A Constitutional View,* II, 329-33).

62. *Confederate Journal,* I, 40. 63. *Ibid.*

wrote: "we have swallowed it with as good grace as we could. The man who has fought against our rights and liberty is selected to wear the laurels of our victory." Cobb was correct in seeing the election as a "disposition to conciliate the Union men by giving the second place in the Confederacy to a cooperationist. . . ."[64] Moreover, the election of Stephens satisfied the claim of Georgia to one of the top offices in the new government.

At one o'clock on the following Monday afternoon, February 11, a group of some five hundred ladies and gentlemen gathered in the Senate chamber of the Capitol. Stephens stood behind the rostrum to give his response to the official notification of his election. Many of the spectators had come in the hope that Stephens would offer a formal speech on the issues of the day but, since Davis would be inaugurated in only seven days, Stephens considered such a course improper.[65] He tendered his appreciation to his colleagues and closed with a few remarks of a general nature. At that time, the President of the Congress administered to Stephens the oath prescribed by the Provisional Constitution. The Vice President was moved by the occasion, by the honor, and by the fact that it was the anniversary of his birth.[66]

Jefferson Davis arrived in Montgomery on Saturday, February 16. That evening a very large crowd gathered before the Exchange Hotel and, in response to enthusiastic calls, the President-elect appeared on the balcony. Davis was introduced to Montgomery by William L. Yancey who, on this occasion, said: "The man and the hour have met. We may now hope that prosperity, honor and victory await his administration."[67] Davis delivered a few brief remarks to the crowd and retired to his rooms.

On Monday morning, February 18, 1861, Montgomery was ready for the inauguration of the first President of the Confederacy. A Committee on Arrangements had been appointed by the Congress, and preparations had been in progress for some days. At ten o'clock in the morning, upwards of ten thousand persons lined the main street and stood in front of the white Capitol building. In front of the Exchange Hotel, Davis,

64. T. R. R. Cobb to his wife, February 9, 1861.
65. Alexander H. Stephens to Linton Stephens, February 11, 1861.
66. *Ibid.*
67. Montgomery *Weekly Advertiser,* February 20, 1861.

Stephens, the Reverend Dr. Basil Manly, and a military aide got into a finely fashioned carriage that was drawn by six iron grey horses. With a signal from the marshal, the parade began. A local newspaper described the occasion: "As the procession moved up Market street, amid the roar of cannon, the inspiring strains of martial music, and the cheers of the multitude, the scene was beyond description."[68] After the procession arrived at the Capitol, Davis, accompanied by Howell Cobb and followed by Stephens, Dr. Manly, and the Committee on Arrangements, walked to the Hall of Congress and was escorted to the chair. Upon a formal motion, the Congress "repaired, in company with the President-elect, to the front of the Capitol for the purpose of inaugurating the President."[69] Howell Cobb presented Davis to the Congress, who occupied the seats under the portico and behind the speaker's rostrum, and Dr. Manly gave the invocation. Then, Davis came forward to give his inaugural address.

Near the end of his speech, Davis referred to the Provisional Constitution. He said: "We have changed the constituent parts, but not the system of our government. The Constitution formed by our fathers is that of these Confederate States, in their exposition of it, and in the judicial construction it has received, we have a light which reveals its true meaning."[70] He concluded his address by asking for divine guidance for himself and his people. Howell Cobb came forward, administered the oath prescribed by the Constitution, whereupon Jefferson Davis became Provisional President of the Confederate States of America.

The Congress had assembled at noon, an hour before the inauguration ceremonies. At that time, Shorter of Alabama, the Chairman of the Committee on Engrossments, reported that the Provisional Constitution had been duly enrolled on parchment, and that it was ready for the signatures of the members.[71] Shorter then moved that the members proceed to affix their signatures to the document before the inauguration. The enrolled Constitution was laid out on the table in front of the rostrum, at which time Howell Cobb came down from his chair and signed his name as President of the Congress. He then ordered that the delegations

68. *Ibid.*

69. *Confederate Journal,* I, 63.

70. *Ibid.,* p. 66.

71. *Ibid.,* p. 63.

come forward in the order of their appearance in the Preamble, that is, according to the geographic location of the state, from east to west. The members signed the Provisional Constitution in the following order: those from South Carolina, first; Georgia, second; Florida, third; Alabama, fourth; Mississippi, fifth; and those from Louisiana last. The President announced that the Constitution had been duly signed by all of the members present.

After the inauguration ceremonies, the Congress reassembled. Several of the delegates who had been absent at the noon session came forward and affixed their names to the document. On March 2, 1861, when the Texas delegation was admitted to the Congress, its seven members were allowed to sign the Constitution. A total of fifty men placed their signatures to the Provisional Constitution.[72]

Although the Montgomery Convention had drafted, debated, and adopted a Provisional Constitution, and had, as a Congress, elected a President and a Vice President, its most important work was still ahead. Continuing its role as a constituent assembly, the Montgomery Convention still had to frame a Permanent Constitution of the Confederate States.

72. The original Provisional Constitution of the Confederate States of America is in the Confederate Museum at Richmond, Virginia.

CHAPTER V

The Permanent Constitution: Part I

The two great vital powers of all governments are the laying of taxes and the expenditure of taxes. These powers decide the character of every government, whether it is limited or unlimited, federal or consolidated. . . .

Robert Barnwell Rhett

The first step toward the erection of a permanent government was taken by the convention when it adopted Robert Barnwell Rhett's motion of February 9, 1861, that called for the appointment of a committee to consider "a constitution for a permanent government of the States represented in this convention."[1] On February 9, 1861, the Congress appointed a Second Committee of Twelve to draft a Permanent Constitution. The members of the committee were Rhett and Chesnut of South Carolina, Clayton and Harris of Mississippi, Morton and Owens of Florida, Walker and Smith of Alabama, Toombs and T. R. R. Cobb of Georgia, and DeClouet and Sparrow of Louisiana.[2]

The Second Committee of Twelve compared favorably in maturity and experience with the First Committee of Twelve. The group that drafted the Permanent Constitution numbered nine college graduates, two who had attended college, Rhett and Smith, and one, Clayton, who had no college training. Nine were trained lawyers, three were planters, and, like the first committee, eight men combined the pursuits of law and plantation life. The Second Committee of Twelve was moderate in nature having six Democrats and six Whigs; only Morton, Smith, and Walker had opposed secession. All of the members had legislative experience on the state level, five had served in the United States Con-

1. *Journal of the Congress of the Confederate States of America, 1861-1865,* 7 volumes (Washington: Government Printing Office, 1904-1905), I, 41. (Hereinafter cited as *Confederate Journal.*)

2. *Ibid.,* p. 42. Harris, Owens, Walker, and Smith had served on the First Committee of Twelve.

gress, and four had served in judicial capacities. The principal difference between the two committees was that the Second Committee of Twelve included more men who had served in a legislative capacity on the national level.

The committee chose Rhett of South Carolina to be its chairman. But Rhett had not come to Montgomery with a draft already prepared, as had Memminger. Rhett's participation in the debates on the Permanent Constitution indicates, however, that he brought to the committee meetings a series of provisions which he sought to have included in the draft. He apparently used his influence to urge the inclusion, in the draft, of provisions which would establish free trade, abolish the three-fifths clause for representation, prohibit the appropriation of money for internal improvements, define the right of secession, exclude the admittance of non-slave states, restrict the term of the president, abolish the federal review of decisions by the state courts, and define an amendment process more in line with the philosophy of John C. Calhoun. The draft presented to the convention contained some of these provisions; Rhett presented the others to the delegates during the debates on the Permanent Constitution.

The Second Committee of Twelve had some significant documents to guide their work. The most important of these was the United States Constitution. The Federal Constitution was of more value to Rhett's committee than it had been to Memminger's committee, inasmuch as the former group of men were preparing a framework for a permanent government.

The Provisional Constitution of the Confederacy was another important guide for Rhett's committee. As a temporary document, it often pointed the way for needed corrections and additions. Moreover, the first constitution contained provisions, such as those concerning the item veto and the district court system, which could, with ample justification, be carried over to the Permanent Constitution. Finally, on the day that the Second Committee of Twelve was appointed, the state of Alabama placed its Supreme Court Library at the disposal of the committee.[3] The library not only served as a place for reference work, but also

3. *Ibid.*, p. 31.

as a convenient place where the committee could meet from time to time.

Rhett and his eleven colleagues were very busy men. While drafting the Permanent Constitution, these men had to continue in their capacity as working members of the Provisional Congress. T. R. R. Cobb gives an intimate picture of the tight schedule under which many of the delegates functioned when he refers to his own activities in a letter to his wife. On February 13, he wrote: "I am working *hard.* Immediately after breakfast the Judiciary Committee meets [Cobb was a member]. We work until 12 o'clock. Congress then sits until 3 or 4. From that time until night I work on my Committee on Printing [Cobb was chairman]. At 7:30 o'clock P.M. the Committee on the Constitution meets and works until 10. Then I have my correspondence to bring up."[4] And again on the fourteenth, he wrote: "The Committee [of Twelve] work on it every night. . . . We have agreed to go over it by paragraphs for revisals and then we shall report it. I am sure it will be adopted by the last of next week and then I am for *love* and *home.*"[5] Cobb and his colleagues worked from nine to twelve hours a day. This exhausting schedule was necessary in order to complete a time table which included the drafting of the Permanent Constitution by February 28, and holding debate on and adopting this document by March 11, 1861.

During the nineteen days that the Second Committee of Twelve worked to draft a Permanent Constitution, the Provisional Government forged ahead in its task of establishing an operational government. On the day that the committee was appointed, a bill was passed which continued in force all of the laws of the United States not inconsistent with the Provisional Constitution.[6] A few days later, an act was adopted which continued the important customs service in the ports of the Confederacy.

A third significant legislative measure was enacted during

4. Thomas Reade Rootes Cobb to his wife, February 13, 1861, in Thomas Reade Rootes Cobb Papers, Special Collections Division, University of Georgia. (Hereinafter cited as T. R. R. Cobb to his wife.)

5. T. R. R. Cobb to his wife, February 14, 1861.

6. *Confederate Journal,* I, 41. Harris of Mississippi, who introduced this bill, had unsuccessfully attempted to have such a statement included in the Provisional Constitution.

this time. The states whose commerce depended on the free navigation of the Mississippi River were concerned at the establishment of a new Confederacy. The delegates at Montgomery from Mississippi, Louisiana, and Alabama had been instructed by their state conventions to seek early approval and assurance of unrestricted commerce on the great river. On February 25, President Davis signed an act "to declare and establish the free navigation of the Mississippi River."[7]

These early acts not only sought to oil the wheels of the new government, but also to assure other nations of the peaceful intentions of the Confederacy. To transmit this peaceful attitude, Confederate commissioners were accredited to Washington, D. C., London, and Paris. President Davis nominated and the Congress confirmed the appointment of three men to the Washington post, in the words of Davis, "to the end that by negotiation all questions between the two Governments might be so adjusted as to avoid war. . . ."[8] The following day the appointment of two commissioners to London and one to Paris was confirmed.[9] These men sought the early recognition of the Confederacy by Great Britain and France. William L. Yancey, the most able of the three commissioners, was probably nominated by Davis because the President felt that the Alabamian was too influential to ignore in the formation of the government and too troublesome to keep nearby. Significantly, Yancey is never once mentioned by name in Davis' *The Rise and Fall of the Confederate Government.*

A significant development during the time that the Permanent Constitution was being drafted was the organization of the Cabinet. On the afternoon of his inauguration, Davis met with Robert W. Barnwell of South Carolina. Later the same day, Barnwell wrote to his wife saying, "though quite confidentially he offered me the place of Secretary of State . . . I declined it most peremp-

7. *Ibid.*, p. 82.

8. Jefferson Davis, *The Rise and Fall of the Confederate Government*, 2 volumes (New York: Thomas Yoseloff, 1958), I, 246. (Hereinafter cited as Davis, *Rise and Fall.*) The three commissioners were A. B. Roman of Louisiana, Martin J. Crawford, a delegate to the Montgomery Convention from Georgia, and John Forsyth of Alabama.

9. *Confederate Journal*, I, 93. William L. Yancey of Alabama and A. Dudley Mann of Georgia were sent to London, and Pierre A. Rost of Louisiana was sent to Paris.

torily."[10] Barnwell declined Davis' offer because the delegates from South Carolina had decided to recommend Christopher G. Memminger for Secretary of the Treasury. Barnwell and his colleagues were successful as Memminger was appointed to the Treasury post, even though President Davis preferred Robert Toombs.[11]

Davis then asked Toombs to join his Cabinet as Secretary of State. Toombs wrote the President a lengthy letter on February 20, explaining his reasons for declining the Cabinet position. The Georgian felt that he could best serve his country in a legislative capacity; he wrote: "The formation of our permanent Constitution, next to the preservation of our national existence is unquestionably our greatest work. . . . I should be much weakened in the advocacy of the changes which I propose, both in Congress and before our State Convention, by occupying an executive department."[12] Upon the entreaty of the President, however, Toombs allowed his nomination to be affirmed by the Congress two days later.

On the same day that Toombs and Memminger were confirmed in their appointments, Leroy Pope Walker of Alabama became Secretary of War. A few days later, other members of Davis' Cabinet were nominated and confirmed by the Congress. Stephen Russell Mallory of Florida became Secretary of the Navy, Judah Philip Benjamin of Louisiana became Attorney General, and John Henninger Reagan of Texas became Postmaster General. Of the six men who formed the first Cabinet of the Confederacy, three (Toombs, Memminger, and Reagan) were delegates to the Montgomery Convention and therefore members of the Provisional Congress.[13]

While the Congress and the President were giving form and direction to the Provisional Government, the Second Committee

10. Robert Woodward Barnwell to his wife, February 18, 1861, in Charles Colcock Jones, "Autograph Letters and Portraits of the Signers of the Constitution of the Confederate States of America" (Augusta, Georgia, 1884), a scrapbook, Manuscript Department, Duke University.

11. Davis, *Rise and Fall*, I, 242.

12. Robert Toombs to Jefferson Davis, February 20, 1861, in Jones, "Letters and Portraits of the Signers."

13. See Rembert Wallace Patrick, *Jefferson Davis and His Cabinet* (Baton Rouge: Louisiana State University Press, 1944).

of Twelve was making steady progress on the draft for the Permanent Constitution. Chairman Rhett reported to the Congress on February 26 that the draft was nearing completion. He explained to his colleagues that one half of the draft had been sent to the printer, and that he hoped to present the completed document in a few days.[14]

On the day following Rhett's interim report, the Congress resolved to include the recently arrived Texas delegation when the constitutional draft was debated, even though Texas would not be formally admitted to the Confederacy until March 2. And, on the afternoon of February 28 while in secret session, the Congress voted to have the Secretary of the Congress keep a separate journal of the debates on the Permanent Constitution.[15]

Rhett presented the completed draft to the Congress on the same afternoon. This document was not, however, to be debated by the Congress. On a motion by Jackson Morton of Florida, the Congress resolved that each day at noon it would resolve itself back into convention in order to consider the draft of the Permanent Constitution, "until the same shall be disposed of."[16] Thus, between February 28 and March 11, 1861, the delegates to Montgomery acted as a Provisional Congress in the mornings and as a convention or constituent assembly in the afternoons. The long and often heated convention debates were held in secret session.

Rhett's committee supplied each member of the convention with a copy of the draft of the Permanent Constitution. Each copy was printed on legal size paper, was twenty-seven pages long, and was triple spaced to allow for corrections and additions by the members. The printed copy was a reproduction of the manuscript copy of the committee draft which was drawn up by T. R. R. Cobb of Georgia. This manuscript draft of the Permanent Constitution was retained by the Cobb family after the Civil War and presented to the University of Georgia Library in 1908.[17] This manuscript is certified by Secretary of the Con-

14. *Confederate Journal,* I, 87.

15. *Ibid.,* p. 95.

16. *Ibid.,* p. 94.

17. "Thomas Reade Rootes Cobb Original Draft of the Permanent Constitution of the Confederate States of America, 1861," Special Collections Division, University of Georgia.

gress J. J. Hooper as "the original draft of the Permanent Constitution"[18] and, with the exception of three pages,[19] is in T. R. R. Cobb's handwriting. Several mistakes appear in the manuscript draft. On three different pages, Cobb wrote the word United and then crossed it out and wrote the words Confederate States. These mistakes are indicative of the pressure under which the committee worked and, perhaps subconsciously, how attached the delegates were to the old Union.

The constitutional draft that was presented to the convention for debate was entitled, "The Constitution of the Confederate States of America."[20] No doubt as to the name of the new nation was left since the words "Confederate States" appeared sixty-seven times and "Confederacy" nine times. Upon the presentation of this draft, the convention members decided to consider the document article by article.

The first debate was devoted to the Preamble. The principal source of contention was the first line of the proposed Preamble which stated: "We, the people of the Confederate States, each State acting for itself. . . ."[21] The phraseology was very similar to that of the United States Constitution, and it had been a source of controversy for many years. The Preamble, as finally adopted, reads as follows:

> We, the people of the Confederate States, each State acting in its sovereign and independent character, in order to form a permanent federal government, establish justice, insure domestic tranquility, and secure the blessings of liberty to ourselves and our posterity—invoking the favor and guidance of Almighty God—do ordain and establish this Constitution for the Confederate States of America.[22]

18. *Ibid.*

19. *Ibid.* The grandson of T. R. R. Cobb, Augustus Longstreet Hull, in his article "The Making of the Confederate Constitution," *Publications of the Southern History Association*, IX (1905), p. 286, states that a few pages are in the hand of Edward Sparrow of Louisiana. A comparison of the fine, almost feminine, handwriting on the three pages of the Cobb manuscript with a sample of Sparrow's thick and angular handwriting indicates that Hull is incorrect. It seems more probable that the three pages were written by Robert H. Smith of Alabama, also a member of the drafting committee. A comparison of Smith's handwriting with that of the three pages of the manuscript led this writer to this determination.

20. *Confederate Journal*, I, 851.

21. *Ibid.*

22. *Ibid.*, p. 909.

In words very similar to those of Curry of Alabama when he described the phraseology of the Provisional Preamble, Stephens wrote of the Permanent Preamble: "In this, the words 'each State acting in its Sovereign and Independent Character' were introduced to put at rest forever the argument of the Centralists, drawn from the old Constitution, that it had been made by the people of all the States collectively, or in mass, and not by the States in their several Sovereign character."[23] Although the adopted Preamble reads much like the Preamble of the United States Constitution, there are two significant differences. First, the introductory paragraph of the Confederate Constitution affirms the state sovereignty concept of its framers and, second, like the Provisional Preamble, it acknowledges the dependence of its framers upon the Deity.

The remainder of the first day of debate was spent on Article I. Indeed, fifty per cent of all the changes made in the draft of the Permanent Constitution were made in the first article. In addition to the first day, March 1-5, and half of March 6 and 9, were spent debating this article. Thus, six of the ten days devoted to debating the Permanent Constitution were spent on Article I alone. Because of the importance attributed to the first article by the convention, the remainder of this chapter will be devoted to that article which defines the legislative branch of the Confederate Government.[24]

In the years preceding 1860, the South was not dissatisfied with the United States Constitution; it was, however, quite unhappy with the interpretation of that document by the Congress and the Supreme Court. In such congressional legislation as that establishing a national bank, a protective tariff, and federal aid to internal improvements, and in the supreme court decisions of John Marshall, the South saw the steadily increasing power of the central government as an infringement of state rights. Curry of Alabama wrote: "The permanent Constitution was framed on the States Rights theory to take from a majority in

23. Alexander Hamilton Stephens, *A Constitutional View of the Late War Between the States,* 2 volumes (Philadelphia: National Publishing Company, 1868 and 1870), II, 335.

24. Articles II-VII will be treated in the following chapter.

Congress unlimited control. . . ."[25] The Southern states had lost their majority in the House of Representatives before 1820, and they lost equality in the Senate in 1850. The attitude of the convention at Montgomery on the federal legislative process is made quite evident in the first section of Article I. It states: "All legislative powers herein delegated [not granted, as in the United States Constitution] shall be vested in a Congress of the Confederate States, which shall consist of a Senate and a House of Representatives."[26] Like the Federal Congress, the Confederate Congress would be a bicameral legislature, not a unicameral body as was the case in the Provisional Congress. The word "delegated" in this section leaves no doubt as to the source of Confederate legislative power.

Not the derivative powers of the Congress, but the subject of citizenship was the first part of Article I to be debated. Most of the first day and all of the second day were devoted to this subject. Under the United States Constitution, the right to vote was not correlative to or dependent on national citizenship. The convention members determined, however, to require the voters in each state to be citizens of the Confederacy as well as citizens of their respective states. Moreover, persons of foreign birth, not citizens of the Confederacy, could not vote for any office, civil or political, state or federal. The delegates perhaps felt that such a provision would do a great deal toward protecting and perpetuating the South's particular way of life. The Congress could enact laws that would provide for the naturalization of such persons.[27] Thus, the first provision of the Permanent Constitution to be debated enlarged the power of the federal government instead of restricting such power and asserting the concept of state rights. Taking the debates as a whole, this was the exception rather than the rule.

A subject that was hotly debated at Philadelphia in 1787 concerned the apportionment of members of the lower branch of Congress and of direct taxes. The delegates to the Philadelphia Convention decided to count three-fifths of other persons (slaves)

25. Jabez Lamar Monroe Curry, *Civil History of the Government of the Confederate States of America with Some Personal Reminiscences* (Richmond: B. F. Johnson Publishing Company, 1901), p. 69.

26. *Confederate Journal,* I, 909. 27. *Ibid.,* pp. 859 ff.

for such purposes. On the second day of the debate at Montgomery, Keitt of South Carolina, a state with a large slave population, sought to include in the Permanent Constitution the following statement: "Representatives and direct taxes shall be apportioned among the several States according to their respective numbers, excluding Indians not taxed."[28] Apparently Keitt was willing for his state to pay greater taxes in return for increased representation in the Congress. The majority of the convention did not share this logic. Keitt's amendment was voted down, and the committee draft provision calling for the counting of only three-fifths of slaves was retained. Since all of the states of the Confederacy were slave states, perhaps the convention felt that the adopted provision would balance itself with respect to representation and taxation; or perhaps the wealthy slaveholding convention delegates felt that giving themselves full representation for their slaves would arouse significant opposition from the small farmers, whose number was steadily increasing. Because of the general population increase, the convention did agree to a provision which stated: "The number of Representatives shall not exceed one for every fifty thousand. . . ."[29] The United States Constitution had used the number thirty thousand.

The committee draft, like the United States Constitution, gave the House of Representatives the sole power of impeachment. On March 2, the third day of debate, T. R. R. Cobb introduced a resolution which, when adopted, amended this power. Cobb's resolution stated: "any judicial or other Federal officer, resident and acting solely within the limits of any State, may be impeached by a vote of two-thirds of both branches of the Legislature thereof."[30] The state authority did not extend to trying the officer since the Senate of the Confederate States had the sole power to try such and all other impeachments. Robert H. Smith of Alabama said of this provision: "It is but the inquest of the grand jury which is given to the State."[31] Nevertheless, a federal judge, for example, faced with deciding between the national in-

28. *Ibid.*, p. 861.

29. *Ibid.*, p. 910.

30. *Ibid.*, p. 910.

31. Robert Hardy Smith, *An Address to the Citizens of Alabama on the Constitution and Laws of the Confederate States of America* (Mobile: Mobile Daily Register Print, 1861), p. 21.

terests and the interests of a state would be placed in a precarious position. Although this provision was not implemented during the brief life of the Confederacy, it appeared in the Permanent Constitution as a significant embodiment of the theory of state rights.

The delegates took Sunday, March 3, as a day of rest, but they returned to their desks on March 4 more determined than ever to complete their task for on that day Abraham Lincoln was inaugurated as President of the United States. In anticipation of that event, the Montgomery delegates had worked long and exhausting hours to establish a new government. While Lincoln was delivering his inaugural address in Washington, D. C., in which he affirmed his constitutional duty to preserve, protect, and defend the Union, the Provisional Congress in Montgomery adopted a flag for the Confederate States of America.[32] Shortly after three o'clock, the Congress adjourned to join an enthusiastic crowd that watched Miss Letitia Christian Tyler, grand-daughter of ex-President John Tyler, raise the first Confederate flag.

Later that evening, the convention reassembled to continue deliberations on the Permanent Constitution. Two days previously, the convention had decided to meet in evening sessions until the constitution was completed. It is not known whether the thoughts of the members on that evening returned to the Republican platform of 1860 and, in particular, to the two planks concerning the tariff and internal improvements. For the next two days, however, the debates of the convention centered around these issues which involved the powers of the Congress.

The South had long been keenly interested in and watchful of national fiscal policy including taxation, protective tariffs, and internal improvements particularly as it affected the sovereignty of the several states. Certainly most of the members of the Provisional Congress agreed with Robert Barnwell Rhett, who wrote: "The two great vital powers in all governments are the laying of taxes and the expenditure of taxes. These powers decide the character of every government, whether it is limited or unlimited, federal or consolidated; hence, from the commencement of the

32. *Confederate Journal,* I, 102.

Government of the United States, strife arose as to the extent of these powers."[33]

On the evening of March 4, T. R. R. Cobb wrote to his wife: "The tariff question is troubling us a good deal. The absolute free trade principal is very strongly advocated."[34] The tariff question had been a thorny issue in national politics for many years, especially since 1816. Under the leadership of South Carolina, this subject came close to causing the disruption of the Union in 1832-1833. For the following ten years, there was a gradual reduction of duties which was more acceptable to the South. After a brief return to a strong protective tariff under the Whigs, the Democratic Walker Tariff of 1846 emphasized the concept of tariff for revenue. In 1857, Howell Cobb, as Secretary of the Treasury, secured an even greater reduction of duties so that there was as near an approach to free trade as this country had had since 1816.[35] Under the existing political and prosperous economic conditions in 1860, the South was generally satisfied with the current duties which embodied the concept of tariff for revenue only.

By a general statute adopted on February 9, the Provisional Congress continued in force the United States Tariff Act of 1857. This act was amended nine days later to allow free trade in foods, railroad iron, and other enumerated manufactured products.[36] If not absolute free trade, then a low tariff was necessary in the minds of many Southerners, for as one Montgomery editorial put it: "As cotton states, almost all we produce is consumed by others, and almost all we consume is produced by others."[37] The subsequent acts of the Congress concerning the tariff caused Robert H. Smith to state: "we have sent our diplomats to Europe with the Constitution in one hand and a low tariff in the other. . . ."[38]

The position of many of the Southern secessionists was substantiated when the Federal Congress, just two days before the

33. Robert Barnwell Rhett, "The Confederate Constitution," *DeBow's Review* (November, 1869), VI, 931.
34. T. R. R. Cobb to his wife, March 4, 1861.
35. Frank William Taussig, *The Tariff History of the United States* (New York: G. P. Putnam's Sons, 1928), p. 115.
36. *Confederate Journal*, I, 63.
37. Montgomery *Weekly Advertiser*, February 20, 1861.
38. Smith, *An Address*, p. 22.

convention at Montgomery debated the tariff issue and passed the Morrill Tariff Act which "began a change toward a higher range of duties and a stronger application of protection."[39] With this act and the echoes of past tariff controversies as an incentive, a majority of the delegates at Montgomery were determined to settle this issue once and for all.

The leading free trade advocates as well as the leaders of the debates on the tariff in the convention were the delegates from South Carolina. The South Carolinians were supported by members in all the delegations, although several Louisiana delegates favored a tariff that would protect the sugar industry in their state. The adoption of an amendment offered by Rhett ended the discussion on this subject. The Permanent Constitution gave the Congress the power "to lay and collect taxes, duties, imposts, and excises, for revenue necessary to pay the debts, provide for the common defense, and carry on the government of the Confederate States. . . ." Rhett's motion also provided: "but no bounties shall be granted from the treasury; nor shall any duties or taxes on importations from foreign nations be laid to promote or foster any branch of industry; . . ."[40] With the inclusion of this statement in the Permanent Constitution, the issue of the protective tariff was laid to rest, as far as the Confederacy was concerned.

In addition to the above provision on imports, the convention members agreed to a provision concerning exports. The United States Constitution prohibited the laying of any duties on articles exported from the several states. The Confederate Constitution, however, contained a provision which stated: "No tax or duty shall be laid on articles exported from any State except by a vote of two thirds of both Houses."[41] The reason for such a modification was the need for revenue by the federal government, especially in view of the acceptance of the principle of low import duties.

The above prohibition of the protective tariff nowhere includes a statement giving the Congress the power to provide for

39. Taussig, *The Tariff History,* p. 158.

40. *Confederate Journal,* I, 864. A comprehensive tariff bill was approved on May 21, 1861, embodying this principle.

41. *Ibid.,* p. 915.

the general welfare. The convention was well aware of the extension of the authority of the Federal Government under the doctrine of implied powers. The general welfare clause was not included in the constitutional draft of the committee, and it was not debated in the convention. The exclusion of this clause represents another manifestation of the philosophy of state rights. In this connection, it is interesting to note that the Permanent Constitution does give the Congress the power "to make all laws which shall be necessary and proper for carrying into execution the foregoing powers. . . ."[42] This was done in the belief that Southern judges would look closely when considering any legislation based on implied powers.

Internal improvements, like the tariff, had been a controversial issue during the first half of the nineteenth century. The authority of the Federal Congress to appropriate money from the treasury for the purpose of internal improvements was construed from the constitutional power of the Congress to regulate commerce with foreign nations and among the states. In general, the South opposed such appropriations for internal improvements as it felt that such action was unconstitutional, that it tended to make the central government more powerful, and that it was a threat to state sovereignty. Different presidents from James Madison to James Knox Polk, for these and other reasons, used the executive veto to arrest appropriations for internal improvements. There were delegates at Montgomery who wanted to have the commerce power of Congress more clearly defined and more closely delimited. Alexander H. Stephens expressed the view of his colleagues on this issue when he wrote: "The true principle is to subject the commerce of every locality to whatever burdens may be necessary to facilitate it. If Charleston harbor needs improvement, let the commerce of Charleston bear the burden."[43] This philosophy was implemented in the Permanent Constitution by an amendment introduced by Robert Toombs.

Robert Toombs had been a watchdog over Federal fiscal policy in Washington for years. At Montgomery, his influence

42. *Ibid.*, p. 914.

43. Henry Cleveland, *Alexander H. Stephens, In Public and Private* (Philadelphia: National Publishing Company, 1866), p. 719.

was apparent and welcome in the fashioning of the financial provisions of the constitution. The committee draft as presented to the convention contained a statement, as did the United States Constitution, giving Congress the power to regulate foreign and domestic commerce. During the debates on March 5, Toombs introduced an amendment to this provision. It reads: "But neither this, nor any other clause contained in the constitution shall ever be construed to delegate the power of Congress to appropriate money for any internal improvement intended to facilitate commerce."[44] Toombs' motion was tabled but was reconsidered on the last day of debates. With the aid of Rhett, T. R. R. Cobb, and Henry Marshall of Louisiana, Toombs' amendment was accepted, but with an amendment. The addition gave the Congress the power to appropriate money for internal improvements, but only for the purpose of aiding navigation and improving harbors. Moreover, duties would be laid on the transportation enjoying these improvements. This latter provision was an exact implementation of the concept expressed by Stephens.

The Permanent Constitution, like the United States Constitution, prohibited states from laying tonnage duties without the consent of the Congress. The Confederate document did allow such duties on sea-going vessels for the improvement of rivers and harbors navigated by the vessels, if such action did not conflict with existing treaties of the Confederacy. It provided that "when any river divides or flows through two or more States, they may enter into compacts with each other to improve the navigation thereof."[45] The original amendment to the commerce clause, made by Toombs, laid the issue of internal improvements to rest along side that of the tariff.

Before debating the tariff and internal improvements issues, the delegates discussed briefly a provision in the draft of the Permanent Constitution that had been omitted from the Provisional Constitution. The Provisional Constitution did not prohibit congressmen from holding other offices under the federal government. Because of this omission, Alexander H. Stephens, who sponsored the idea, could be elected Vice President, and Memminger,

44. *Confederate Journal,* I, 865.

45. *Ibid.,* p. 917.

Toombs, and Reagan could serve in the Cabinet. The draft of the Permanent Constitution, like the United States Constitution, did prohibit dual office holding.

Robert Toombs, like his colleague Stephens, greatly admired the British cabinet system. Indeed, in 1855, Toombs had observed the British Parliament in operation. During a debate in the United States Senate in 1859, the colorful Georgian had said: "My opinion is, that it would be a great improvement on our own system . . . if the Cabinet officers should be on the floor of both Houses and should participate in the debates. I have no doubt that we should thus get rid of one of the very greatest difficulties in our Constitution."[46] Toombs had strongly urged the adoption of a provision embodying the British cabinet system upon the committee drafting the Permanent Constitution. His efforts resulted in an amendment to the prohibitory clause which stated: "Congress may, by law, grant to the principal officer in each of the Executive Departments a seat upon the floor of either House, with the privilege of discussing any measures appertaining to his department."[47] On March 4, Toombs and Stephens sought to have a more compulsory provision included in the constitution, because they were fearful of congressional inaction, but they were not successful.

Although the adopted amendment did not completely satisfy either Stephens or Toombs, it was designed, if implemented by the Congress, to have constructive effects. As Robert H. Smith wrote: "The want of facility of communication between the Executive and Legislature, has, it is believed, been a serious impediment to the easy and harmonious working of Government."[48] Stephens, Toombs, and Smith believed that the provision would enhance better understanding and cooperation between these two branches of government. Moreover, this concept, borrowed from the British Constitution, would give the legislature a closer check upon the executive, it would keep the Congress better informed as to administrative policy, and finally, it would place more direct responsibility upon the department heads. These

46. *Congressional Globe,* 35 Cong., 2 Sess. (Washington: John C. Rives, 1859), 286.

47. *Confederate Journal,* I, 853.

48. Smith, *An Address,* p. 9.

benefits were, of course, dependent upon favorable action by the Congress. President Davis subsequently wrote: "This wise and judicious provision, which would have tended to obviate much delay and misunderstanding, was, however, never put into execution by the necessary legislation."[49] In January 1863 and again in February, 1865, bills were introduced in the Senate to give seats in the Permanent Congress to Cabinet members. The first bill was defeated and the second bill was buried in committee.[50]

The reason Congress failed to give seats in the House and Senate to Cabinet members is not clearly evident. Under the Provisional Constitution, Cabinet members functioned effectively from their seats in Congress; however, their legislative status was questioned. Secretary Memminger felt it necessary to introduce a resolution to admit the heads of departments to secret and open sessions of Congress.[51] Moreover, the records do not disclose any nonmember secretaries being seated in the Provisional Congress.

Probably the best explanation for the failure of the Permanent Congress to give seats to Cabinet members is suggested by a statement of Walter Bagehot, a nineteenth century authority on British parliamentary government: "The efficient secret of the English Constitution may be described as the close union, the nearly complete fusion, of the executive and legislative powers."[52] As the pressures of war increased, the executive policies of President Davis came under increasing attack by the Congress and, in lieu of the uncertainty of the effect of the "Cabinet in Congress" practice upon the theory of the separation of powers, Congress determined to maintain the independence of the legislative branch of government.

The executive budget and the item veto were closely related

49. Davis, *Rise and Fall,* I, 224. Had Congress passed favorable legislation there would have been one significant difference between the British and Confederate systems in that the British Cabinet was directly responsible to the Parliament.

50. *Confederate Journal,* III, 24, 44, 45, 146, 153; IV, 533.

51. *Ibid.,* I, 82.

52. Walter Bagehot, *The English Constitution, and other Political Essays* (New York: D. Appleton and Company, 1877), p. 78. A later day American who much admired the British parliamentary system, and who was influenced by Bagehot, was Woodrow Wilson. See Woodrow Wilson, *Congressional Government, A Study in American Politics,* Fifteenth Edition (Boston: Houghton, Mifflin and Company, 1900).

to the "Cabinet in Congress" provision of Article I. These two provisions concerned fiscal responsibility, and both had been incorporated in the Provisional Constitution. Stephens' executive budget provision stated: "Congress shall appropriate no money from the treasury unless it be asked for by the President or some one of the heads of department, except for the purpose of paying its own expenses and contingencies."[53] His model for this provision was the British Constitution which he so much admired. Stephens wrote: "The object of this was to make, as far as possible, each administration responsible for the public expenditures."[54] Stephens and his Southern colleagues had too long witnessed what they considered to be the fiscal irresponsibility of the majority in the Federal Congress. With this provision, the principal responsibility would be placed in the hands of the executive.

The desire of the members of the Second Committee of Twelve for a more economical and efficient government and their memory of "pork-barrel legislation" and "log-rolling" caused them to include Stephens' executive budget provision in their draft. When this section of the first article was presented to the convention for debate, some of the members feared that a belligerent president might bring ruin to the government by refusing to ask for appropriations. This possibility was rectified to the satisfaction of the convention by the adoption of an amendment, offered by Curry of Alabama, which reintroduced Congress into the appropriation process. As adopted on March 6, the executive budget provision of the Permanent Constitution reads: "Congress shall appropriate no money from the treasury except by a vote of two-thirds of both Houses, taken by yeas and nays, except it be asked for or estimated for by some one of the heads of Department. . . ."[55] Thus, the executive was made the primary guardian of the treasury with the Congress having a balancing power.

The incorporation of the item veto feature into the Provisional Constitution was explained in the previous chapter. Robert H.

53. *Confederate Journal,* I, 27.
54. Stephens, *A Constitutional View,* II, 336.
55. *Confederate Journal,* I, 872.

Smith has described the evil that he sought to eliminate: "Bills necessary for the support of the Government are loaded with items of the most exceptionable character, and are thrown upon the President at the close of the session, for his sanction, as the only alternative for keeping the Government in motion."[56] As part of Stephens' plan to adapt British budget principles to American conditions, the item veto was also adopted to protect the budget estimations of the President.[57] During the debates on the Permanent Constitution, the wordy phraseology in the Provisional Constitution was changed so as to read: "The President may approve any appropriation and disapprove any other appropriation in the same bill."[58]

Also on March 6 the convention adopted two other provisions which concerned the clarification of the legislative process. The first provision, proposed by Conrad and Kenner of Louisiana, stated: "All bills appropriating money shall specify in federal currency the exact amount of each appropriation and the purpose for which it is made."[59] This clause supported the other provisions of the constitution that defined and clarified fiscal responsibility. The second provision stated: "Every law, or resolution having the force of law, shall relate to but one subject, and that shall be expressed in the title."[60] Both provisions sought to reform old legislative evils. This latter clause, in addition to clarifying an important part of the legislative process, would remedy the practice of inserting a number of subjects in one bill, some of which could not be passed standing alone.

The soundness of federal finances was the subject of yet another provision. Once again the influence and experience of Robert Toombs was decisive in the drafting of a provision concerning the Confederate Post Office. Toombs wrote into the committee draft, and the convention adopted, a clause giving the Congress power "To establish post-offices and post-routes; but the expenses of the Post-Office Department shall be paid out of its own revenues."[61] The convention did, upon the motion of Wil-

56. Smith, *An Address,* p. 8.

57. It is interesting to note that Smith, who introduced the item veto, opposed the executive budget provision of the Provisional Constitution.

58. *Confederate Journal,* I, 864.

59. *Ibid.,* p. 872.

60. *Ibid.,* p. 874.

61. *Ibid.,* p. 867.

liam Porcher Miles of South Carolina, adopt an amendment to this provision which gave the Post Office Department two years to become self-sufficient.[62] As Postmaster General, John H. Reagan of Texas accomplished the near impossible by not only showing no annual deficits, but by showing annual profits. The constitutional requirement of self-sufficiency was in practice a burden to Reagan, and was accomplished only at the expense of good service.

On March 5, the attention of the convention was turned from matters of a financial nature to a brief debate on the slave trade. The slave trade provision in the committee draft was taken, almost verbatim, from the Provisional Constitution. It prohibited foreign slave trade and required Congress to pass legislation that would effectively prevent this trade.[63] Just as they had done during the debates on the Provisional Constitution, Rhett and Keitt once again sought to give the Congress the power to prohibit the foreign slave trade; they did not want the Congress required to do so. Once again they were unsuccessful. The convention realized the significance of the prohibitory statement to Europe and the border states.

On the last of six consecutive days of debate on Article I, a subject of fundamental importance was introduced before the convention. Some members of the convention wanted to see the right of secession defined and included in the Permanent Constitution. William W. Boyce of South Carolina introduced a provision which, in part, stated: "That the right of secession of any State from this Confederacy is expressly admitted, to be exercised by any State according to its pleasure. . . ."[64] Debate on this issue was postponed until the following day at which time Hill of Georgia presented an elaborate substitute provision. Hill's plan denied the right of nullification, but did set up a system of conventions and courts whereby the several states could air their grievances and, if not satisfied with the results, secede.[65] Following Hill's motion, Chesnut of South Carolina offered a suggestion that took the middle ground between the Boyce and Hill plans. The convention as a whole did not wish to debate this subject, and it was postponed, not to be reconsidered. In a sense,

62. *Ibid.*

63. *Ibid.*, p. 868.

64. *Ibid.*, p. 873.

65. *Ibid.*, pp. 876-77.

the Confederacy was founded upon the right of secession and yet it evoked little debate in the convention and does not appear in either of the Confederate Constitutions. The right of secession was, however, implied in the specific phraseology of the Preamble to the Permanent Constitution.

The Bill of Rights was not taken for granted in 1787. Four years later, these rights became the first ten amendments to the United States Constitution. Between that time and 1861, two additional amendments were added to the constitution. The first eight of these amendments were appropriately written into the first article of the Permanent Constitution of the Confederacy. The remaining four were incorporated into the remaining six articles.

After six strenuous days of debate, the convention completed its deliberations on Article I of the Permanent Constitution. In the Preamble and in such provisions as those concerning the impeachment of federal officials by state legislatures, the tariff, and internal improvements, the convention exhibited its determination to protect and define the sovereignty of the several states. In such provisions as those concerning citizenship, the "Cabinet in Congress," the executive budget, the item veto, and the post office, the delegates gave substance to significant governmental reforms.

After completing Article I, the convention, in point of time, was past the half-way mark in its deliberations on the Permanent Constitution. Six articles were yet to be presented to and debated by the convention. This final portion of the Permanent Constitution would challenge the patience, intelligence, and ingenuity of the delegates at least as much as had the first portion.

CHAPTER VI

The Permanent Constitution: Part II

The restrictions thrown around amendments to the organic law by the Constitution of the United States proved to be a practical negation of the power to alter the instrument.

Robert H. Smith of Alabama

After March 6, the convention continued its deliberations until the Permanent Constitution was adopted on the evening of March 11, 1861. During that time, the members considered and debated such significant subjects as the executive and judiciary branches of government, slavery, the admission of new states, the acquisition of new territory, the amendment process, and the ratification of the Permanent Constitution. On the sixth day of debates, however, the attention of the convention was directed toward the second article of the constitution, concerning the executive branch of government.

One of the most perplexing problems that faced the delegates to the Philadelphia Convention in 1787 was the method of electing a chief executive. The convention finally decided on the electoral college system, which was borrowed from the constitution of the state of Maryland. In the years that followed, the hope that the electoral college would intelligently and judiciously select the most able candidate floundered with the rise of political parties. The delegates to the Montgomery Convention in 1861 felt that the great party struggles, the spoils system, and the many political pressures had seriously challenged the effectiveness of the electoral college. In committee and during the debates, most delegates favored some change in the method of electing the chief executive.[1] On the sixth day of debates on the Permanent Consti-

1. Jabez Lamar Monroe Curry, *Civil History of the Government of the Confederate States of America with Some Personal Reminiscences* (Richmond: B. F. Johnson Publishing Company, 1901), p. 73. (Hereinafter cited as Curry, *Civil History.*)

tution, Walter Brooke of Mississippi and William Porcher Miles of South Carolina offered alternatives to the electoral college system.[2] Neither plan, nor indeed any suggestion that was offered, was free from objections. The convention failed to agree on any change and, a few weeks later, Smith of Alabama said: "I regret to say that the chief defect of the Constitution of the Confederate States is, in my opinion, the retention of the old mode of electing the President."[3] The hope of the convention was, wrote Curry of Alabama, "that the reluctant acquiescence in the retention of what none favored was in the strong hope that what was temporary might be adjusted under more favorable circumstances."[4] The short and violent life of the Confederacy did not see any such adjustment.

Both the Philadelphia Convention and the Montgomery Convention wrestled with the problem of the term of office of the president. At Montgomery, many of the delegates were concerned about the situation presented by an incumbent president seeking re-election. Rhett of South Carolina, the Chairman of the Second Committee of Twelve, wrote: "The re-eligibility of the President was not without danger, as the re-eligibility of the Consuls of Rome opened the way to the Roman empire."[5] In an effort to negate any possibility of presidential tyranny and to keep the chief executive from using his patronage for the purpose of re-election, Rhett introduced a provision to the drafting committee that proposed the extension of the term of service of the president and vice president to six years, and the requirement that the president should be ineligible for re-election. The committee accepted the six-year term for the president; however, some disagreement was apparent as to whether the president

2. *Journal of the Congress of the Confederate States of America, 1861-1865*, 7 volumes (Washington: Government Printing Office, 1904-1905), I, 875. (Hereinafter cited as *Confederate Journal.*)

3. Robert Hardy Smith, *An Address to the Citizens of Alabama on the Constitution and Laws of the Confederate States of America* (Mobile: Mobile Daily Register Print, 1861), p. 14. (Hereinafter cited as Smith, *An Address.*) The Twelfth Amendment to the United States Constitution, providing for separate balloting for President and Vice President, was appropriately written into Article II of the Confederate Constitution.

4. Curry, *Civil History*, p. 73.

5. Robert Barnwell Rhett, "The Confederate Constitution," *DeBow's Review*, VI (November, 1869), 933.

should be absolutely or conditionally ineligible to stand for re-election.

The executive article, as presented to the convention on March 6, stated only that the two executive officers would hold their offices for a term of six years. Immediately, Rhett gained the floor and offered an amendment which stated: "The President shall not be eligible again to the Presidency until six years after the expiration of his term of service."[6] Rhett explained: "By this policy, the President would have no motive to use his patronage in the election, and the services of a very able man might be obtained for a second term."[7] During the convention debates, Nisbet of Georgia proposed a term of eight years for the president, and Memminger of South Carolina proposed seven years. Rhett's original suggestion of six years was retained. Boyce of South Carolina was successful in having the conditional re-eligibility of the president stricken from the provision. Thus, Rhett's original suggestion to the drafting committee, that the president serve a term of six years and be ineligible for re-election, was adopted by the convention.

According to the wording of the accepted provision, the vice president was eligible to succeed himself. An editorial in the Charleston *Mercury*, published only a few days before the convention debates began, suggested that the constitution should contain a provision whereby the vice president would automatically succeed the president. This article held that the next president should be chosen six years ahead of time, "so that the *man*, rather than his *party*, will be considered by the electors, and the officer will have time and opportunity to educate and fit himself for his high duties."[8] Although this editorial was probably read by some of the convention members, there is no evidence that it received serious consideration.

On the seventh day of debates, the power of executive removal came before the convention. The United States Constitution indicates the manner by which federal executive officers shall be appointed, but it makes no mention as to their removal except

6. *Confederate Journal*, I, 875.
7. Rhett, "The Confederate Constitution," p. 933.
8. The Charleston *Mercury*, February 19, 1861.

by impeachment. Between 1789 and 1861, Congresses and Presidents had speculated over the many questions concerning the problem of executive removal.[9] A provision authored by Rhett and somewhat clarified by Barry of Mississippi during the debates made the Confederate Constitution clear on this question. The adopted provision, in a general statement, reads: "The principal officer in each of the executive departments, and all persons connected with the diplomatic service, may be removed from office at the pleasure of the President. . . ." Becoming more specific, the provision continues: "All other civil officers of the executive department may be removed at any time by the President, or other appointing power, when their services are unnecessary, or for dishonesty, incapacity, inefficiency, misconduct, or neglect of duty; and when so removed, the removal shall be reported to the Senate together with the reasons thereof."[10] By this definition, the convention restricted the removal power of the president by giving the Senate a check upon the exercise of this power in connection with most civil executive offices.

The convention accepted a further restriction of the power of the executive. In the past, executives had given recess appointments to men whose original confirmation had been rejected by the United States Senate. Unlike the United States Constitution, the Confederate Constitution gave the Senate the final word on presidential appointments when it stated: "But no person rejected by the Senate shall be reappointed to the same office during their ensuing recess."[11]

The significant changes made by the Montgomery Convention in the executive article tend to give the impression that the constitutional powers at the disposal of the Confederate President were less extensive than those at the disposal of the President of the United States. The Confederate innovations or reforms, the term of the executive, his ineligibility to succeed himself, and his removal and appointive power are all of a restrictive nature. Taken as a whole, however, the Confederate President probably had more authority than his Federal counterpart, particularly in

9. It was not until Myers v. United States, 272 U.S. 52 (1926) that a case clearly involving the President's removal power came before the Supreme Court. Even then, the government's case was based on implied powers.

10. *Confederate Journal*, I, 877.

11. *Ibid.*, p. 856.

view of the executive budget and the item veto provisions of the Confederate Constitution.

After completing the debates on the executive article on March 7, the convention proceeded to a brief discussion of the article pertaining to the judiciary branch of government. Article III of the Provisional Constitution was considerably altered and enlarged for the Permanent Constitution. With the exception of a few minor differences, however, Article III in the Permanent Constitution of the Confederacy and Article III in the United States Constitution were identical.

During the debates, the convention, at the suggestion of Stephens of Georgia, struck from the committee draft the provision allowing federal jurisdiction to extend to controversies "between citizens of different States."[12] One of the major functions of the federal courts under the United States Constitution was to protect citizens bringing suit outside their own state from local prejudices and pressures. Apparently, the members at Montgomery excluded this provision as an expression of state rights.

Another significant omission from the judiciary article of the Permanent Constitution was the phrase "in law and equity."[13] The judicial power of the Confederate government did not extend to all cases in law and equity. With this omission, constitutional recognition of the distinction between the law and equity sides of the federal courts was withdrawn. It was thus left to the Congress to regulate the enforcement of legal rights, as well as the quest of suitable remedies. The English concept of dual jurisdiction had long been in conflict with the Roman concept of single jurisdiction in Louisiana and Texas.[14] This omission of the fundamental difference between law and equity suits, like the withdrawal of jurisdiction over suits dependent upon the diversity of citizenship, was a manifestation of the state rights philosophy of the convention.

A significant inclusion in the Permanent Constitution that does not appear in the Provisional Constitution states: "The judicial

12. *Ibid.*, pp. 878-79.

13. *Ibid.*, p. 920.

14. See William Morrison Robinson, Jr., *Justice in Grey* (Cambridge: Harvard University Press, 1941), pp. 43 ff.

power shall extend to all cases arising under this Constitution . . . between a State and citizens of another State, *where the State is the plaintiff . . . but no State shall be sued by a citizen or subject of any foreign state.*"[15] The italicized words in the above provision represent in effect the Eleventh Amendment to the United States Constitution. The adoption of this amendment in 1798 curtailed the jurisdiction of the federal judiciary, thus making a concession to the sovereignty of the states. The writing of this amendment into the judiciary article of the Permanent Constitution was a natural and consistent action on the part of the convention.

With the exception of the few differences mentioned above, Article III of the Permanent Constitution and the United States Constitution were the same. Both documents provided for the establishment of a Supreme Court. Where the judiciary branches of the two governments greatly differed was in the implementation of the third article of the respective constitutions. The Confederate States of America did not establish a supreme court during its lifetime. Because of the absence of the high court, "the supreme courts of the several states [not the federal District Courts] . . . were elevated to an authority unknown under the Constitution of the United States."[16] These state supreme courts were the courts of last resort.

A key to the absence of a supreme court in the Confederacy is found in the debates held on the eighth day. Memminger of South Carolina introduced a motion to include in the Permanent Constitution the following phrase: "but the appellate Jurisdiction of the Supreme Court shall not extend to any case which shall have been adjudged in any court of a State."[17] Although this motion failed it indicated a strong state rights persuasion concerning the judiciary branch of the federal government.

After the debates, indeed after the adoption of the Permanent Constitution by the convention, the question of the establishment

15. *Confederate Journal,* I, 920. The italics were inserted by this writer and do not appear in the Permanent Constitution.

16. Joseph Gregoire de Roulhac Hamilton, "The State Courts and the Confederate Constitution," *The Journal of Southern History,* IV (November, 1938), 425.

17. *Confederate Journal,* I, 880.

of the Supreme Court still faced the government. The Congress implemented Article III of the Provisional Constitution by passing the Judiciary Act of March 16, 1861.[18] This act called for the first meeting of the Supreme Court, which would be made up of the various District Judges, in January of 1862. Shortly thereafter, this meeting date was rescinded, primarily because the Congress realized the difficulties involved in constituting the high court with District Judges who were located some distance from each other. Also, the Congress looked forward to the implementation of Article III of the Permanent Constitution after February 18, 1862.

From 1862 until the end of the war, every Congress considered a bill to establish a supreme court; however, none of the bills passed both houses. On each occasion, the debate as to the appellate jurisdiction of the Supreme Court killed the bill. The high point of the Supreme Court controversy came on February 4, 1863, when Benjamin H. Hill of Georgia, somewhat excited, threw an inkstand at his colleague from Alabama, Senator William L. Yancey.[19] As Chairman of the Senate Judiciary Committee, Hill led the administration forces favoring the establishment of a Supreme Court with appellate jurisdiction over the state courts. Yancey's eloquent and fiery oratory led the opposition. Thus, the state rights reasoning manifested in Memminger's motion of March 8, 1861, prevailed in sufficient strength throughout the life of the Confederacy to prevent the establishment of a supreme court.

Although the state rights philosophy was the principal cause of the non-establishment of a Confederate Supreme Court, there were other contributing causes. Some delegates opposed a high court for fear President Davis would appoint John Archibald Campbell of Alabama, an Associate Justice of the United States Supreme Court from 1853 to 1861, as Chief Justice. Campbell's opponents were afraid that he would follow in the nationalistic footsteps of John Marshall. The tendency of the state Supreme

18. James Muscoe Matthews, ed., *The Statutes at Large of the Provisional Government of the Confederate States of America* (Richmond: R. M. Smith, 1864), pp. 75-87.

19. Some of Yancey's followers held that this attack led to his early death in 1863.

Courts to sustain the acts of the Confederate government, and not to emphasize state rights, helps explain why the movement for a federal supreme court did not become stronger. And finally, the war itself drew the attention of most men to matters that they considered of greater importance than the establishment of a supreme court.[20] It seems likely, however, that the Confederate government would have been stronger and more efficient had it relied upon one high court instead of several courts for the interpretation of the organic law.

On the seventh, eighth, and ninth days of the debates on the Permanent Constitution, Article IV, containing miscellaneous provisions, was under consideration. The last of the four sections of this article, which guaranteed the several states a republican form of government, was added to the committee draft upon a motion by Alexander M. Clayton of Mississippi on March 8.[21] The three most significant provisions of this article, however, concerned fugitive slaves, the acquisition of new territory, and the admission of new states. The feature that all three of these provisions had in common was the domestic institution of Negro slavery.

On March 21, 1861, after the adoption of the Permanent Constitution, Alexander H. Stephens appeared at the Athenaeum in Savannah to speak on the state of public affairs. To an over-flow audience he gave his famous "corner-stone speech." Concerning the institution of Negro slavery, Stephens said: "This was the immediate cause of the late rupture and the present revolution." He continued by saying of the newly established government: "Its foundations are laid, its cornerstone rests upon the great truth, that the negro is not equal to the white man; that slavery—subordination to the superior race—is his normal condition."[22]

These expressions by Stephens were echoed and expanded upon about a week later by Robert H. Smith before an enthusiastic audience in Mobile, Alabama. Speaking of the longevity of the

20. See Robinson, *Justice in Grey*, pp. 490 ff., and Bradley Tyler Johnson, John V. Wright, Jehu Amaziah Orr, and L. Quinton Washington, "Why the Confederate States of America Had No Supreme Court," *Southern History Association*, IV (March, 1900), 81-101.

21. *Confederate Journal*, I, 887.

22. Henry Cleveland, *Alexander H. Stephens* (Philadelphia: National Publishing Company, 1886), p. 721.

slavery issue in American life, Smith said: "The question of negro slavery has been the apple of discord in the government of the United States since its foundation. The strife has now and then lulled, but has not ceased. All observing men must have felt, for at least ten years, that this fanatical agitation was the death knell of the Union."[23] Being more specific, Smith said: "We have dissolved the late Union chiefly because of the negro quarrel."[24]

It is evident from the words of Stephens and Smith that they, and indeed all of the delegates to the Montgomery Convention, came to Montgomery with a determination to recognize openly and to protect the South's "peculiar institution" in the Confederate Constitution.

On the seventh day of debates, Stephen F. Hale of Alabama introduced a motion that was specifically directed toward the protection of slavery. The original committee draft provision held that the citizens of each state were entitled to all the privileges and immunities of the citizens of the several states. Hale's amendment, when adopted, stated that the citizens of the several states "shall have the right of transit and sojourn in any state of this Confederacy, with their slaves and other property; and the right of property in said slaves shall not be thereby impaired."[25] It seems likely that the convention had the particulars of the Dred Scott case in mind when it accepted this amendment.

A further protection of slavery was involved in the fugitive slave provision of the Permanent Constitution. The recapture and return of fugitive slaves had been a serious source of controversy between the North and the South for generations. One of the bases of the preservation of the Federal Union in 1850, at least as far as the South was concerned, was the faithful observance of the terms of the Fugitive Slave Act of that year by the North.[26] The failure of the North in this respect is evidenced by the passage of Personal Liberty Laws in many of the states that made the recovery of fugitive slaves extremely difficult.

It is evident from the convention debates of March 7 that the

23. Smith, *An Address*, p. 16.

24. *Ibid.*, p. 19.

25. *Confederate Journal*, I, 882.

26. See the Georgia Platform in *Journal of the State Convention, Held in Milledgeville, in December 1850* (Milledgeville: R. M. Orme, State Printer, 1850), pp. 18-23.

members sought to make the fugitive slave provision of the Permanent Constitution as specific and extensive as possible. Perhaps with the Personal Liberty Laws in mind, Rhett introduced an amendment which stated that "in the case of the failure of the executive to deliver up a slave, or of any abduction or forcible rescue, full compensation (including the value of the slave and all costs and expenses) shall be made to the party by the State to which said slave may have fled."[27] Hill of Georgia introduced a similar amendment, but made the Confederate government responsible for compensation in such cases. Neither of these two amendments was adopted.

The fugitive slave provision of the committee draft was identical to that contained in the United States Constitution. After the convention accepted the amendments to the draft provision made by Hale, and two brief changes in phraseology offered by Stephens and Keitt, the fugitive slave provision of the Permanent Constitution was more specific and more extensive than that of the Federal Constitution. Past experience had taught the convention the advisability of such action.

The Philadelphia Convention of 1787 failed to include in the United States Constitution a provision authorizing the acquisition of new territory. Because of this omission, President Thomas Jefferson wanted an amendment to the constitution in 1803 to legalize the purchase of Louisiana. In 1820, the heated issue of slavery in new territory was interjected into the Congressional debate over the admission of Missouri. The flame aroused by that debate was reduced to coals by agreement on a compromise line of 36° 30′ whereby slavery would be prohibited above that line except in the state of Missouri. The prospect of acquiring new territory as a result of the Mexican War caused the coals to burst into flames once again. More specifically, the situation was caused by the introduction of the Wilmot Proviso. The general position of the North, as expressed in the Proviso, was that slavery should be excluded from all new territories acquired by the United States from Mexico. The South wanted the extension of slavery into new territories constitutionally guaranteed. Many people hoped that the concept of popular sovereignty as em-

27. *Confederate Journal,* I, 882.

bodied in the Compromise of 1850 would solve this problem. This solution was tested by the Kansas-Nebraska Act of 1854. The result was bloody Kansas, a prelude to the Civil War.

The past forty years of conflict over slavery in the territories was still a vivid memory in the minds of many of the members of the convention who drafted and debated the Permanent Constitution. The Second Committee of Twelve presented a provision to the convention concerning the acquisition of territory which is not found in the United States Constitution. The first part of this provision stated: "The Confederate States may acquire new territory; and Congress shall have power to legislate and provide governments for the inhabitants of all territory belonging to the Confederate States, lying without the limits of the several States; and may permit them, at such times and in such manner as it may by law provide, to form States to be admitted into the Confederacy." The last part of the provision concerned the institution of slavery and the right of transit and sojourn. It stated: "In all such territory, the institution of negro slavery, as it now exists in the Confederate States, shall be recognized and protected by Congress and by the territorial government; and the inhabitants of the several Confederate States and Territories shall have the right to take to such territory any slaves lawfully held in any of the States or Territories of the Confederate States."[28] With the adoption of this provision by the convention, the Confederate Constitution specifically answered the controversial question of the status of slaves in the territories. At the same time, the institution of Negro slavery received its ultimate constitutional protection.

The day before Article IV was introduced to the convention, T. R. R. Cobb wrote to his wife, and said in part: "I found out yesterday why George Sanders was here. He is an agent from [Stephen Arnold] Douglass [*sic*] and is working to keep out of the Constitution any clause which will exclude 'Free States.' The game now is to reconstruct [the Federal Union] *under our Constitution. . . .*" Cobb concluded his letter by saying: "Stephens and Toombs are both for leaving the door open. . . . Confidentially and to be kept secret *from the public,* Mr. Davis is opposed

28. *Ibid.*, p. 922.

to us on this point also and wants to keep the door open. . . . I am much afraid of the result."[29]

Cobb and other staunch secessionists had been fearful, during the writing of and the debates on both constitutions, that the ex-Unionists and the cooperationists would try to reconstruct or reunify the Federal Union. As indicated by Cobb's letter, this fear reached its highest point during the debates on the provision of Article IV defining the admission of new states. Indeed, the better part of March 7, 8, and 9 was devoted to a discussion of this provision. On the second day of debates on this subject, Stephens of Georgia wrote: "The most exciting of all questions we have had was decided today. If we have no motion made to reconsider that tomorrow I shall be glad. That was the clause relating to the admission of other States."[30] The debates on this issue were continued over to a third day. The three days spent debating this provision involved the longest and most intense sessions on any single provision during the consideration of the two Confederate Constitutions.

Before and during the "Great Debate," George Nicholas Sanders was in Montgomery. He was a Kentuckian by birth and an adventurer and opportunist by profession. During the 1850's, he had been a confidant and adviser of Stephen A. Douglas. A recent biographer of the "Little Giant" has written: "With reconstruction in mind—and as an alternative to war—Douglas at one point drew up a plan for a commercial union with the Confederacy which may actually have been presented in Montgomery by his old crony George Sanders."[31] Douglas' biographer describes the commercial union as follows: "The plan called for uniform trade and tariff regulations between the two republics under a super-council consisting of one member from each of their states. Surplus revenue would be divided by the two on a basis of population, and neither could add territory without the

29. Thomas Reade Rootes Cobb to his wife, March 6, 1861, in Thomas Reade Rootes Cobb Papers, Special Collections Division, University of Georgia.

30. Alexander Hamilton Stephens to Linton Stephens, March 8, 1861, in Alexander Hamilton Stephens Papers (microfilm), Southern Historical Collection, University of North Carolina.

31. Gerald Mortimer Capers, *Stephen A. Douglas: Defender of the Union* (Boston: Little Brown and Company, 1959), p. 217. During the Civil War, Sanders served as a Confederate agent in Europe and Canada.

others consent."[32] It is quite likely that Sanders discussed this plan with members of the Montgomery Convention, particularly since some of the delegates favored some form of commercial arrangement with the old Union. It is doubtful, however, that many of the delegates would have favored the specifics of the Douglas plan, particularly that concerning the addition of new territories.

It is more certain that Sanders was lobbying for a constitutional provision allowing the admission of free states into the Confederacy. Cobb's letter indicates this, as does an item in the Charleston *Mercury* which stated: "Friends of Mr. Douglas, including the near and dear George N. Sanders, are already declaring that the Northwestern States should apply for admission into the Confederate States."[33] Perhaps Sanders saw the admission of free states into the Confederacy as a necessary preliminary step to the acceptance of the Douglas plan for commercial union. It is certain that Cobb, Rhett, and other staunch secessionists opposed Sanders, who advocated the admission of non-slaveholding states into the new Confederacy.

Rhett and Miles of South Carolina, Perkins of Mississippi, and Harris of Louisiana introduced amendments before the convention which were variations of the amendment offered by T. R. R. Cobb of Georgia. It stated: "But no State shall be admitted which, by its constitution or laws, denies the right of property in negro slaves, or the right of the master to recapture his slaves."[34] These men and others who opposed the admission of non-slaveholding states well remembered the slave-state versus free-state controversy of the past forty years. The free states increased in number until they constituted a majority of the states of the Union. The free states then captured the presidency of the United States and threatened the very existence of the slave states. As a recourse, the slave states had seceded. Cobb, Rhett, and their adherents accepted this logic and sought to exclude free states from the new Confederacy in an effort to prevent the past forty years of history from repeating itself.

32. *Ibid.*
33. Charleston *Mercury,* April 1, 1861.
34. *Confederate Journal,* I, 885.

Stephens and Toombs of Georgia, who led the opposition in the convention, also looked to the future. They felt that to limit the horizons of the Confederacy by excluding free states would seriously delimit the growth, prosperity, and security of the new nation. This view is pictured by Smith of Alabama, who said: "Looking to the future with full confidence . . . I earnestly hope that not only will the kindred States join us, but abide in the confidence that some of the great Northwestern States, watered by the Mississippi, will be drawn . . . to swell the number and power of this Confederation."[35]

With both factions equally convinced of the propriety of their argument, the "Great Debate" continued for three stormy days. At the end of this time, this question, which came as close as any to causing serious defection in the convention, was answered by a compromise. John G. Shorter of Alabama introduced a compromise motion that was adopted. It stated: "Other States may be admitted into this Confederacy by a vote of two-thirds of the whole House of Representatives and two-thirds of the Senate, the Senate voting by States."[36] The words "Other States" were used instead of "New States" inasmuch as the convention anticipated that the states of the upper South might wish to join the Confederacy. Thus, the "Great Debate" ended with the Stephens' faction satisfied that free states could join the Confederacy, and the Rhett-Cobb faction at least partially satisfied with an extra-majority vote being required for the admission of such non-slave-holding states.

In addressing the Washington Peace Conference a month before the "Great Debate," ex-President John Tyler spoke of the amendment provision of the United States Constitution. He said: "Our ancestors probably committed a blunder in not having fixed upon every fifth decade for a call of a General Convention to amend and reform the Constitution. On the contrary, they have made the difficulties next to insurmountable to accomplish amendments to an instrument which was perfect for five millions of people, but not wholly so as to thirty millions."[37] Many of the dele-

35. Smith, *An Address*, p. 20.

36. *Confederate Journal,* I, 895.

37. *The American Annual Cyclopedia and Register of Important Events,* 15 volumes (New York: D. Appleton and Company, 1869), I, 564.

gates at the Montgomery Convention agreed with these words of the venerable ex-President. Smith of Alabama wrote: "The restrictions thrown around amendments to the organic law by the Constitution of the United States proved to be a practical negation of the power to alter the instrument."[38] Smith was referring to the fact that only twelve amendments had been adopted since the ratification of the United States Constitution. Ten of these amendments, the Bill of Rights, had been ratified in 1791, and the eleventh in 1798. Thus, only one amendment had been added to the constitution in the nineteenth century, and that had been in 1804. To the convention membership, these facts of history were sufficient reason for a revision of the amendment process, the vital heart of any written constitution.

The first part of Article V of the Permanent Constitution reads: "Upon the demand of any three States, legally assembled in their several conventions, the Congress shall summon a convention of all the States, to take into consideration such amendments to the Constitution as the said States shall concur in suggesting at the time when the said demand is made. . . ."[39]

The first significant feature of this Confederate provision is that the Congress is excluded from the proposal of amendments. Under the Provisional Constitution, the entire amendment process operated within the Congress. The United States Constitution provided that the Congress, whenever two-thirds of both houses deem it necessary, may propose amendments to the constitution. The Confederate "Founding Fathers" decided that the proposal of amendments would be the exclusive function of a national convention. Delegates to such a convention, elected specifically for the purpose of amending the basic document of government, would, they felt, more accurately reflect the sovereign will of the people.

The United States Constitution, when two-thirds of the legislatures of the several states made application, also provided for the calling of a national convention for the proposal of amendments. The United States Constitution does not, however, contain a delimiting clause as to the amendments that such a con-

38. Smith, *An Address,* p. 14. 39. *Confederate Journal,* I, 922.

stitutional convention might consider. Such a convention could loosely construe Article V and, if its proposals were ratified by three-fourths of the states, rewrite the constitution in the form of amendments. Perhaps because of this possibility, a national convention was not called into session before 1861; indeed, such a convention has never been convened during the history of this country.

Article V of the draft of the Permanent Constitution was subject to the construction that the national constitutional convention could submit for ratification any amendment proposed to that body. To avoid the possibility inherent in the amendment provision of the United States Constitution, DeClouet of Louisiana offered a qualifying clause to the Constitution. When this motion was adopted by the convention, Article V provided that the national convention could consider only such amendments suggested by the states at the time demand was made on the Congress that such a convention be convened.[40]

The second significant feature of the first part of this Confederate provision is that three state conventions could initiate the amendment process. Application by two-thirds of the state legislatures was required to call a national convention under the United States Constitution. Whereas an extra-majority was necessary for such action under the Federal Constitution, a minority of the states could do so under the Confederate Constitution. For some years before his death, John C. Calhoun had been much concerned with what he called "the numerical or absolute majority and the concurrent or constitutional majority."[41] He felt that this latter group, which was a numerical minority, should have its rights constitutionally protected. In an incisive work entitled "A Discourse on the Constitution of the United States," Calhoun wrote: "I call it the constitutional majority because it is an essential element in every constitutional government, be its form what it may."[42] Thus, the Confederate amendment process embodied the constitutional protection of the rights of the

40. *Ibid.*, p. 887.

41. John Caldwell Calhoun, *The Works of John C. Calhoun*, 6 volumes, edited by Richard Kenner Cralle (New York: D. Appleton and Company, 1853-1855), I, 28.

42. *Ibid.*

minority or "constitutional majority" and gave this group an effective voice in the expression of its sovereign will.

The Confederate ratification process also differs from that of the Federal system. Under the United States Constitution, ratification occurs after three-fourths of the state legislatures or state conventions concur. The Confederate amendment provision requires only that two-thirds of the state legislatures or state conventions ratify. The reduction of the ratification requirement from three-fourths to two-thirds, in addition to the reduction of the proposal requirements, greatly increased the flexibility of the amendment provision.

With this new flexibility in mind, the author of Article V of the Permanent Constitution, Robert Barnwell Rhett, made the following statement: "If it had been part of the Constitution of the United States the vast discontent which preceded the war, and made it inevitable, would have been easily arrested and allayed; and the states in convention would have settled amicably their differences."[43] Although the validity of Rhett's statement is questionable, his words do indicate the significance that Rhett, and indeed others, attached to the amendment provision of the Confederate Constitution.

The heart of the Confederate Constitution was so constructed as to be more responsive to the will of the sovereign people. In summing up his remarks on the amendment provision, and at the same time making an evaluation, Smith of Alabama said: "The substituted provision imparts a wholesome flexibility to our Constitution and, at the same time, assures us against an assembling of the States for light or transient causes, or hopeless purposes, and the consultive body, when convened, will be confined to action on propositions put forth by three States."[44]

The first section of Article VI of the Permanent Constitution made the newly established government the successor of the Provisional Government. It validated all the laws of the temporary government until they were modified or repealed, and continued

43. Rhett, "The Confederate Constitution," p. 934.

44. Smith, *An Address*, p. 14. The final clause of Article V of the Permanent Constitution, like the United States Constitution, provides that no state, without its consent, may be deprived of its equal representation in the Senate by an amendment.

in office the provisional officials until such time as their successors were qualified and took office. The second section provided that all debts contracted and engagements entered into under the Provisional Constitution be valid against the Confederacy under the Permanent Constitution.[45] This section embodied the same responsibility as did the corresponding section of the United States Constitution, which validated obligations assumed under the Articles of Confederation. And the last two sections of this article, that concerning the enumeration of certain rights which shall not deny others retained by the people and that concerning the reserve powers of the states,[46] are but a slight rephrasing of the last two sections of the Bill of Rights.

The committee draft of Article VI contained a provision that caused the Confederacy to recognize its ultimate liability for such proportion of the debts of the United States as was contracted prior to December 20, 1860 (the day South Carolina seceded), as the representative population of the Confederacy bore to that of the United States according to the 1860 census. On a motion by Hale of Alabama, on March 8, this generous provision was stricken from the Permanent Constitution.[47] The convention took the position that the Confederacy had neither legal nor moral responsibility for the debts of the old Union.

The final article of the Permanent Constitution defined the procedure of ratification, a process absent from the Provisional Constitution. This article was added to the constitution on the ninth day of debates upon a motion by T. R. R. Cobb.[48] Life would be given to the Permanent Constitution when it was ratified by five states. In addition, Cobb's provision also provided that the Provisional Congress fix a time for holding an election of a Permanent President and Vice President, for the meeting of the electoral college, for the election of a Permanent Congress, and for a time for its assemblage. Moreover, the Provisional Congress retained legislative power until the organization of the first elective Congress.

On the day preceding Cobb's introduction of Article VII, Kenner of Louisiana introduced a resolution which stated: "That

45. *Confederate Journal*, I, 922.
46. *Ibid.*, p. 923.
47. *Ibid.*, p. 888.
48. *Ibid.*, p. 895.

the Committee on the Permanent Constitution appoint from their number a subcommittee of three, to whom shall be referred the Constitution, with instructions to perfect its style and arrangement, and have the same printed and reported for revisal at the earliest possible day."[49] Although there is no positive indication as to who the three committee members were, scattered evidence indicates that T. R. R. Cobb, Robert H. Smith, and possibly Edward Sparrow of Louisiana made up the committee. On Saturday evening, March 9, the report of the Committee of Three was ordered spread on the convention journal upon a motion by Robert H. Smith.[50]

Although the report of the Committee of Three does not appear in the convention journal, it has been preserved in its original form. In preparing their report, the committee used the services of Alexander Birch Clitherall who was Assistant Secretary of the Congress to J. J. Hooper.[51] Clitherall was an experienced jurist and state legislator and, at the time of the meeting of the Montgomery Convention, was a resident of Montgomery. While serving the Provisional Congress, Clitherall briefly acted as secretary to President Davis; later he was appointed Register of the Treasury.[52] Clitherall had worked with Rhett's Second Committee of Twelve from the beginning, having had the committee draft printed for use by the convention during the debates. He noted all forty-two changes in phraseology and amendments made by the convention. When the Committee of Three met, it probably used Clitherall's annotated copy of the committee draft as the basis for its report. Since the convention made the necessary changes and corrections in verbiage, the committee was primarily concerned with appropriately arranging the Permanent Constitution. The report of the committee, including the changes made during the debates on the afternoon of March 9, was presented to the convention on the evening of the ninth.

The following day, Sunday, the convention did not meet. On

49. *Ibid.*, p. 888.

50. *Ibid.*, p. 896.

51. What is called the "Alexander Birch Clitherall Scratcher Copy of the Permanent Constitution of the Confederate States of America" is in the possession of the Alabama State Department of Archives and History, Montgomery, Alabama.

52. *Confederate Journal,* I, 69, 143, 153.

Monday afternoon, March 11, 1861, Howell Cobb, as President of the Convention, asked his fellow members: "Shall the Constitution be passed and adopted."[53] After the yeas and nays of the entire body were taken, the President announced that the Permanent Constitution of the Confederacy had been unanimously passed and adopted.

The Second Committee of Twelve had reported a draft after nineteen hectic days and, after ten days of heated debate, the Confederate "Founding Fathers" adopted a Permanent Constitution.

After the adoption of the constitution, the convention resolved itself back into session as the Provisional Congress and the Montgomery Convention as a constituent assembly passed into history. The work of the convention, however, faced an essential test. The Permanent Constitution had to be submitted to the several states for ratification.

53. *Ibid.*, p. 896.

CHAPTER VII

The Constitution Completed

I see no strong necessity for referring its action back to the people. They could have limited the power, . . . and as there were many weighty reasons for prompt action, I feel authorized to vote for immediate ratification.

Alexander M. Clayton of Mississippi

On the last day of the first session of the Provisional Congress, the members affixed their signatures to the Permanent Constitution. On March 16, 1861, the enrolled document, transcribed in the traditional Spencerian style, was reported and laid on the long table in front of the speaker's rostrum. The procedure for the signing was similar to that followed in the signing of the Provisional Constitution. After Howell Cobb affixed his signature as President of the Congress, the delegations from South Carolina, Georgia, Florida, Alabama, Mississippi, Louisiana, and Texas came forward and signed their names. Upon the completion of this significant action, the convention adopted a motion made by Rhett which ordered the President of the Congress to have the signed constitution lithographed and copies thereof sent to each of the Confederate States.[1]

The lithographing of the Permanent Constitution was delayed for several months since all of the delegates were not present at the signing. Seven men had been absent four days earlier when the constitution had been adopted.[2] These same delegates were absent at the signing. Shortly after the second session of the Provisional Congress reassembled on April 20, Rhett moved that

1. *Journal of the Congress of the Confederate States of America, 1861-1865,* 7 volumes (Washington: Government Printing Office, 1904-1905), I, 150. (Hereinafter cited as *Confederate Journal.*)

2. Those absent were: Crawford, Kenan, and T. R. R. Cobb of Georgia (before leaving Montgomery on March 9, Cobb ordered that an affirmative vote be placed beside his name pursuant to the adoption); Chilton and Lewis of Alabama; Campbell of Mississippi, and Wigfall of Texas.

the members of the Congress who had not signed the enrolled Permanent Constitution be requested to do so.[3] This motion prevailed and the seven men came forward to affix their signatures. The following day T. R. R. Cobb wrote to his wife and said: "Yesterday . . . I signed the Permanent Constitution of the Confederate States and have thus perfected my 'rebellion.' I trust that my children hereafter may recur with pride to it, whether by others I am cannonized as a saint or hung as a traitor."[4] With the addition of the last seven of the fifty signatures, the signing of the constitution was completed.[5]

On the evening of March 16, just prior to the adjournment of the Provisional Congress, Rhett introduced a resolution complimentary to Howell Cobb for the manner in which he had discharged his duties as President of the Congress. Rhett commented upon the uniqueness of his resolution, inasmuch as such resolutions were not usually introduced until the completion of the services of a presiding officer at the termination of a legislative body. He said: "we are not in ordinary times. This Congress is the most important political body which has assembled in this country, since the Revolutionary Congress of 1776. Perhaps it exceeds in importance the great Revolutionary Congress of the last Century." Rhett concluded his brief remarks by saying: "Let us treat it as a great event marked in the calendar of time—complete in itself; and turning to him who has presided over our deliberations with so much efficiency and dignity, award to him the just meed of our cordial approbation."[6]

Before announcing the adjournment, Cobb made a brief and eloquent response to the compliment paid him by the convention. In his opening remarks, Cobb said: "To have presided over such a body, engaged in such duties, I regard as the highest honor which ever has been or ever will be conferred upon me." Referring to

3. *Confederate Journal,* I, 170.

4. Thomas Reade Rootes Cobb to his wife, April 30, 1861, in Thomas Reade Rootes Cobb Papers, Special Collections Division, University of Georgia.

5. The original Permanent Constitution of the Confederate States of America is in the Special Collections Division of the University of Georgia Library at Athens, Georgia. This vellum document is twenty-seven inches wide, twelve feet long, and kept in a copper cylinder about three feet long. In 1951, the constitution was insured for $50,000.

6. Montgomery *Weekly Advertiser,* March 27, 1861.

the constitution just signed, he said: "Having completed the great work for which we assembled—the formation of a permanent Constitution for the Confederate States—we rest for a period from our labors, to receive the judgment of our constituents upon our action."[7] Looking to the future, Cobb commented: "Whatever may be the criticism of the hour upon the Constitution we have formed, I feel confident that the judgment of our people, and indeed the world, will in the end, pronounce it the ablest instrument ever prepared for the government of a free people."[8] After extending the appreciation of a grateful heart, the distinguished Georgian announced the adjournment of the Congress.

When Cobb referred to the submission of the constitution to his countrymen for ratification, he was referring to an action that had already transpired. On March 12, the day following the adoption of the Permanent Constitution, Cobb sent printed copies of the constitution to the conventions of the several states. This action was in accordance with the original instructions of the state conventions to their delegations. The Permanent Constitution, after adoption, was to be referred back to the several states for ratification or rejection.

Cobb's letter accompanying the printed constitution manifested a positive approach to ratification by stating only that the Permanent Constitution was submitted to the state for its approval and ratification. In an open effort to encourage favorable action, Cobb explained that the enclosed document was patterned after the United States Constitution. He further explained that the departures from the parent document were suggested by the experience of the past and were intended to guard against the evils and dangers which had led to the disruption of the late Union. Cobb's letter concluded with the following statement: "This Constitution is now submitted with confidence to the State Conventions for their action."[9]

The first state convention to receive Cobb's communication was that of Alabama. The second session of the Alabama Secession Convention had been meeting for a week prior to the adop-

7. *Confederate Journal,* I, 152. 8. *Ibid.,* p. 153.

9. *Journal of the State Convention and Ordinances and Resolutions Adopted in March, 1861* (Jackson: E. Barksdale, 1861), p. 4. (Hereinafter cited as *Journal of the Mississippi Convention.*)

tion of the Permanent Constitution. The state convention had anticipated the early adoption of the constitution and wanted to be ready to give the new document immediate attention. On the day after the Montgomery Convention adopted the constitution, the Alabama Secession Convention received a printed copy of the document along with Cobb's letter. The ratification debates took place in the House of Representatives Chamber of the state capitol building, just across the hall from the Senate Chamber in which the Permanent Constitution had been debated and adopted.

On the afternoon of March 12, the Confederate Constitution was read to the Alabama convention while a second person held a copy of the United States Constitution and declared the differences between the two seriatim. At the conclusion of the readings, a vigorous discussion of ratification began and lasted for the balance of the day. Almost every member favored the ratification of the Permanent Constitution; the difficulty came as to what method would be employed. The cooperationists favored either submitting the constitution directly to the people or to a new convention. The immediate secessionists wanted the constitution ratified immediately.

The principal argument for immediate ratification was based on the necessity for unity in the face of the uncertainty of the future. Members favoring this argument were fearful that delay would cause the public mind to again become agitated and would cause new divisions to spring up among the people. Lewis Maxwell Stone of Pickens County said: "Our divisions would be exposed and magnified in the face of our enemies; our friends, at home and abroad, would despair of ever seeing us a united people; and all this, sir, at a time when union, harmony, brotherly feeling, and concerted action among ourselves, are so much needed to secure the great objects of the Southern movement."[10]

Although the desire for unanimity was uppermost in the thoughts of those favoring immediate ratification, other telling points were put forward in support of their position. The members who advocated immediate action held that the Provisional

10. William Russell Smith, *The History and Debates of the Convention of the People of Alabama* (Montgomery: White, Pfister, and Company, 1861), p. 332. Stone had been a supporter of immediate secession.

Constitution and government were not sufficient to encourage needed cooperation at home or abroad. While preparing the Permanent Constitution, the Montgomery Convention had often had the border states and Europe in mind. Those members in the Alabama convention who supported immediate ratification felt that delay might jeopardize the early cooperation of the border states. Moreover, they argued that to delay ratification might also affect the respect and early recognition of the Confederacy. the major powers of Europe.

A further point concerned the credit of the new Confederacy. Speaking honestly and bluntly, Stone argued: "Bonds, with the endorsement of a Permanent Government, can be much more readily disposed of to capitalists, and will command much higher rates than the bonds of a mere temporary or Provisional Government."[11] After mentioning the financial security of the Confederacy, Stone attacked the unnecessary heavy expense that would be incurred by the state of Alabama to hold an election of delegates to another convention. Why, he challenged, was it necessary to call a second convention "to do precisely what we were authorized and required to do, but what it is proposed we shall leave undone."[12]

A final argument of the members favoring immediate ratification asserted that prompt action would greatly strengthen the new nation. Looking to the days ahead, Stone argued for a permanent government by saying: "Such a Government would be more powerful in war, and more persuasive to peace."[13] Security through strength was a vital requirement, he said, to the growth and prosperity of the infant Confederacy.

The secession convention members were proud of the fact that Montgomery was the capital of the Provisional Government of the Confederacy. They wanted the capital to remain in Montgomery. Indeed, during the meeting of the Montgomery Convention some Alabamians had advocated the granting of an area of land in or near Montgomery to be named the District of Davis. Although the question of the site of the Confederate capital did not arise during the debates on ratification, it is quite

11. *Ibid.*, p. 335.
12. *Ibid.*, p. 336.
13. *Ibid.*, p. 334.

likely that the members felt that immediate ratification by Alabama would aid Montgomery's chances of becoming the permanent capital of the Confederacy.

At the outset of the debates on ratification in the Alabama Secession Convention, Robert Jamison, Jr. of Tuscaloosa County, President of the convention, relinquished his chair to take the floor. He offered a resolution which provided that the Permanent Constitution be submitted for ratification or rejection to a convention of the people. In speaking for his resolution, Jamison said: "So far as I am individually concerned, I have no great preference for the plan that I propose, and I am moved to it by the respect that I have for the people, as well as by what I conceive to be my duty to them. I should have no hesitation whatever to vote for ratification now."[14] William Russell Smith of Tuscaloosa County, another cooperationist, did have strong feelings concerning the submission of the constitution to a convention. He lashed out against the credit argument of those favoring immediate ratification by saying: "Between poverty and liberty there can be no debate." Relative to foreign recognition, he said: "It is a sad day, sir, when an American has to admit that he depends upon *foreign allies* for his *protection*."[15]

A group of cooperationists, even more adamant than Smith, advocated submitting the new constitution directly to the people of the state. These members countered the argument that action other than immediate ratification would be unnecessarily expensive by saying, in effect, what price liberty. These cooperationists denied that delay would impair the credit of the Confederate States, or that submitting the constitution would create significant divisions among the people. James S. Clarke of Lawrence County said: "There is no necessity for the immediate ratification of the Constitution. . . . The strength, power and resources of the Provisional Government render haste not only unnecessary, but absolutely unexcusable." Concluding the argument for this group of cooperationsts, Clarke stated: "The people, if they ratify it, will love it and submit to it cheerfully, because it will then be the

14. *Ibid.*, p. 323.

15. *Ibid.*, p. 349. Smith later authored and edited *The History and Debates of the Convention of the People of Alabama*, which records the proceedings to which he was a part.

Government of their own selection. But, sir, if you impose it upon them what assurances have you that it will survive the first wave of popular indignation?"[16]

The small group of convention delegates who favored ratification by a popular vote did not bring a resolution embodying their philosophy to a vote. Instead, they rallied behind Jamison's resolution which advocated ratification by a newly called convention. When this resolution came to a vote, it was defeated 36-53.[17] Immediately after the vote, Jamison rose and, in a move designed to bring unanimity, said: "I would not only be proud to see a unanimous vote in favor of Ratification, but I would be proud of the privilege of marching up side by side with all of those who have not yet signed the Ordinance of Secession, and sign it."[18] The motion for immediate ratification was then presented and was adopted by a decisive vote of 87-5.[19]

The Alabama Secession Convention which had been instrumental in the calling of the Montgomery Convention was the first to ratify the Permanent Constitution.[20] This convention received the constitution on March 12, and debated and ratified it on the same day. Alabama set an example for her sister states by the swift ratification of the new constitution. The convention debates in Alabama were significant in yet another respect. These debates incorporated the principal arguments that were to be voiced for immediate ratification in the Georgia convention; moreover, they incorporated the principal arguments for and against immediate ratification in the conventions of Louisiana, Texas, and Mississippi.

16. *Ibid.*, p. 329.
17. *Ibid.*, p. 363.
18. *Ibid.*
19. *Ibid.*

20. After hearing a speech by Robert H. Smith of Alabama at Mobile on the evening of March 31, 1861, Howell Cobb wrote his wife and said: "It will be published and I advise everyone to read it. It was really a finished and eloquent defense of our new Constitution." Ulrich Bonnell Phillips, ed., *The Correspondence of Robert Toombs, Alexander H. Stephens and Howell Cobb*, American Historical Association, *Annual Report, 1911*, II (Washington: Government Printing Office, 1913), 557. Cobb refers to what this writer believes to be not only the most eloquent but also the most incisive contemporary defense of the Permanent Constitution. Smith's speech has been liberally quoted in the preceding chapters. It was delivered after the Permanent Constitution was ratified by the requisite five states. Because the speech is a defense of the work of the Montgomery Convention, and not an appeal for ratification, it is mentioned instead of being discussed in this chapter.

Although the Georgia Secession Convention reconvened at Savannah on March 7, the Permanent Constitution along with Cobb's official letter did not arrive for presentation to the convention until the fifteenth. After the communication was read, the convention agreed to consider the constitution at the morning session the following day. On the morning of March 16, in secret session, the new constitution was read. With little discussion, the document was referred to a committee with instructions to frame and report, during the morning session, an ordinance to accept and ratify the Permanent Constitution. Later the same morning, an ordinance of ratification was reported and unanimously adopted by a vote of 276-0.[21]

The debates in the Georgia Secession Convention upon the introduction of an ordinance of ratification were more perfunctory than had been the case in Alabama. No attempt was made to introduce an amendment which would cause the constitution to be submitted to a new convention, nor was any move made to submit the constitution to the people of the state. A desire to avoid delay and achieve unity was the overriding consideration during the brief morning session of the convention. Thus, Georgia was the second state to ratify the Permanent Constitution, and the first to do so by a unanimous vote.[22]

Three days before the Louisiana Secession Convention received the Permanent Constitution, an ordinance was introduced providing for the submission of the constitution to the people for ratification or rejection. This ordinance, which was proposed on March 13, came to a vote three days later and was defeated by a count of 26-74.[23] The Confederate Constitution was received and read to the convention on March 19, but consideration of the document was delayed until Thursday, March 21. A second effort was then made to block immediate ratification. An ordinance to

21. Allen D. Chandler, ed., *The Confederate Records of the State of Georgia,* 6 volumes (Atlanta: Charles P. Byrd, 1909), I, 458.

22. On the evening of March 21, Alexander H. Stephens gave his famous "corner-stone speech" at the Athenaeum in Savannah. His eloquence was directed toward an examination and defense of the new constitution, as opposed to an argument for ratification, since Georgia had adopted the Permanent Constitution five days earlier.

23. *Official Journal of the Proceedings of the Convention of the State of Louisiana* (New Orleans: J. O. Nixon, 1861), p. 70.

provide for the calling of a new convention to consider ratification was proposed. This attempt to thwart immediate ratification failed when a motion to table the ordinance was adopted by the decisive vote of 94-10.[24]

A small but vocal minority in the Louisiana Secession Convention, like that in Alabama, sought to delay the ratification process by offering two alternative plans. After pressing its position upon the convention and meeting defeat, most of the minority joined ranks with the majority who favored immediate ratification. The third state to ratify the Permanent Constitution presented a united front, as had Alabama and Georgia, by adopting an ordinance of immediate ratification by the decisive vote of 102-7.[25]

Because Austin, Texas, was the convention city most distant from Montgomery, William B. Ochiltree presented a resolution to the Provisional Congress on March 12, which provided for a special messenger to take the constitution to the Texas Secession Convention.[26] The resolution was adopted and, on March 19, the messenger arrived in Austin, and presented the documents under his charge to the convention. A letter, signed by the Texas delegation in the Montgomery Convention, encouraging immediate ratification was read to the convention, as well as Cobb's letter and the new framework of government. After a brief discussion, the consideration of the constitution was delayed until March 23. At that time, a resolution to submit the Confederate Constitution to the people of Texas was lost when a motion to table the resolution passed by a vote of 93-32.[27] Immediately thereafter, an ordinance of ratification was adopted by a vote of 126-2.[28]

A few weeks after ratification, the Texas convention published a document entitled "An Address to the People of Texas." It detailed some of the familiar arguments for the immediate ratification of the Confederate Constitution. Evidencing the opinion of a large majority of the convention, this document also echoed

24. *Ibid.*, p. 74.

25. *Ibid.*, p. 76.

26. *Confederate Journal*, I, 130.

27. *Journal of the Secession Convention of Texas 1861, Edited from the Original* by Ernest William Winkler (Austin: Austin Printing Company, 1912), p. 233. (Hereinafter cited as *Texas Convention Journal.*)

28. *Ibid.*, p. 235.

some arguments unique to Texas. After suggesting that prompt action by Texas would encourage the Confederate government to adopt more effective and permanent measures for the defense of the state, particularly the desolate Texas frontier, the address continued by stating: "In connection with the defense of Texas, the appearance of uncertainty as to its political position would embarrass the pending arrangements for an alliance between the Confederacy, as one party, and the Choctaw, Chickasaw, Creek and Cherokee nations, in concert as the other party."[29] Concerning the effect of the action of Texas upon her neighbors, the address declared: "Such hesitation on the part of Texas would tend to produce similar hesitation in Arizona and New Mexico, as to their connection with the Confederacy. Such procrastination would operate unfavorably on the neighboring government and people of Mexico, as to desirable negotiations and intercourse."[30]

Texans were aware of the necessity of unity, credit, and recognition to the new Confederacy and, indeed, used these arguments to support the cause of immediate ratification. Because Texas was sparsely settled and located on the vulnerable flank of the Confederacy, the delegates in the Austin Secession Convention were probably more impressed by the defense needs of their state. In the hope that prompt action would contribute to the solution of the principal concern of the state, Texas became the fourth state to ratify the Confederate Constitution, less than two weeks after the adoption of the document by the Montgomery Convention.

The next state to ratify the Permanent Constitution would have the honor of establishing the permanent basic framework of the new government. Both the Mississippi Secession Convention, which convened on March 25, and the South Carolina Secession Convention, which convened on the next day, were called specifically to consider ratification or rejection of the constitution. The honor went to the home state of the President of the Confederacy.

A committee on ratification was appointed, on the day that the Mississippi convention assembled. Resolutions instructing the

29. *Ibid.*, p. 258. President Davis presented treaties recently made with these tribes of Indians on December 12, 1861, and they were ratified on December 12 and 24. *Confederate Journal*, I, 591, 610, 611.

30. *Texas Convention Journal*, p. 258.

committee to report an ordinance for immediate ratification, for ratification by a new convention, for ratification by a vote of the people of the state were introduced. All were referred to the committee for its consideration. After only one day, the committee made its report. A majority report was embodied in an ordinance for immediate ratification by the convention. A minority report provided for the ratification or rejection of the constitution by the people at the ballot box. For the next three days, the two reports were debated along the lines set down in the debates of the Alabama convention.

On March 28, Alexander M. Clayton, who had recently returned from the Montgomery Convention, made an impassioned plea for immediate ratification. Until this speech, one of the major points of conflict within the convention was whether or not the convention had the right and power to ratify the Permanent Constitution. Clayton addressed himself to this controversy by saying: "I feel no strong necessity for referring its action back to the people. They could have limited the power, and have required the Constitution to be referred to them, . . . but as they had imposed no limitation, and as there were many weighty reasons for prompt action, I feel authorized to vote for immediate action."[31] Clayton's speech came at the climax of the Mississippi debates on ratification and apparently was very influential in convincing many undecided members.

The next day the minority report came up for consideration and was defeated by a vote of 13-66.[32] A great majority of the members agreed with Clayton and another Montgomery delegate, Wiley Pope Harris, who wrote: "When we brought back from Montgomery the Constitution which had been framed then, I opposed its submission to the people because it involved delay and imperiled the whole undertaking. I felt that the defection of one state would be fatal."[33] The vote on the majority report was

31. Speech of Alexander Mosby Clayton before the Mississippi Convention of March 28, 1861, in Claiborne Papers, Southern Historical Collection, University of North Carolina.

32. *Mississippi Convention Journal*, p. 34.

33. "Autobiography of Wiley P. Harris," in Dunbar Rowland, *Courts, Judges, and Lawyers of Mississippi, 1798-1935* (Jackson: State Department of Archives and History, 1935), p. 325.

78-7.[34] With this vote on March 26, 1861, the fifth and last required state ratified the Permanent Constitution of the Confederacy.

Following ratification in Mississippi, favorable action in South Carolina and Florida was still required to unify the new nation upon a permanent government. The debates in the conventions of the first five states to ratify the constitution centered upon the propriety of immediate ratification. In South Carolina, the focal point of debate shifted dramatically to the defects of the new constitution. This state, which had done so much to make the Permanent Constitution possible, was the state least satisfied with the finished document. The ensuing debates at Charleston were the most extended and the most heated of any in the seven states of the Confederacy. During the early months of the secession movement, South Carolina had often voiced an appeal for unity; during the Charleston debates on ratification, however, this state posed a serious threat to the unity of the Confederacy.

When the South Carolina Secession Convention reassembled in St. Andrews Hall in Charleston at noon on March 26, the first order of business was the reading of Howell Cobb's official letter. Then, Robert Barnwell Rhett introduced a motion to have five hundred copies of the new Confederate Constitution printed in parallel columns with the United States Constitution. This motion, along with a second one by Rhett providing that the ratification debates be held in secret session, was adopted.

Although Rhett had played a significant role in the framing of the Permanent Constitution, some provisions that he considered critical were excluded from the finished document. One such provision was the exclusion of non-slave holding states from the Confederacy. Because of his strong feelings in this matter, he had been an outspoken leader in the "Great Debate" at Montgomery. Rhett continued his fight for a slaveholding Confederacy at Charleston. On the first day, he introduced an ordinance that required the governor of the state to call a convention of the people upon the admission of a non-slaveholding state into the Confederacy. Included in the ordinance was Rhett's reason for introducing such a measure. It stated: "experience has proved

34. *Mississippi Convention Journal,* p. 35.

that the slaveholding and non-slaveholding States cannot live in peace under the same government. . . ."[35] This ordinance was laid on the table and was not reconsidered. The subject of Rhett's ordinance did, however, come before the convention again.

On the second day, Gabriel Manigault, an ardent secessionist planter, introduced a series of resolutions. The preface to these resolutions stated: "That before this Convention ratifies the Constitution adopted at Montgomery, we feel bound to express our conviction that it is imperfect and objectionable, and ought to be amended. . . ."[36] Manigault's amendments pointed to five defects in the constitution, namely, the failure to prohibit the admission of non-slaveholding states, the adoption of the three-fifths basis for calculating representation, the granting of unlimited power to the federal government over indirect taxes, the prohibition of the African slave trade without giving this prerogative to the Congress, and the continuation of the post office monopoly in the hands of the federal government. In the closest significant vote during the debates, Manigault's resolutions were defeated 60-94.[37] Montgomery delegates Rhett, Chesnut, and Keitt voted for the resolutions, while Barnwell, Withers, and Miles opposed them.[38]

On March 29, the day Mississippi ratified the constitution, the Confederate and United States Constitutions were read to the Charleston convention. Thereafter and for the next few days, the debates revolved around whether to proceed immediately to ratification or first to discuss necessary amendments to the constitution. The climax came on April 2, when Rhett introduced an amendment to an ordinance of ratification which stated: "That in ratifying and adopting the above Constitution, they suppose that it established a Confederacy of Slaveholding States; and this State does not consider itself bound to enter or continue in confederation with any State not tolerating the institution of

35. *Journal of the Convention of the People of South Carolina, Held in 1860-'61* (Charleston: Evans and Cogswell, Printers to the Convention, 1861), p. 211. (Hereinafter cited as *Journal of South Carolina.*)

36. *Ibid.*, p. 219.

37. *Ibid.*, p. 220.

38. Boyce was absent from the convention because of illness in his family and Memminger was busy directing the operation of the Treasury Department in Montgomery.

slavery. . . ."[39] Rhett's radical amendment was defeated 41-89.[40] On the same day, one of the members, ex-Governor John Laurence Manning, wrote to his wife: "A vast deal of time has been consumed in giving the opponents of ratification an opportunity to express their views—but I think their arguments are convincing the Convention in a contrary way."[41] The following day, April 3, with the situation in Charleston Harbor becoming more critical each day, the convention adopted an ordinance of ratification by a vote of 138-21.[42] Rhett, along with his fellow delegates to Montgomery, voted in favor of ratification.

With ratification accomplished, the Charleston convention continued to discuss the amendment problem for another two days. The convention adopted a resolution which called for the meeting of a national convention, when the permanent government was securely established and in peaceful operation, for the purpose of considering amendments to the constitution. Four amendments, finally agreed upon, were: (1) to repeal the three-fifths clause and count Negroes in full; (2) to prohibit the admission of non-slaveholding states into the Confederacy except by the consent of all the states; (3) to repeal the constitutional provision prohibiting the foreign slave trade and to give such power to Congress; and (4) to prohibit the Congress from contracting any debt except for war purposes, and to require that all expenditures in excess of revenues from imports (not to exceed 15% ad valorem) be met from direct taxes laid by the Congress making the appropriation.[43] These resolutions, adopted by a vote of 117-15,[44] indicate the general opinion of the convention that the defects in the constitution needed amending, but that such action should be postponed until a more suitable time. The time of the secure establishment and peaceful operation of the Confederate government never arrived, and the implementation of the South Carolina resolutions never took place.

39. *Journal of South Carolina,* p. 241. 40. *Ibid.*

41. John Laurence Manning to his wife, April 2, 1861, in Williams–Chesnut–Manning Papers, Southern Historical Collection, University of North Carolina.

42. *Journal of South Carolina,* p. 249. Six negative votes were later changed to the affirmative, three affirmative and one negative votes were cast late; thus, the final vote was 147-16. Among the most prominent men who voted against ratification were Gabriel Manigault, Leonidas William Spratt, Maxcy Gregg, and John Izard Middleton.

43. *Ibid.,* pp. 256 ff. 44. *Ibid.,* p. 274.

The last of the original seven Confederate states to ratify the Permanent Constitution was Florida. A called session of the Florida Secession Convention reassembled in Tallahassee on April 18. By this date, not only had Florida's six sister states already ratified the constitution, but the firing on Fort Sumter was history. The introduction of the constitution and its subsequent ratification were perfunctory. On April 22, 1861, by a vote of 54-0,[45] the Florida convention made the ratification of the Confederate Constitution unanimous.

The most significant single feature of the Confederate ratification process was the speed and ease with which it took place. Only eighteen days elapsed between the adoption of the Permanent Constitution by the Montgomery Convention and the establishment of the document upon the ratification of Mississippi. Indeed, the seventh state to ratify the constitution did so only forty-two days after adoption in Montgomery.

The secession conventions of three states entertained resolutions to refer the Confederate Constitution either to the people or to new conventions. The Texas convention considered a resolution to submit the constitution to the people at the ballot box. Only in South Carolina was there any serious opposition to ratification. The ratification issue was before the conventions of Alabama, Georgia, Louisiana, Texas, Mississippi, and Florida from one to five days. Even in Charleston, the stormy sessions on ratification ended after only nine days. After a short period of debate, the advocates of immediate ratification won their case in all seven conventions.

Attesting to the ease with which the ratification of the Confederate Constitution was achieved are the convention votes: Alabama 87-5; Georgia 276-0; Louisiana 102-7; Texas 126-2; Mississippi 78-7; and Florida 54-0. Only in the South Carolina Secession Convention was the vote (138-21) indicative of any sizeable minority opposition. Less than five per cent of the combined membership of the seven state conventions opposed immediate ratification of the constitution.

Although newspapers played an important role in the ratification of the United States Constitution, such was not the

45. *Journal of the Proceedings of the Convention of the People of Florida* (Tallahassee: Dyke and Carlisle, 1861), p. 36.

case in the Confederacy. Prior to ratification, an Alabama editorial briefly mentioned how foolish and unnecessary it would be to submit the new constitution to a vote of the people.[46] In South Carolina, the Charleston *Mercury* tersely reflected Rhett's dissatisfaction with parts of the constitution.[47] In general, however, Confederate newspapers happily noted the occasion of ratification, instead of offering detailed opinions before the fact.

The ratification of the Confederate Constitution was achieved quickly and easily and, like the United States Constitution, it floated on a wave of economic prosperity. A more significant catalyst to the Confederate ratification process was the desire for unity. The conventions believed that in unity there was strength and that in strength there was the best hope of realizing the destiny of southern nationalism. Certainly the leaders of the Confederacy were encouraged to have an established permanent constitution on April 12, 1861, after which unity was vital to the survival of the Confederacy.

After the firing on Fort Sumter, and following President Lincoln's appeal to arms, the four border states of Virginia, Arkansas, Tennessee, and North Carolina determined to share the future of the Confederacy. During the summer months of 1861, the actions of these states brought the number of states ratifying the Confederate Constitution to eleven.

Arkansas, after seceding on May 6, 1861, ratified the Confederate Constitution on June 1, 1861, by acclamation.[48] North Carolina adopted an Ordinance of Secession on May 20 and quickly followed the lead of Arkansas by ratifying the Confederate Constitution by a unanimous vote on June 6.[49] Virginia seceded on April 17 and was the third border state to ratify the new constitution on June 19, by a vote of 92-0.[50] The General

46. The Selma *Weekly Issue*, March 13, 1861. The editorial was written the day before the Alabama convention ratified the Constitution.

47. Charleston *Mercury*, March 15, 1861.

48. *Journal of the Convention of the State of Arkansas* (Little Rock: Johnson and Yerkes, State Printers, 1861), p. 455.

49. *Journal of the Convention of the People of North Carolina Held on the 20th Day of May, A.D. 1861* (Raleigh: J. W. Syme, Printer to the Convention, 1862), p. 73.

50. *Journal of the Acts and Proceedings of a General Convention of the State of Virginia Assembled at Richmond on Wednesday, the Thirteenth Day of February, Eighteen Hundred and Sixty-One* (Richmond: Wyatt M. Elliott, Printer, 1861), p. 256.

Assembly of Tennessee, after adopting a secession ordinance on May 6, passed an act that provided for the submission of the question of the ratification of the Confederate Constitution to the voters of the state at the next election.[51] This act also provided that the governor would proclaim the results of the election. On August 1, the vote was 85,753 for ratification and 30,863 against,[52] the majority for the constitution being 54,890. Tennessee was the only state of the Confederacy to submit the Permanent Constitution to the people for ratification or rejection, and the governor did not issue a formal proclamation of ratification.

Although Missouri and Kentucky were the last of the border states to join the Confederacy, in neither state was the Confederate Constitution formally ratified either by a secession convention or a General Assembly. Before the end of September 1861, internecine warfare was a fact in Missouri and Kentucky's policy of neutrality had proven untenable.

Claiborne Jackson, Missouri's secessionist governor, called a special session of the General Assembly to meet at Neosho, in southwestern Missouri, on October 21.[53] Seven days later the General Assembly acted upon the governor's recommendations, even though a quorum was not present, by passing an ordinance of secession and an act ratifying the Provisional Confederate Constitution.[54] This action fulfilled the requirements of the Confederate Congress, and Missouri was admitted as the twelfth state on November 28.[55] The following day the Congress passed an act requiring Missouri to ratify the Permanent Constitution before electing members to the House of Representatives.[56] Al-

51. *Public Acts of the State of Tennessee Passed at the Extra Session of the Thirty-Third General Assembly, April, 1861* (Nashville: J. O. Griffith and Company, Public Printers, 1861), p. 55. Secession and ratification were acted upon by secession conventions in Arkansas, North Carolina, and Virginia. The voters of Tennessee rejected the proposition to call a secession convention; thus, the General Assembly acted in its stead.

52. Nashville *Union and American,* August 18, 1861.

53. *Journal of the Senate, Extra Session of the Rebel Legislature, called together by a Proclamation of C. F. Jackson, begun and held at the town of Neosho, Newton County, Missouri, on the Twenty-First Day of October, Eighteen Hundred and Sixty-One* (Jefferson City: Emory S. Foster, 1865), pp. 3-4.

54. *Ibid.,* pp. 8-9, 42-43.

55. *Confederate Journal,* I, 488.

56. James Muscoe Matthews, ed., *The Statutes at Large of the Provisional Government of the Confederate States of America* (Richmond: R. M. Smith, 1864), p. 221.

though Missouri was represented in the Permanent Congress at Richmond, a study of the records does not show that Missouri ratified the Permanent Constitution. Apparently the Confederate Congress overlooked their ratification requirement because of the flight of the Jackson government and the subsequent Union occupation of southern Missouri.

President Davis and President Lincoln held more than a sentimental attachment to the pivotal state of Kentucky. Within a month after Missouri seceded, and while Union troops occupied northern and part of central Kentucky, delegates from sixty-eight counties assembled at Russellville to organize a provisional government of Kentucky. The Russellville convention, meeting in southwestern Kentucky from November 18 to 21, established a provisional government, located the state capital at nearby Bowling Green, and on November 20 passed an ordinance of secession, or what they called a "Declaration of Independence."[57] On December 10 the council of the provisional government proclaimed that the Provisional Constitution, all laws passed by the Provisional Congress, and the Permanent Constitution of the Confederacy were adopted and ratified.[58] On the same day in Richmond the Congress was informed that President Davis had just signed an act admitting his native state to the Confederacy.[59]

Although the formal ratification process of the Confederate Constitution ended in August with the action of Tennessee, Missouri's rump legislature ratified the Provisional Constitution in October, and Kentucky concluded her ratification by irregular means in December. The secession governments of the latter two states were soon in flight and their states under Union control; nevertheless, the action of these governments served to legalize the position of those citizens who served the Confederacy. Even though the loyalties of Missouri and Kentucky remained divided, the momentous year of 1861 ended with the Confederate States claiming thirteen stars in their flag. Thirteen states had once fought successfully for their independence; the Confederate "Founding Fathers" believed that history would repeat itself.

57. *Proceedings of the Convention Establishing Provisional Government of Kentucky* (Augusta: Steam Press of Chronicle and Sentinel, 1863), p. 5.

58. *Ibid.*, p. 23.

59. *Confederate Journal,* I, 554.

CHAPTER VIII

Conclusion

The problem which all federated nations have to solve is how to secure an efficient central government and preserve national unity, while allowing free scope for the diversities and free play to the authorities, of the members of the federation.

James Bryce

The greatest constitutional question in the United States between 1787 and 1861 was: "What is the nature of the Union under the Constitution?" Basic to this question was the location of sovereignty in the Federal Union. Expressing the Southern view, William S. Oldham, a Texas delegate to the Montgomery Convention, wrote: "I have defined sovereignty to be the inherent power to establish, organize, sustain, and administer government. This power always rests primarily in the State—the people constituting the political community."[1] A natural concomitant to the theory of the sovereignty of the states was the Southern belief in the compact theory of government. Oldham again expressed the Southern view when he described the United States Constitution as "an agreement, a compact, a treaty, entered into by and between sovereign States, creating a common agent, and delegating to that agent certain specified powers, to be exercised in common for the good of all."[2]

The constitutional concept as defined by Oldham in the 1860's was neither so clearly articulated nor so specifically relevant in 1787. The compact theory of government as understood during the latter part of the eighteenth century called for the establishment of government by the consent of the people. Whether such a compact was a voluntary or binding agreement between

1. William Simpson Oldham, "True Causes and Issues of the Civil War," *DeBow's Review,* VII (September, 1869), 738.

2. *Ibid.,* p. 735. The following discussion of the growth of federal power is necessarily abbreviated and attempts only to establish historical perspective pursuant to treating the significance of the two Confederate Constitutions.

the states or between the people was of little concern in 1787. In an effort to write a practical as well as a generally acceptable constitution, the members of the Philadelphia Convention left several significant questions unanswered in the United States Constitution. By failing to make it indisputably clear that the federal government had the sole power to interpret the constitution, the Philadelphia Convention opened the way for the states to assert their right to interpret the nature and the extent of their powers under the constitution.

As the new nation grew and prospered, the federal government necessarily became more powerful through the interpretation of the constitution by the Congress, the Supreme Court, and the President. The contribution of the Congress to the power and prestige of the federal government is especially evident after the War of 1812. In 1816, the Congress adopted legislation that established the Second United States Bank, a protective tariff, and a permanent fund for internal improvements. All three measures, which were adopted during a time of strong nationalism, were vigorously supported by the Southern spokesman, John C. Calhoun.

The Supreme Court under Chief Justice John Marshall greatly added to the power of the federal government. Marshall's most significant decision in this respect was rendered in McCulloch v. Maryland, 4 Wheaton 316 (1819). Vigorously asserting the doctrine of implied powers and the loose construction of the constitution, Marshall defended the act of Congress establishing the Second United States Bank; thus, he asserted the supremacy of the federal government within its sphere of action.

Various presidents increased the power and prestige of the federal government. Andrew Jackson was especially significant in this respect. By acting as the direct representative of the people, by making extensive use of the removal and veto power, and by assuming the leadership of his political party, Jackson made the Presidency the most dominant force in the government, during his term of office. He was strong enough to ignore a Supreme Court decision rendered by John Marshall in Worcester v. Georgia, 6 Peters 515 (1832), without any repercussions.

After 1820, the South became less and less satisfied with the state of the Union as the power and prestige of the federal government increased. At the same time that the power and influence of the federal government was steadily increasing, the power and influence of the South in the federal government was steadily decreasing. The reason for this situation has been succinctly stated by the historian Jesse Thomas Carpenter: "Geography made the South a section; population relegated that section to a minority role in the American Union."[3] The population of the United States increased by leaps and bounds between 1789 and 1861. The greatest growth of population during this time took place outside of the South. Thus, as the power of the federal government was increasing, largely in response to the needs fostered by a rapidly growing population, the South was steadily losing the position of strength in the federal government that it held in 1789.

While population was relegating the South to a minority role in the Union, the South sought to protect and maintain its position. The Missouri Controversy in 1820 made the South especially conscious of its minority position. The South attempted to secure its interests against the inroads of a Northern majority by utilizing the principle of the concurrent voice or concurrent majority; whereby the South would be given, in the words of John C. Calhoun, "either a concurrent voice in making and executing the laws or a veto on their execution."[4] By vigorously supporting the system of checks and balances, and by seeking to control at least one of the three branches of government, the South might veto any usurping action by either of the other two branches of government. In the first six decades of the nineteenth century, the South was consistently fortunate in having presidents sympathetic to its section.[5] Having lost its equality in the House of Representatives before 1820, the South lost its concurrent voice in the United States Senate in 1850. During the next decade, the South sought to maintain its strength in a minor-

3. Jesse Thomas Carpenter, *The South As a Conscious Minority* (New York: The New York University Press, 1930), p. 33.

4. John Caldwell Calhoun, *The Works of John C. Calhoun,* 6 volumes, edited by Richard Kenner Cralle (New York: D. Appleton and Company, 1853-1855), I, 25.

5. Only Presidents John Quincy Adams, Martin Van Buren, and William Henry Harrison showed significant opposition to Southern interests.

ity role by demanding constitutional guarantees. Primarily, this effort took the form of constitutional justification of the position of the South on slavery in the territories. Also, it took the form of constitutional protection of fugitive slaves. The South viewed the election of Lincoln in 1860 as the final victory of the Northern majority. The federal government had fallen into the hands of a man and a party alien to the interests of the South, and, in the minds of a majority of Southern leaders, the last recourse of the South was secession.

During the seventy years preceding the secession of the lower South, there grew up in the United States a minority constitutional philosophy. The ambiguity of the constitution allowed the states to assert their right to interpret the nature and extent of their authority. The motivation for the development of this philosophy in the South was its decline in power and influence in the federal government, or its relegation to a minority role in the Union. The same motivation had caused the articulation of this philosophy in New England, at the time of the Louisiana Purchase, during the War of 1812, and during the controversy over the annexation of Texas. The philosophy of extreme state rights and the concept of the sovereignty of the states were, however, developed to their most complete degree in the South.

Thomas Jefferson viewed the constitution as a document or instrument of government whose major purpose was the protection of the states. Jefferson's Kentucky Resolutions, as well as James Madison's Virginia Resolutions, adopted in 1798 and 1799, challenged the authority of the federal government and argued in favor of state sovereignty. Judge Spencer Roane of Virginia attacked several decisions of Chief Justice Marshall, in particular Cohens v. Virginia, 6 Wheaton 264 (1821), as threatening the sovereign power of the states. Another Virginian, John Taylor of Caroline, argued elaborately in favor of state sovereignty and strict constructionism in such pamphlets as *Construction Construed* (1820) and *New Views of the Constitution* (1823) during the period of intense nationalism following the War of 1812. And finally, the most complete, the most incisive, and the most rigid expression of state sovereignty and the state rights philosophy of the South was articulated by John C. Calhoun of South Carolina in his *A Disquisition on Government* and *A Discourse on the Constitution and Government of the United States,* written shortly before his death. Calhoun's political philosophy was almost universally accepted in the South in 1860.

The culmination of the Southern belief in the Union as a compact between the individually sovereign states was the secession of the seven states of the lower South (and ultimately four border states) and the formation of the Confederate States of America. The most significant constitutional expression or definition of the South's answer to the enigmatic question on the nature of the Union is embodied in the Confederate Constitutions.

The Preambles of the Confederate Constitutions describe a confederation of sovereign states and not a sovereign confederation of people. The words "each State acting in its sovereign and independent character . . ."[6] expressed the state sovereignty concept of the Confederate "Founding Fathers" and constituted the central theme of the constitutions. Although the Confederate Constitutions were framed by the delegates of sovereign states which had recently seceded from the Federal Union, the two documents did not contain any provision for secession. The right of the states of the Confederacy to secede is implied in the phraseology of the Preambles of the Confederate Constitutions.

Manifestations of the state sovereignty concept of the Confederate "Founding Fathers" were the provisions of the constitutions which fostered a greater degree of local self-government. Local autonomy was strengthened by the exclusion of the general welfare clause from the Preamble and from Article I of the Permanent Constitution. Expansion of the power of the central government by implied powers was thus limited. In such provisions as those restricting the appropriation of money by the Congress for internal improvements and prohibiting a protective tariff, the reserved power of the several states was expanded. The power of the states was also expanded in the judiciary provision allowing the impeachment of Confederate officials acting solely within the limits of any state by the state legislatures. By refusing to extend the jurisdiction of the Confederate courts in

6. *Journal of the Congress of the Confederate States of America, 1861-1865,* 7 volumes (Washington: Government Printing Office, 1904-1905), I, 909.

cases between citizens of different states, local autonomy was again strengthened. And finally, although the constitutions provided for a Confederate Supreme Court, a sufficient number of congressmen espousing the state rights philosophy united to prevent the establishment of a high court.

Inherent in the provisions of the Confederate Constitutions was an effort to secure the extension of minority rights. From 1820 to 1850, the South had sought to protect its position by vigorously supporting the system of checks and balances. The Confederate Constitutions contain three innovations to further delineate the separation of powers or checks and balances. Taxes or duties laid on exports from the several states were prohibited except by a vote of two-thirds of both Houses of Congress; the admission of other states to the Confederacy required a two-thirds majority of the two Houses of Congress; and, Congress, unless recommended by a department head and submitted to the Congress by the president, could appropriate no money except by a vote of two-thirds of the two Houses of Congress. Thus, the extra-majority requirements were an added protection of minority rights.

To protect its minority position after 1850, the South had turned to an argument demanding constitutional guarantees. The Confederate framers extended and applied this plan to the institution of slavery. The Confederate Constitutions recognized, regulated, and protected the South's "peculiar institution." Slaves were recognized as property, the foreign slave trade was prohibited, and the institution of slavery was protected in the several states and the territories of the Confederate States of America.

The provision embodying the most significant constitutional guarantee of the position of the minority, and thus, the most significant provision manifesting the Confederate concept of state sovereignty, was Article V. A minority of three states could initiate a process that might alter or amend the basic document of government.

Among the fifty men who were collectively responsible for the expression of the philosophy of state rights and the concept of state sovereignty in the Confederate Constitutions were a smaller number who represented the leadership of the Montgomery

Convention. Under their leadership, the convention framed two constitutions in only thirty-five days. The principal architects of the Confederate Constitutions were Rhett and Memminger of South Carolina, Stephens, Howell Cobb, Toombs, T. R. R. Cobb, and Hill of Georgia, Smith, Curry, and Walker of Alabama, Harris of Mississippi, and Conrad of Louisiana.

Rhett, Stephens, and Howell Cobb exerted decisive influence. The spokesman for the extreme state rights group in the Montgomery Convention was Rhett. As Chairman of the Second Committee of Twelve, he played a significant role in the drafting and the debating of the Permanent Constitution. Rhett opposed admitting non-slaveholding states into the Confederacy, the closing of the foreign slave trade, and the federal review of decisions of the state courts; and he advocated the inclusion of a secession provision in the Permanent Constitution. He reluctantly accepted the defeat of these four measures. Rhett's major contribution, in addition to his leadership in debate, was in his five provisions that were accepted. They were: (1) the abolition of the protective tariff; (2) the clause of the internal improvements provision concerning the improvement of navigation and harbors; (3) the limiting of the presidential term to a single six year term; (4) executive removal; and (5) the amendment process.

Stephens led the group in the convention at the opposite end of the political spectrum from Rhett. For example, when Rhett led the forces opposing the admission of free states, during the "Great Debate," Stephens led the members favoring such a provision. Stephens was an influential member of the First Committee of Twelve, and he made a significant contribution in drafting the executive budget provision and the provision providing for the seating of the department heads on the floor of Congress.

Howell Cobb's great contribution to the framing of the Confederate Constitutions was as President of the Montgomery Convention. Cobb was a skilled politician and an adept negotiator. His tact and diplomacy tempered the conflicts between the Rhett and Stephens factions. In moderating the debates on and the adoption of the Confederate Constitutions, Cobb played a role equal to, if not greater than, that of Rhett or Stephens.

Next to the influence of the Cobb-Rhett-Stephens leadership was that of Memminger, Toombs, and T. R. R. Cobb. Although Memminger took an active part in the debates on the two constitutions, his major contribution was as Chairman of the First Committee of Twelve. His foresight in bringing a tentative draft for the Provisional Constitution to Montgomery expedited the ease and the speed by which the work of the convention was dispatched. Toombs, who served on the Second Committee of Twelve, was the major contributor in the fashioning of the fiscal provisions of the Permanent Constitution. The leading changes that he proposed were the ones prohibiting bounties, extra allowances, and internal improvements, and the one establishing a self-sustaining Confederate Post Office. Moreover, Toombs was responsible for the "Cabinet in Congress" provision of the Permanent Constitution, where his friend Stephens had been responsible for this provision in the Provisional Constitution. T. R. R. Cobb made his most important contribution in the drafting of the Permanent Constitution as a member of the Second Committee of Twelve, and as a member of the Committee on Style and Arrangements. He was an active debater and was responsible for the ratification provision of the Permanent Constitution.

A final group of major contributors to the framing of the Confederate Constitutions was Smith, Walker, Harris, Hill, Conrad, and Curry. Smith was the author of the item veto provision and served on the Committee on Style and Arrangements, Walker was responsible for the provision combining the Confederate District and Circuit Courts, and Harris was responsible for the validation of all United States laws not in conflict with the Permanent Constitution. Smith, Walker, and Harris were the only members of the Montgomery Convention, with the exception of Owens of Florida, to serve on both the First and Second Committees of Twelve. Hill, Conrad, and Curry did not serve on the constitutional drafting committees, but they were significant contributors in the debates on the two constitutions.

The major contributors to the framing of the Confederate Constitutions, along with their convention colleagues, were faced with a basic problem as to the division of sovereignty. This problem has been clearly stated by the eminent English historian James Bryce: "The problem which all federated nations have to solve is how to secure an efficient central government and preserve national unity, while allowing free scope for the diversities and free play to the authorities, of the members of the federation."[7] The basis for the solution of this problem which was embodied in the Confederate Constitutions was the United States Constitution and past experience within the Federal Union. The Confederate "Founding Fathers" were generally satisfied with the United States Constitution and incorporated most of its provisions in the Confederate Constitutions. The differences between the two constitutions reflect the dissatisfaction of the South with interpretations of the parent document. One of the major differences is in the extended expression of both the philosophy of state rights and the concept of state sovereignty in the Confederate Constitutions. The second major difference is the reform of the machinery of government that is manifested in the Confederate Constitutions.

The reforms in the two constitutions were included for two reasons: (1) to help correct the harmful effects of the spoils system that had accompanied the growth of the federal government, and particularly, that had attended the growth of political parties; and (2) to insure the fiscal integrity of the government. The single six-year term of the president and the constitutional provision concerning executive removal attempted to reduce the harmful effects of partisan politics. Also attacking the spoils system was the provision curtailing the president's appointment power of senators whereby the chief executive could not reappoint a person rejected by the Senate during the ensuing recess, and the requirement that every law relate to but one subject.

Stephens and Toombs hoped to keep the Congress better informed as to the policies of the administration, and to place more direct responsibility upon the department heads by advocating the "Cabinet in Congress" provision. Integral to this reform was the executive budget and item veto provisions which directly affected the fiscal policy and integrity of the govern-

7. James Bryce, *The American Commonwealth,* New Edition, 2 volumes (New York: The Macmillan Company, 1915 and 1916), I, 356.

ment. The executive budget placed the responsibility for fiscal policy upon the president and the item veto protected his budget estimates. The provision defining a self-sufficient post office department after March 1, 1863, and the provision requiring that all appropriation bills specify the amount and purpose of the appropriations also sought to encourage fiscal responsibility.

The reforms in the Confederate Constitutions represent a significant constitutional legacy. For example, the executive budget concept is today an integral feature of our national government. The Twenty-Second Amendment, much like the limitation upon the Confederate President to one six-year term, limits the president today to two four-year terms. The item veto provision is much used in the states of the United States today. The president does not have the use of the item veto, but in 1953, Tennessee became the fortieth state to adopt this provision.[8]

The Confederate Constitutions were quickly framed and were baptized in a bloody war. Where the United States Constitution enjoyed almost a quarter of a century of peace before being tested by a war, the Confederate Constitutions enjoyed no such luxury.

Although the Confederate Constitutions were buried at Appomattox on April 9, 1865, they are significant documents deserving of study today. They offer insight into the critical events of 1861-1865, and they mark a milestone in the constitutional development of the United States.

The Confederate Constitutions are principally significant for two reasons: (1) they represent the ultimate constitutional expression of the state rights philosophy and the state sovereignty concept in nineteenth century America; and (2) they make a valuable contribution through the legacy of governmental reform.

8. Frank Williams Prescott, "A Footnote on Georgia's Constitutional History: The Item Veto of the Governors," *The Georgia Historical Quarterly*, XLII (March, 1958), 3.

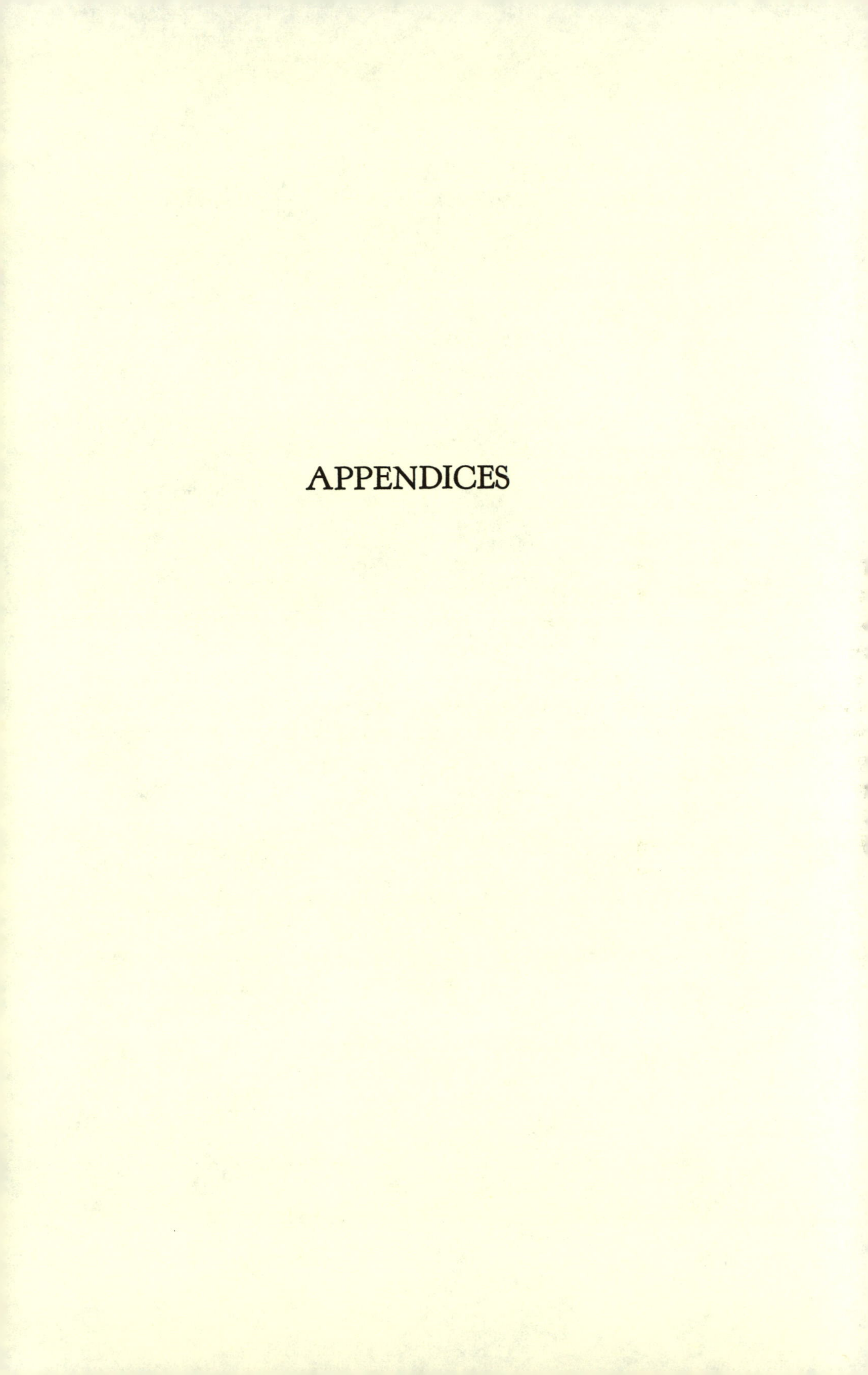

APPENDICES

Appendix A

STATISTICAL TABLES ON THE MEMBERS OF THE MONTGOMERY CONVENTION

The information contained in this appendix was gathered from many sources. Primary sources were used when available. Where more recent research corrected earlier data, secondary sources were used. The number of "Slaves," and the "Real Property" and "Personal Property" figures were gleaned from the voluminous Eighth Census of the United States, 1860, Manuscript Returns of Schedule No. 1, Free Inhabitants, and Schedule No. 2, Slave Inhabitants, for the States of South Carolina, Georgia, Florida, Alabama, Louisiana, Mississippi, and Texas, National Archives, Washington 25, D. C. "Real Property" includes such items as land, buildings, and the improvements thereof. "Personal Property" includes slaves, household goods, farm tools, and livestock.

When the name of a delegate to the Montgomery Convention is in italics, this indicates that he was earlier a delegate to his state secession convention.

A particularly difficult problem was the designation, with consistency, of occupations for the delegates. The terms "Lawyer" or "Lawyer-Planter" are assigned to the forty-two licensed lawyers at the convention, even though a few never practiced. "Planter" or "Lawyer-Planter" designates any delegate owning ten or more slaves according to the Census of 1860. Ulrich Bonnell Phillips in *Life and Labor in the Old South* (Boston: Little, Brown, and Company, 1929), p. 339, considers twenty slaves as a holding of plantation size. Lewis Cecil Gray in *History of Agriculture in the Southern United States to 1860*, 2 volumes (Washington: The Carnegie Institution of Washington, 1933), I, 481-483, accepts ten slaves as a holding of plantation size. Although this writer tends to agree with Phillips, the number ten was decided upon to allow for inaccuracies and obvious errors in the Census of 1860.

An indication of the stature of the members of the Montgomery Convention is that twenty-eight of the fifty delegates are listed in Allen Johnson and Dumas Malone, eds., *Dictionary of American Biography*, 21 volumes (New York: Charles Scribner's Sons, 1928-1937), and twenty-four of the fifty are found in *Biographical Dictionary of the American Congress 1774-1949* (Washington: Government Printing Office, 1950).

For information and statistics differing, in several instances, from this appendix, see Albert N. Fitts, "The Confederate Convention: The Provisional Constitution," *The Alabama Review*, II (April, 1949), 83-101, and Wilfred Buck Yearns, Jr., *The Confederate Congress* (Athens: The University of Georgia Press, 1960).

The South Carolina Delegation to the Montgomery Convention

Name	Birth-Place	Age	Education	Occupa-tion	Political Party	Public Service	Slaves	Real Property	Personal Property
Barnwell, R. W.	S.C.	59	Harvard	Planter	Demo.	Legis. U.S. Cong. U.S. Senate	158	$ 16,000	$ 27,000
Boyce, W. W.	S.C.	42	S.C. Col. U. of Va.	Lawyer-Planter	Demo.	Legis. U.S. Cong.	9	$ 24,169	$ 34,390
Chesnut, J. Jr.	S.C.	46	Princeton	Lawyer-Planter	Demo.	Legis. U.S. Senate	76	—	—
Keitt, L. M.	S.C.	36	S.C. Col.	Lawyer	Demo.	Legis. U.S. Cong.	—	—	—
Memminger, C. G.	Ger-many	58	S.C. Col.	Lawyer-Planter	Demo.	Legis.	15	$ 25,000	$150,000
Miles, W. P.	S.C.	38	College of Charleston	College Professor	Demo.	Mayor of Charleston U.S. Cong.	—	—	—
Rhett, R. B.	S.C.	60	Attended Beaufort College (S.C.)	Lawyer-Planter	Demo.	Legis. U.S. Cong. U.S. Senate	16	$ 9,000	$ 25,000
Withers, T. J.	S.C.	56	S.C. Col.	Lawyer-Planter	Demo.	Circuit Judge	23	$ 7,000	$100,000

The Mississippi Delegation to the Montgomery Convention

Name	Birth-Place	Age	Education	Occupa-tion	Political Party	Public Service	Slaves	Real Property	Personal Property
Barry, W. T. S.	Miss.	39	Yale	Lawyer	Demo.	Legis. U.S. Cong.	7	$ 50,000	$ 65,000
Brooke, W.	Va.	47	U. of Va.	Lawyer	Whig	Legis. U.S. Senate	5	$ 10,000	$ 75,000
Campbell, J. A. P.	S.C.	30	Davidson (N.C.)	Lawyer-Planter	Demo.	Legis.	11	$ 8,500	$ 30,000
Clayton, A. M.	Va.	58	—	Lawyer-Planter	Demo.	Fed. Judge U.S. Consul to Havana Asso. Jus. of Miss. Sup. Ct.	142	$160,000	$150,000
Harris, W. P.	Miss.	42	U. of Va.	Lawyer	Demo.	Cir. Judge U.S. Cong.	—	$ 5,000	$ 31,000
Harrison, J. T.	S.C.	49	S.C. Col.	Lawyer-Planter	Demo.	—	13	$700,000	$750,000
Wilson, W. S.	Md.	44	—	Lawyer	—	Legis.	—	—	$600,000

The Florida Delegation to the Montgomery Convention

Name	Birth-Place	Age	Education	Occupation	Political Party	Public Service	Slaves	Real Property	Personal Property
Anderson, J. P.	Tenn.	38	Jefferson Col. (Pa.)	Lawyer-Planter	Demo.	Legis. (of Miss.) U.S. Cong.	30	$ 3,500	$ 35,000
Morton, J. C.	Va.	66	William & Mary Col.	Planter	Whig	Legis. U.S. Senate	132	$ 51,000	$150,000
Owens, J. B.	S.C.	44	Furman Col. (S.C.)	Planter	Demo.	Legis.	89	$ 30,000	$ 88,000

The Alabama Delegation to the Montgomery Convention

Name	Birth-Place	Age	Education	Occupation	Political Party	Public Service	Slaves	Real Property	Personal Property
Chilton, W. P.	Ky.	49	—	Lawyer	Whig	Legis. Ch. Jus. Ala. Sup. Ct.	8	—	—
Curry, J. L. M.	Ga.	35	Franklin Col.; Harvard	Lawyer-Planter	Demo.	Legis. U.S. Cong.	47	$ 10,000	$ 37,335
Fearn, T.	Va.	71	Wash. Col.; Phila. Med.	Physician Planter	Demo.	Legis.	14	$ 46,000	$128,000
Hale, S. F.	Ky.	44	Cumberland; Lexington Law School	Lawyer-Planter	Whig	Legis.	12	$ 8,000	$ 47,000
Lewis, D. P.	Va.	40	—	Lawyer-Planter	Demo.	Legis.	23	$ 20,000	$ 42,185
McRae, C. J.	N.C.	48	Catholic Col. (Miss.)	Cotton-Factor	Demo.	Legis. (of Miss.)	2	$ 75,000	$ 3,000
Shorter, J. G.	Ga.	42	Franklin College	Lawyer-Planter	Demo.	Legis. Cir. Judge	10	$ 45,000	$125,000
Smith, R. H.	N.C.	47	Attended West Point	Lawyer-Planter	Whig	Legis.	15	$ 10,000	$ 50,000
Walker, R. W.	Ala.	37	Princeton	Lawyer-Planter	Whig	Legis. Asso. Jus. of Ala. Sup. Ct.	38	$ 30,000	$ 50,000

The Georgia Delegation to the Montgomery Convention

Name	Birth-Place	Age	Education	Occupa-tion	Political Party	Public Service	Slaves	Real Property	Personal Property
Bartow, F. S.	Ga.	44	U. of Ga.	Lawyer-Planter	Whig	Legis.	99	$ 14,000	$ 20,000
Cobb, H.	Ga.	45	U. of Ga.	Lawyer-Planter	Demo.	Speaker of U.S. House Gov. of Ga. U.S. Sec. of the Treas.	9	$ 8,000	$ 7,500
Cobb, T. R. R.	Ga.	37	U. of Ga.	Lawyer-Planter	Demo.	Recorder of Ga. Sup. Ct.	23	$ 40,000	$ 80,000
Crawford, M. J.	Ga.	40	Attended Mercer Col. (Ga.)	Lawyer	Demo.	Legis. Cir. Judge U.S. Cong.	8	—	—
Hill, B. H.	Ga.	37	U. of Ga.	Lawyer-Planter	Whig	Legis.	57	$ 30,000	$ 70,000
Kenan, A. H.	Ga.	55	Orange-on-the-Hudson (N.Y.)	Lawyer	Whig	Legis.	3	$ 3,000	$ 6,000
Nisbet, E. A.	Ga.	57	S.C. Col.; U. of Ga.	Lawyer-Planter	Whig	Legis. U.S. Cong. Ga. Sup. Ct.	16	$ 30,000	$ 30,000
Stephens, A. H.	Ga.	48	U. of Ga.	Lawyer-Planter	Whig	Legis. U.S. Cong.	31	$ 18,000	$ 35,000
Toombs, R. A.	Ga.	50	Union Col. (N.Y.)	Lawyer-Planter	Whig	Legis. U.S. Cong. U.S. Senate	16	$200,000	$350,000
Wright, A. R.	Ga.	47	Attended U. of Ga.	Lawyer	Demo.	Cir. Judge U.S. Cong.	—	—	—

The Louisiana Delegation to the Montgomery Convention

Name	Birth-Place	Age	Education	Occupa-tion	Political Party	Public Service	Slaves	Real Property	Personal Property
Conrad, C. M.	Va.	56	—	Lawyer	Whig	Legis. U.S. Senate U.S. Cong. Sec. of War	—	—	—
DeClouet, A.	La.	48	St. Joseph (Ky.)	Planter	Whig	Legis.	275	$323,000	$ 26,000
Kenner, D. F.	La.	47	Miami U. (Ohio)	Lawyer-Planter	Whig	Legis.	473	$190,000	$250,000
Perkins, J. Jr.	Miss.	41	Yale Col.; Harvard Law	Lawyer-Planter	Demo.	Dis. Judge U.S. Cong.	319	$500,000	$ 20,000
Sparrow, E.	Ireland	50	Kenyon Col. (Ohio)	Lawyer-Planter	Whig	Legis.	226	$665,500	$582,500
Marshall, H.	S.C.	54	Union Col. (N.Y.)	Planter	—	Legis.	201	$ 40,000	$116,110

The Texas Delegation to the Montgomery Convention

Name	Birth-Place	Age	Education	Occupa-tion	Political Party	Public Service	Slaves	Real Property	Personal Property
Gregg, J.	Ala.	32	La Grange College (Ala.)	Lawyer-Planter	Demo.	District Judge	13	$ 2,800	$ 13,560
Hemphill, J.	S.C.	57	Jefferson Col. (Pa.)	Lawyer	Demo.	Ch. Jus. of Texas Sup. Ct. U.S. Senate	—	—	—
Ochiltree, W. B.	N.C.	49	—	Lawyer	Whig	Dis. Judge Sec. of Treas. Atty. Gen. Legis.	9	$ 14,000	$ 18,900
Oldham, W. S.	Tenn.	47	—	Lawyer	Demo.	Legis. & Sup. Ct. of Arkansas	—	—	—
Reagan, J.	Tenn.	42	—	Lawyer	Demo.	Legis. U.S. Cong.	5	$ 2,500	$ 14,350
Waul, T. N.	S.C.	46	Attended S.C. Col.	Lawyer	Demo.	Cir. Judge (of Miss.)	—	—	—
Wigfall, L. T.	S.C.	44	S.C. Col.; U. of Va.	Lawyer-Planter	Demo.	Legis. U.S. Senate	10	$ 200	$ 5,000

Statistical Table on the Montgomery Convention

	S.C.	Miss.	Fla.	Ala.	Ga.	La.	Tex.	Convention
Total Delegates	8	7	3	9	10	6	7	50
Native State	14	3	0	2	12	2	0	—
College Trained	8	5	3	7	10	5	4	42
Occupation								
Lawyer	6	7	1	7	10	4	7	42
Planter	6	3	3	7	7	5	2	33
College Prof.	1	—	—	—	—	—	—	1
Physician	—	—	—	1	—	—	—	1
Cotton-Factor	—	—	—	1	—	—	—	1
Political Party								
Democrat	8	5	2	5	4	1	6	31
Whig	—	1	1	4	6	4	1	17
Unknown	—	1	—	—	—	1	—	2
Public Service								
Judicial Office	1	2	0	3	4	1	5	16
State Legislature	8	6	3	9	8	6	5	45
U.S. Congress	6	3	2	1	6	2	3	23
House	5	2	1	1	6	2	1	18
Senate	3	1	1	0	1	1	2	9
Both	2	0	0	0	1	1	0	4
Other	—	—	—	—	1	1	—	2

Appendix B

CONSTITUTION FOR THE PROVISIONAL GOVERNMENT OF THE CONFEDERATE STATES OF AMERICA[1]

We, the Deputies of the Sovereign and Independent States of South Carolina, Georgia, Florida, Alabama, Mississippi, and Louisiana, invoking the favor of Almighty God, do hereby, in behalf of these States, ordain and establish this Constitution for the Provisional Government of the same: to continue one year from the inauguration of the President, or until a permanent Constitution or Confederation between the said States shall be put in operation, whichsoever shall first occur.

ARTICLE I.

SECTION 1.—All legislative powers herein delegated shall be vested in this Congress now assembled until otherwise ordained.

SECTION 2.—When vacancies happen in the representation from any State, the same shall be filled in such manner as the proper authorities of the State shall direct.

SECTION 3.—1. The Congress shall be the judge of the elections, returns, and qualification of its members; any number of Deputies from a majority of the States, being present, shall con-

1. This is an exact copy taken from the *Journal of the Congress of the Confederate States of America, 1861-1865,* 7 volumes (Washington: Government Printing Office, 1904-1905), I, 899-909.

stitute a quorum to do business; but a smaller number may adjourn from day to day, and may be authorized to compel the attendance of absent members; upon all questions before the Congress, each State shall be entitled to one vote, and shall be represented by any one or more of its Deputies who may be present.

2. The Congress may determine the rules of its proceedings, punish its members for disorderly behavior, and with the concurrence of two-thirds, expel a member.

3. The Congress shall keep a journal of its proceedings, and from time to time publish the same, excepting such parts as may in their judgment require secrecy; and the yeas and nays of the members on any question, shall, at the desire of one-fifth of those present, or at the instance of any one State, be entered on the journal.

SECTION 4.—The members of Congress shall receive a compensation for their services, to be ascertained by law, and paid out of the treasury of the Confederacy. They shall in all cases, except treason, felony and breach of the peace, be privileged from arrest during their attendance at the session of the Congress, and in going to and returning from the same; and for any speech or debate, they shall not be questioned in any other place.

SECTION 5.—1. Every bill which shall have passed the Congress, shall, before it become a law, be presented to the President of the Confederacy; if he approve, he shall sign it; but if not, he shall return it with his objections to the Congress, who shall enter the objections at large on their journal, and proceed to reconsider it. If, after such reconsideration, two-thirds of the Congress shall agree to pass the bill, it shall become a law. But in all such cases, the vote shall be determined by yeas and nays; and the names of the persons voting for and against the bill shall be entered on the journal. If any bill shall not be returned by the President within ten days (Sundays excepted) after it shall have been presented to him, the same shall be a law, in like manner, as if he had signed it, unless the Congress by their adjournment, prevent its return, in which case it shall not be a law. The President may veto any appropriation or appropriations, and approve any other appropriation or appropriations, in the same bill.

2. Every order, resolution or vote, intended to have the force and effect of a law, shall be presented to the President, and before the same shall take effect, shall be approved by him, or being disapproved by him, shall be repassed by two-thirds of the Congress, according to the rules and limitations prescribed in the case of a bill.

3. Until the inauguration of the President, all bills, orders, resolutions and votes adopted by the Congress shall be of full force without approval by him.

Section 6.—1. The Congress shall have power to lay and collect taxes, duties, imposts and excises, for the revenue necessary to pay the debts and carry on the Government of the Confederacy; and all duties, imposts and excises shall be uniform throughout the States of the Confederacy.

2. To borrow money on the credit of the Confederacy:

3. To regulate commerce with foreign nations, and among the several States, and with the Indian tribes:

4. To establish a uniform rule of naturalization, and uniform laws on the subject of bankruptcies throughout the Confederacy:

5. To coin money, regulate the value thereof and of foreign coin, and fix the standard of weights and measures:

6. To provide for the punishment of counterfeiting the securities and current coin of the Confederacy:

7. To establish post offices and post roads:

8. To promote the progress of science and useful arts, by securing, for limited times to authors and inventors the exclusive right to their respective writings and discoveries:

9. To constitute tribunals inferior to the Supreme Court:

10. To define and punish piracies and felonies committed on the high seas, and offences against the law of nations:

11. To declare war, grant letters of marque and reprisal, and make rules concerning captures on land and water:

12. To raise and support armies; but no appropriation of money to that use shall be for a longer term than two years:

13. To provide and maintain a navy:

14. To make rules for the government and regulation of the land and naval forces:

15. To provide for calling forth the militia to execute the laws of the Confederacy, suppress insurrections, and repel invasions:

16. To provide for organizing, arming, and disciplining the militia, and for governing such part of them as may be employed in the service of the Confederacy, reserving to the States respectively the appointment of the officers, and the authority of training the militia according to the discipline prescribed by Congress: and

17. To make all laws that shall be necessary and proper for carrying into execution the foregoing powers and all other powers expressly delegated by this Constitution to this Provisional Government.

18. The Congress shall have power to admit other States.

19. This Congress shall also exercise Executive powers until the President is inaugurated.

SECTION 7.—1. The importation of African negroes from any foreign country other than the slaveholding States of the United States, is hereby forbidden; and Congress are required to pass such laws as shall effectually prevent the same.

2. The Congress shall also have power to prohibit the introduction of slaves from any State not a member of this Confederacy.

3. The privilege of the writ of Habeas Corpus shall not be suspended unless, when in case of rebellion or invasion, the public safety may require it.

4. No Bill of Attainder, or *ex post facto* law shall be passed.

5. No preference shall be given, by any regulation of commerce or revenue, to the ports of one State over those of another; nor shall vessels bound to or from one State be obliged to enter, clear, or pay duties, in another.

6. No money shall be drawn from the treasury, but in consequence of appropriations made by law; and a regular statement and account of the receipts and expenditures of all public money shall be published from time to time.

7. Congress shall appropriate no money from the treasury unless it be asked and estimated for by the President or some one of the heads of Departments, except for the purpose of paying its own expenses and contingencies.

8. No title of nobility shall be granted by the Confederacy; and no person holding any office of profit or trust under it, shall, without the consent of the Congress, accept of any present, emolument, office, or title of any kind whatever, from any king, prince or foreign State.

9. Congress shall make no law respecting an establishment of religion or prohibiting the free exercises thereof; or abridging the freedom of speech, or of the press; or the right of the people peaceably to assemble and to petition the Government for a redress of such grievances as the delegated powers of this Government may warrant it to consider and redress.

10. A well regulated militia being necessary to the security of a free State, the right of the people to keep and bear arms shall not be infringed.

11. No soldier shall, in time of peace be quartered in any house without the consent of the owner; nor in time of war, but in a manner to be prescribed by law.

12. The right of the people to be secure in their persons, houses, papers, and effects against unreasonable searches and seizures, shall not be violated; and no warrants shall issue but upon probable cause, supported by oath or affirmation, and particularly describing the place to be searched, and the persons or things to be seized.

13. No person shall be held to answer for a capital or otherwise infamous crime, unless on a presentment or indictment of a grand jury, except in cases arising in the land or naval forces, or in the militia, when in actual service in time of war or public danger; nor shall any person be subject for the same offense to be twice put in jeopardy of life or limb; nor shall be compelled in any criminal case to be a witness against himself; nor be deprived of life, liberty, or property, without due process of law; nor shall private property be taken for public use without just compensation.

14. In all criminal prosecutions, the accused shall enjoy the right to a speedy and public trial by an impartial jury of the State and district wherein the crime shall have been committed, which district shall have been previously ascertained by law, and to be informed of the nature and cause of the accusation; to be con-

fronted with the witness against him; to have compulsory process for obtaining witnesses in his favor; and to have the assistance of counsel for his defense.

15. In suits at common law, where the value in controversy shall exceed twenty dollars, the right of trial by jury shall be preserved; and no fact tried by a jury shall be otherwise re-examined in any court of the Confederacy, than according to the rules of the common law.

16. Excessive bail shall not be required, nor excessive fines imposed, nor cruel and unusual punishment inflicted.

17. The enumeration, in the Constitution, of certain rights, shall not be construed to deny or disparage others retained by the people.

18. The powers not delegated to the Confederacy by the Constitution, nor prohibited by it to the States, are reserved to the States respectively, or to the people.

19. The judicial power of the Confederacy shall not be construed to extend to any suit in law or equity, commenced or prosecuted against one of the States of the Confederacy, by citizens of another State, or by citizens or subjects of any foreign state.

SECTION 8.—1. No State shall enter into any treaty, alliance, or confederation; grant letters of marque and reprisal; coin money; emit bills of credit; make anything but gold and silver coin a tender in payment of debts; pass any bills of attainder, *ex post facto* law, or law impairing the obligation of contracts; or grant any title of nobility.

2. No State shall, without the consent of the Congress, lay any imports or duties on imports or exports, except what may be absolutely necessary for executing its inspection laws; and the nett produce of all duties and imposts, laid by any State on imports or exports, shall be for the use of the treasury of the Confederacy, and all such laws shall be subject to the revision and control of the Congress. No State, shall, without the consent of Congress, lay any duty on tonnage, enter into any agreement or compact with another State, or with a foreign power, or engage in war, unless actually invaded, or in such imminent danger as will not admit of delay.

ARTICLE II.

SECTION 1.—1. The Executive power shall be vested in a President of the Confederate States of America. He, together with the Vice President, shall hold his office for one year, or until this Provisional Government shall be superceded by a Permanent Government, whichsoever shall first occur.

2. The President and Vice-President shall be elected by ballot by the States represented in this Congress, each State casting one vote, and a majority of the whole being requisite to elect.

3. No person, except a natural-born citizen, or a citizen of one of the States of this Confederacy at the time of the adoption of this Constitution, shall be eligible to the office of President; neither shall any person be eligible to that office who shall not have attained the age of thirty-five years, and been fourteen years a resident of one of the States of this Confederacy.

4. In case of the removal of the President from office, or of his death, resignation, or inability to discharge the powers and duties of the said office, (which inability shall be determined by a vote of two-thirds of the Congress,) the same shall devolve on the Vice-President; and the Congress may by law provide for the case of removal, death, resignation, or inability, both of the President and Vice-President, declaring what officer shall then act as President; and such officer shall act accordingly, until the disability be removed or a President shall be elected.

5. The President shall at stated times receive for his services, during the period of the Provisional Government, a compensation at the rate of twenty-five thousand dollars per annum; and he shall not receive during that period any other emolument from this Confederacy, or any of the States thereof.

6. Before he enters on the execution of his office, he shall take the following oath or affirmation:

I do solemnly swear (or affirm) that I will faithfully execute the office of President of the Confederate States of America, and will, to the best of my ability, preserve, protect, and defend the Constitution thereof.

SECTION 2.—1. The President shall be Commander-in-Chief of the Army and Navy of the Confederacy, and of the militia of the several States, when called into the actual service of the Confederacy; he may require the opinion, in writing, of the principal officer in each of the Executive Departments, upon any subject relating to the duties of their respective offices; and he shall have power to grant reprieves and pardons for offences against the Confederacy, except in cases of impeachment.

2. He shall have power, by and with the advice and consent of the Congress, to make treaties; provided two-thirds of the Congress concur: and he shall nominate, and by and with the advice and consent of the Congress, shall appoint ambassadors, other public ministers and consuls, judges of the courts, and all other officers of the Confederacy whose appointments are herein otherwise provided for and which shall be established by law. But the Congress may, by law, vest the appointment of such inferior officers as they think proper in the President alone, in the courts of law, or in the heads of departments.

3. The President shall have power to fill up all vacancies that may happen during the recess of the Congress, by granting commissions which shall expire at the end of their next session.

SECTION 3.—1. He shall, from time to time, give to the Congress information of the state of the Confederacy, and recommend to their consideration such measures as he shall judge necessary and expedient; he may, on extraordinary occasions, convene the Congress at such times as he shall think proper; he shall receive ambassadors and other public ministers; he shall take care that the laws be faithfully executed; and shall commission all the officers of the Confederacy.

2. The President, Vice-President, and all civil officers of the Confederacy shall be removed from office on conviction by the Congress of treason, bribery, or other high crimes and misdemeanors; a vote of two-thirds shall be necessary for such conviction.

ARTICLE III.

SECTION 1.—1. The judicial power of the Confederacy shall be vested in one Supreme Court, and in such inferior courts as are herein directed, or as the Congress may from time to time ordain and establish.

2. Each State shall constitute a District,[2] in which there shall

2. Amended on May 21, 1861.

be a court called a District Court, which, until otherwise provided by the Congress, shall have the jurisdiction vested by the laws of the United States, as far as applicable, in both the District and Circuit Courts of the United States, for that State; the Judge whereof shall be appointed by the President, by and with the advice and consent of the Congress, and shall, until otherwise provided by the Congress, exercise the power and authority vested by the laws of the United States in the Judges of the District and Circuit Courts of the United States, for that State, and shall appoint the times and places at which the courts shall be held. Appeals may be taken directly from the District Courts to the Supreme Court, under similar regulations to those which are provided in cases of appeal to the Supreme Court of the United States, or under such regulations as may be provided by the Congress. The commissions of all the judges shall expire with this provisional Government.

3. The Supreme Court shall be constituted of all the District Judges, a majority of whom shall be a quorum, and shall sit at such times and places as the Congress shall appoint.

4. The Congress shall have power to make laws for the transfer of any causes which were pending in the courts of the United States, to the courts of the Confederacy, and for the execution of the orders, decrees and judgments heretofore rendered by the said courts of the United States; and also all laws which may be requisite to protect the parties to all such units, orders, judgments, or decrees, their heirs, personal representatives, or assignees.

SECTION 2.—1. The judicial power shall extend to all cases of law and equity, arising under this Constitution, the laws of the United States, and of this Confederacy, and treaties made, or which shall be made, under its authority; to all cases affecting ambassadors, other public ministers and consuls; to all cases of admiralty and maritime jurisdiction; to controversies to which the Confederacy shall be a party; controversies between two or more States; between citizens of different States; between citizens of the same States claiming lands under grants of different States.

2. In all cases affecting ambassadors, other public ministers and consuls, and those in which a State shall be a party, the Supreme Court shall have original jurisdiction. In all the other

cases before mentioned, the Supreme Court shall have appellate jurisdiction, both as to law and fact, with such exceptions and under such regulations as the Congress shall make.

3. The trial of all crimes except in cases of impeachment, shall be by jury, and such trial shall be held in the State where the said crimes shall have been committed; but when not committed within any State, the trial shall be at such place or places as the Congress may by law have directed.

SECTION 3.—1. Treason against this Confederacy shall consist only in levying war against it, or in adhering to its enemies, giving them aid and comfort. No person shall be convicted of treason unless on the testimony of two witnesses to the same overt act, or on confession in open court.

2. The Congress shall have power to declare the punishment of treason; but no attainder of treason shall work corruption of blood, or forfeiture, except during the life of the person attained.

ARTICLE IV.

SECTION 1.—1. Full faith and credit shall be given in each State to the public acts, records, and judicial proceedings of every other State. And the Congress may, by general laws, prescribe the manner in which such acts, records, and proceedings shall be proved, and the effect of such proof.

SECTION 2.—1. The citizens of each State shall be entitled to all privileges and immunities of citizens in the several States.

2. A person charged in any State with treason, felony, or other crime, who shall flee from justice, and be found in another State, shall, on demand of the executive authority of the State from which he fled, be delivered up, to be removed to the State having jurisdiction of the crime.

3. A slave in one State, escaping to another, shall be delivered up on claim of the party to whom said slave may belong by the executive authority of the State in which such slave shall be found, and in case of any abduction or forcible rescue, full compensation, including the value of the slave and all costs and expenses, shall be made to the party, by the State in which such abduction or rescue shall take place.

SECTION 3.—1. The Confederacy shall guarantee to every State in this union, a republican form of government, and shall protect each of them against invasion; and, on application of the legislature, or of the executive, (when the legislature can not be convened,) against domestic violence.

ARTICLE V.

1. The Congress, by a vote of two thirds, may, at any time, alter or amend this Constitution.

ARTICLE VI.

1. This Constitution, and all laws of the Confederacy which shall be made in pursuance thereof, and all treaties made, or which shall be made, under the authority of the Confederacy, shall be the supreme law of the land; and the judges in every State shall be bound thereby, anything in the Constitution or laws of any State to the contrary notwithstanding.

2. The Government hereby instituted shall take immediate steps for the settlement of all matters between the States forming it, and their other late confederates of the United States, in relation to the public property and public debt at the time of their withdrawal from them; these States hereby declaring it to be their wish and earnest desire to adjust everything pertaining to the common property, common liability, and common obligations of that union upon the principles of right, justice, equity, and good faith.

3. Until otherwise provided by the Congress, the city of Montgomery in the State of Alabama, shall be the seat of Government.

4. The members of the Congress and all executive and judicial officers of the Confederacy shall be bound by oath or affirmation to support this Constitution; but no religious test shall be required as a qualification to any office or public trust under this Confederacy.

Done in the Congress, by the unanimous consent of all the said States, the Eighth day of February, in the year of our Lord, One Thousand Eight Hundred and Sixty-One; and of the Confederate States of America, the first. In witness whereof, we have hereunto subscribed our names.

Howell Cobb,
President of the Congress.

AMENDMENT TO THE PROVISIONAL CONSTITUTION OF THE CONFEDERATE STATES.

An Ordinance of the Convention of the Congress of the Confederate States.

Be it ordained by the Congress of the Confederate States of America, That the second paragraph of the first section of the third Article of the Constitution of the Confederate States of America, be so amended in the first line of said paragraph, as to read, "Each state shall, until otherwise enacted by law, constitute a district;" and in the sixth line, after the word "judge," add "or judges."

Approved, May 21, 1861.

Appendix C

THE CONSTITUTION OF THE UNITED STATES[1]

WE the People of the United States, in Order to form a more perfect Union, establish Justice, insure domestic Tranquility, provide for the common defence, promote the general Welfare, and secure the Blessings of Liberty to ourselves and our Posterity, do ordain and establish this CONSTITUTION for the United States of America.

ARTICLE I.

SECTION. 1. All legislative Powers herein granted shall be vested in a Congress of the United States,

CONSTITUTION OF THE CONFEDERATE STATES OF AMERICA.[2]

WE, the people of the *Confederate* States, *each State acting in its sovereign and independent character, in order to form a permanent federal government,* establish justice, insure domestic tranquillity, and secure the blessings of liberty to ourselves and our posterity—*invoking the favor and guidance of Almighty God*—do ordain and establish this Constitution for the *Confederate* States of America.

ARTICLE I.

SECTION 1. All legislative powers herein *delegated* shall be vested in a Congress of the *Con-*

1. This is an exact copy, except that interlineations are indicated by enclosing them in angle brackets < >, taken from Max Farrand, ed., *The Records of the Federal Convention,* 3 volumes (New Haven: Yale University Press, 1911), II, 651-664.

2. This is an exact copy, except that italics are used to indicate the differences between this constitution and its parent document, taken from the *Journal of the Congress of the Confederate States of America, 1861-1865* (Washington: Government Printing Office, 1904-1905), I, 909-923.

which shall consist of a Senate and House of Representatives.

federate States, which shall consist of a Senate and House of Representatives.

SECTION. 2. The House of Representatives shall be composed of Members chosen every second Year by the People of the several States, and the Electors in each State shall have [the] Qualifications requisite for Electors of the most numerous Branch of the State Legislature.

SECTION 2. 1. The House of Representatives shall be composed of members chosen every second year by the people of the several States; and the electors in each State shall *be citizens of the Confederate States, and* have the qualifications requisite for electors of the most numerous branch of the State Legislature; *but no person of foreign birth, not a citizen of the Confederate States, shall be allowed to vote for any officer, civil or political, State or Federal.*

No Person shall be a Representative who shall not have attained to the Age of twenty five Years, and been seven Years a Citizen of the United States, and who shall not, when elected, be an Inhabitant of that State in which he shall be chosen.

2. No person shall be a Representative who shall not have attained the age of twenty-five years, and *be a citizen of the Confederate* States, and who shall not, when elected, be an inhabitant of that State in which he shall be chosen.

Representatives and direct Taxes shall be apportioned among the several States which may be included within this Union, according to their respective Numbers, which shall be determined by adding to the whole Number of free Persons, including those bound to Service for a Term of Years, and excluding Indians not taxed, three fifths of all other Persons. The actual Enumeration shall be made within three Years after the first Meeting of the Congress of the United States, and within every subsequent Term of ten Years, in such Manner as they shall by Law direct. The Number of Representatives

3. Representatives and direct taxes shall be apportioned among the several States, which may be included within this *Confederacy,* according to their respective numbers, which shall be determined, by adding to the whole number of free persons, including those bound to service for a term of years, and excluding Indians not taxed, three-fifths of all *slaves.* The actual enumeration shall be made within three years after the first meeting of the Congress of the *Confederate* States, and within every subsequent term of ten years, in such manner as they shall by law direct. The number of Representa-

shall not exceed one for every thirty thousand, but each State shall have at Least one Representative; and until such enumeration shall be made, the State of New Hampshire shall be entitled to chuse three, Massachusetts eight, Rhode-Island and Providence Plantations one, Connecticut five, New-York six, New Jersey four, Pennsylvania eight, Delaware one, Maryland six, Virginia ten, North Carolina five, South Carolina five, and Georgia three.

When vacancies happen in the Representation from any State, the Executive Authority thereof shall issue Writs of Election to fill such Vacancies.

The House of Representatives shall chuse their Speaker and other Officers; and shall have the sole Power of Impeachment.

SECTION. 3. The Senate of the United States shall be composed of two Senators from each State, chosen by the Legislature thereof, for six Years; and each Senator shall have one Vote.

Immediately after they shall be assembled in Consequence of the first Election, they shall be divided as equally as may be into three Classes. The Seats of the

tives shall not exceed one for every *fifty* thousand, but each State shall have at least one Representative; and until such enumeration shall be made, the State of *South Carolina* shall be entitled to choose *six, the State of Georgia ten, the State of Alabama nine, the State of Florida two, the State of Mississippi seven, the State of Louisiana six, and the State of Texas six.*

4. When vacancies happen in the representation from any State, the Executive authority thereof shall issue writs of election to fill such vacancies.

5. The House of Representatives shall choose their Speaker and other officers; and shall have the sole power of impeachment, *except that any judicial or other Federal officer, resident and acting solely within the limits of any State, may be impeached by a vote of two-thirds of both branches of the Legislature thereof.*

SECTION 3. 1. The Senate of the *Confederate* States shall be composed of two Senators from each State, chosen for six years by the Legislature thereof, *at the regular session next immediately preceding the commencement of the term of service;* and each Senator shall have one vote.

2. Immediately after they shall be assembled, in consequence of the first election, they shall be divided as equally as may be into three classes. The seats of the

Senators of the first Class shall be vacated at the Expiration of the second Year, of the second Class at the Expiration of the fourth Year, and of the third class at the Expiration of the sixth Year, so that one third may be chosen every second Year; and if Vacancies happen by Resignation, or otherwise, during the Recess of the Legislature of any State, the Executive thereof may make temporary Appointments until the next Meeting of the Legislature, which shall then fill such Vacancies.

No Person shall be a Senator who shall not have attained to the Age of thirty Years, and been nine Years a Citizen of the United States, and who shall not, when elected, be an Inhabitant of that State for which he shall be chosen.

The Vice President of the United States shall be President of the Senate, but shall have no Vote, unless they be equally divided.

The Senate shall chuse their other Officers, and also a President pro tempore, in the Absence of the Vice President, or when he shall exercise the Office of President of the United States.

The Senate shall have the sole Power to try all Impeachments. When sitting for that Purpose, they shall be on Oath or Affirmation. When the President of the United States [is tried,] the Chief Justice shall preside: And no Person shall be convicted without the Concurrence of two-thirds of the Members present.

Senators of the first class shall be vacated at the expiration of the second year; of the second class at the expiration of the fourth year; and of the third class at the expiration of the sixth year; so that one-third may be chosen every second year; and if vacancies happen by resignation, or otherwise, during the recess of the Legislature of any State, the Executive thereof may make temporary appointments until the next meeting of the Legislature which shall then fill such vacancies.

3. No person shall be a Senator who shall not have attained the age of thirty years, and *be a citizen of the Confederate* States; and who shall not, when elected, be an inhabitant of *the* State for which he shall be chosen.

4. The Vice President of the *Confederate* States shall be President of the Senate, but shall have no vote unless they be equally divided.

5. The Senate shall choose their other officers; and also a President *pro tempore* in the absence of the Vice President, or when he shall exercise the office of President of the *Confederate* States.

6. The Senate shall have the sole power to try all impeachments. When sitting for that purpose, they shall be on oath or affirmation. When the President of the *Confederate* States is tried, the Chief Justice shall preside; and no person shall be convicted without the concurrence of two-thirds of the members present.

Judgment in Cases of Impeachment shall not extend further than to removal from Office, and disqualification to hold and enjoy any Office of honor, Trust or Profit under the United States: but the Party convicted shall nevertheless be liable and subject to Indictment, Trial, Judgment and Punishment, according to Law.

SECTION. 4. The Times, Places and Manner of holding Elections for Senators and Representatives, shall be prescribed in each State by the Legislature thereof; but the Congress may at any time by Law make or alter such Regulations, except as to the places of chusing Senators.

The Congress shall assemble at least once in every Year, and such Meeting shall be on the first Monday in December, unless they shall by Law appoint a different Day.

SECTION. 5. Each House shall be the Judge of the Elections, Returns and Qualifications of its own Members, and a Majority of each shall constitute a Quorum to do Business; but a smaller Number may adjourn from day to day, and may be authorized to compel the Attendance of absent Members, in such Manner, and under such Penalties as each House may provide.

Each House may determine the Rules of its Proceedings, punish its Members for disorderly Behaviour, and, with the Concur-

7. Judgment in cases of impeachment shall not extend further than to removal from office, and disqualification to hold and enjoy any office of honor, trust, or profit, under the *Confederate* States; but the party convicted shall, nevertheless, be liable and subject to indictment, trial, judgment and punishment according to law.

SECTION 4. 1. The times, place, and manner of holding elections for Senators and Representatives, shall be prescribed in each State by the Legislature thereof, *subject to the provisions of this Constitution;* but the Congress may, at any time, by law, make or alter such regulations, except as to the *times and* places of choosing Senators.

2. The Congress shall assemble at least once in every year; and such meeting shall be on the first Monday in December, unless they shall, by law, appoint a different day.

SECTION 5. 1. Each House shall be the judge of the elections, returns, and qualifications of its own members, and a majority of each shall constitute a quorum to do business; but a smaller number may adjourn from day to day, and may be authorized to compel the attendance of absent members, in such manner and under such penalties as each House may provide.

2. Each House may determine the rules of its proceedings, punish its members for disorderly behavior, and, with the concur-

rence of two-thirds, expel a Member.

Each House shall keep a Journal of its Proceedings, and from time to time publish the same, excepting such Parts as may in their Judgment require Secrecy; and the Yeas and Nays of the Members of either House on any question shall, at the Desire of one fifth of those Present, be entered on the Journal.

Neither House, during the Session of Congress, shall, without the Consent of the other, adjourn for more than three days, nor to any other Place than that in which the two Houses shall be sitting.

SECTION. 6. The Senators and Representatives shall receive a Compensation for their Services, to be ascertained by Law, and paid out of the Treasury of the United States. They shall in all Cases, except Treason, Felony and Breach of the Peace, be privileged from Arrest during their Attendance at the Session of their respective Houses, and in going to and returning from the same; and for any Speech or Debate in either House, they shall not be questioned in any other Place.

No Senator or Representative shall, during the Time for which he was elected, be appointed to any civil Office under the Authority of the United States, which shall have been created, or the Emoluments whereof shall have encreased during such time; and no Person holding any Office under the United States, shall be

rence of two thirds of the whole number, expel a member.

3. Each House shall keep a journal of its proceedings, and from time to time publish the same, excepting such parts as may in their judgment require secrecy; and the yeas and nays of the members of either House, on any question, shall, at the desire of one fifth of those present, be entered on the journal.

4. Neither House, during the session of Congress, shall, without the consent of the other, adjourn for more than three days, nor to any other place than that in which the two Houses shall be sitting.

SECTION 6. 1. The Senators and Representatives shall receive a compensation for their services, to be ascertained by law, and paid out of the Treasury of the *Confederate* States. They shall, in all cases, except treason, felony and breach of the peace, be privileged from arrest during their attendance at the session of their respective Houses, and in going to and returning from the same; and for any speech or debate in either House, they shall not be questioned in any other place.

2. No Senator or Representative shall, during the time for which he was elected, be appointed to any civil office under the authority of the *Confederate* States, which shall have been created, or the emoluments whereof shall have been increased during such time; and no person holding any office under the *Confederate* States shall

a Member of either House during his Continuance in Office.

SECTION. 7. All Bills for raising Revenue shall originate in the House of Representatives; but the Senate may propose or concur with Amendments as on other Bills.

Every Bill which shall have passed the House of Representatives and the Senate, shall, before it become a Law, be presented to the President of the United States; If he approve he shall sign it, but if not he shall return it, with his Objections to that House in which it shall have originated, who shall enter the Objections at large on their Journal, and proceed to reconsider it. If after such Reconsideration two thirds of that House shall agree to pass the Bill, it shall be sent, together with the Objections, to the other House, by which it shall likewise be reconsidered, and if approved by two thirds of that House, it shall become a Law. But in all such Cases the Votes of both Houses shall be determined by yeas and nays, and the Names of the Persons voting for and against the Bill shall be entered on the Journal of each House respectively. If any Bill shall not be returned by the President within ten Days (Sundays

be a member of either House during his continuance in office. *But Congress may, by law, grant to the principal officer in each of the executive departments a seat upon the floor of either House, with the privilege of discussing any measures appertaining to his department.*

SECTION 7. 1. All bills for raising revenue shall originate in the House of Representatives; but the Senate may propose or concur with amendments, as on other bills.

2. Every bill which shall have passed *both Houses,* shall, before it becomes a law, be presented to the President of the *Confederate* States; if he approve, he shall sign it; but if not, he shall return it, with his objections, to that House in which it shall have originated, who shall enter the objections at large on their journal, and proceed to reconsider it. If, after such reconsideration, two-thirds of that House shall agree to pass the bill, it shall be sent, together with the objections, to the other House, by which it shall likewise be reconsidered, and if approved by two-thirds of that House, it shall become a law. But, in all such cases, the votes of both Houses shall be determined by yeas and nays, and the names of the persons voting for and against the bill shall be entered on the journal of each House respectively. If any bill shall not be returned by the President within ten days (Sundays excepted) after it shall have been presented to

excepted) after it shall have been presented to him, the Same shall be a law, in like Manner as if he had signed it, unless the Congress by their Adjournment prevent its Return, in which Case it shall not be a Law.

him, the same shall be a law, in like manner as if he had signed it, unless the Congress, by their adjournment, prevent its return; in which case it shall not be a law. *The President may approve any appropriation and disapprove any other appropriation in the same bill. In such case he shall, in signing the bill, designate the appropriations disapproved; and shall return a copy of such appropriations, with his objections, to the House in which the bill shall have originated; and the same proceeding shall then be had as in case of other bills disapproved by the President.*

Every Order, Resolution, or Vote to which the Concurrence of the Senate and House of Representatives may be necessary (except on a question of Adjournment) shall be presented to the President of the United States; and before the Same shall take Effect, shall be approved by him, or being disapproved by him, shall be repassed by two thirds of the Senate and House of Representatives, according to the Rules and Limitations prescribed in the Case of a Bill.

3. Every order, resolution or vote, to which the concurrence of *both Houses* may be necessary (except on a question of adjournment), shall be presented to the President of the *Confederate* States; and, before the same shall take effect, shall be approved by him; or, being disapproved by him, shall be repassed by two-thirds of *both Houses*, according to the rules and limitations prescribed in case of a bill.

Section. 8. The Congress shall have Power

To lay and collect Taxes, Duties, Imposts and Excises, to pay the Debts and Provide for the common Defence and general Welfare of the United States; but all Duties, Imposts and Excises shall be uniform throughout the United States;

Section 8. The Congress shall have power—

1. To lay and collect taxes, duties, imposts, and excises, *for revenue necessary* to pay the debts, provide for the common defence, *and carry on the Government of the Confederate* States; *but no bounties shall be granted from the Treasury; nor shall any duties or taxes on im-*

To borrow Money on the credit of the United States;

To regulate Commerce with foreign Nations, and among the several States, and with the Indian Tribes;

To establish an uniform Rule of Naturalization, and uniform Laws on the subject of Bankruptcies throughout the United States;

To coin Money, regulate the Value thereof, and of foreign Coin, and fix the Standard of Weights and Measures;

To provide for the Punishment of counterfeiting the Securities

portations from foreign nations be laid to promote or foster any branch of industry; and all duties, imposts, and excises shall be uniform throughout the Confederate States:

2. To borrow money on the credit of the *Confederate* States:

3. To regulate commerce with foreign nations, and among the several States, and with the Indian tribes; *but neither this, nor any other clause contained in the Constitution, shall ever be construed to delegate the power to Congress to appropriate money for any internal improvement intended to facilitate commerce; except for the purpose of furnishing lights, beacons, and buoys, and other aid to navigation upon the coasts, and the improvement of harbors and the removing of obstructions in river navigation, in all which cases, such duties shall be laid on the navigation facilitated thereby, as may be necessary to pay the costs and expenses thereof:*

4. To establish uniform *laws* of naturalization, and uniform laws on the subject of bankruptcies, throughout the *Confederate* States; *but no law of Congress shall discharge any debt contracted before the passage of the same:*

5. To coin money, regulate the value thereof and of foreign coin, and fix the standard of weights and measures:

6. To provide for the punishment of counterfeiting the securi-

and current Coin of the United States;

To establish Post Offices and post Roads;

To promote the Progress of Science and useful Arts, by securing for limited Time to Authors and Inventors the exclusive Right to their respective Writings and Discoveries;

To constitute Tribunals inferior to the supreme Court;

To define and punish Piracies and Felonies committed on the high Seas, and Offences against the Law of Nations;

To declare War, grant Letters of Marque and Reprisal, and make Rules concerning Captures on Land and Water;

To raise and support Armies, but no Appropriation of Money to that Use shall be for a longer Term than two Years;

To provide and maintain a Navy;

To make Rules for the Government and Regulation of the land and naval Forces;

To provide for calling forth the Militia to execute the Laws of the Union, suppress Insurrections and repel Invasions;

To provide for organizing, arming, and disciplining, the Militia, and for governing such Part of them as may be employed in the Service of the United States, reserving to the States respectively,

ties and current coin of the *Confederate* States:

7. To establish post-offices and post-*routes; but the expenses of the Post-office Department, after the first day of March, in the year of our Lord eighteen hundred and sixty-three, shall be paid out of its own revenues:*

8. To promote the progress of science and useful arts, by securing for limited times to authors and inventors the exclusive right to their respective writings and discoveries:

9. To constitute tribunals inferior to the Supreme Court:

10. To define and punish piracies and felonies committed on the high-seas, and offences against the law of nations:

11. To declare war, grant letters of marque and reprisal, and make rules concerning captures on land and on water:

12. To raise and support armies, but no appropriation of money to that use shall be for a longer term than two years:

13. To provide and maintain a navy:

14. To make rules for the government and regulation of the land and naval forces:

15. To provide for calling forth the militia to execute the laws of the *Confederate* States, suppress insurrections, and repel invasions:

16. To provide for organizing, arming, and disciplining the militia, and for governing such part of them as may be employed in the service of the *Confederate* States, reserving to the States,

the Appointment of the Officers, and the Authority of training the Militia according to the discipline prescribed by Congress;

To exercise exclusive Legislation in all Cases whatsoever, over such District (not exceeding ten Miles square) as may, by Cession of particular States, and the Acceptance of Congress, become the Seat of the Government of the United States, and to exercise like Authority over all Places purchased by the Consent of the Legislature of the State in which the Same shall be, for the Erection of Forts, Magazines, Arsenals, dock-Yards, and other needful Buildings;—And

To make all Laws which shall be necessary and proper for carrying into Execution the foregoing Powers, and all other Powers vested by this Constitution in the Government of the United States, or in any Department or Officer thereof.

SECTION. 9. The Migration or Importation of such Persons as any of the States now existing shall think proper to admit, shall not be prohibited by the Congress prior to the Year one thousand eight hundred and eight, but a Tax or duty may be imposed on such Importation, not exceeding ten dollars for each Person.

The Privilege of the Writ of Habeas Corpus shall not be sus-

respectively, the appointment of the officers, and the authority of training the militia according to the discipline prescribed by Congress:

17. To exercise exclusive legislation in all cases whatsoever, over such district (not exceeding ten miles square) as may, by cession of *one or more* States and the acceptance of Congress, become the seat of the Government of the *Confederate* States: and to exercise like authority over all places purchased by the consent of the Legislature of the State in which the same shall be, for the erection of forts, magazines, arsenals, dockyards, and other needful buildings: and

18. To make all laws which shall be necessary and proper for carrying into execution the foregoing powers, and all other powers vested by this Constitution in the Government of the *Confederate* States, or in any department or officer thereof.

SECTION 9. 1. The importation of *negroes of the African race, from any foreign country other than the slave-holding States or Territories of the United States of America, is hereby forbidden; and Congress is required to pass such laws as shall effectually prevent the same.*

2. *Congress shall also have power to prohibit the introduction of slaves from any State not a member of, or Territory not belonging to, this Confederacy.*

3. The privilege of the writ of *habeas corpus* shall not be sus-

pended, unless when in Cases of Rebellion or Invasion the public Safety may require it.

No Bill of Attainder or ex post facto Law shall be passed.

No Capitation, or other direct, Tax shall be laid, unless in Proportion to the Census or Enumeration herein before directed to be taken.

No Tax or Duty shall be laid on Articles exported from any State.

No Preference shall be given by any Regulation of Commerce or Revenue to the Ports of one State over those of another: nor shall Vessels bound to, or from, one State, be obliged to enter, clear, or pay Duties in another.

No Money shall be drawn from the Treasury, but in Consequence of Appropriations made by Law; and a regular Statement and Account of the Receipts and Expenditures of all public Money shall be published from time to time.

pended, unless when in case of rebellion or invasion the public safety may require it.

4. No bill of attainder, *ex post facto* law, *or law denying or impa[i]ring the right of property in negro slaves shall be passed.*

5. No capitation or other direct tax shall be laid, unless in proportion to the census or enumeration hereinbefore directed to be taken.

6. No tax or duty shall be laid on articles exported from any State *except by a vote of two-thirds of both Houses.*

7. No preference shall be given by any regulation of commerce or revenue to the ports of one State over those of another.

8. No money shall be drawn from the treasury, but in consequence of appropriations made by law; and a regular statement and account of the receipts and expenditures of all public money shall be published from time to time.

9. *Congress shall appropriate no money from the treasury except by a vote of two-thirds of both Houses, taken by yeas and nays, unless it be asked and estimated for by some one of the heads of departments, and submitted to Congress by the President; or for the purpose of paying its own expenses and contingencies; or for the payment of claims against the Confederate States, the justice of which shall have*

been judicially declared by a tribunal for the investigation of claims against the Government, which it is hereby made the duty of Congress to establish.

10. *All bills appropriating money shall specify in federal currency the exact amount of each appropriation, and the purposes for which it is made; and Congress shall grant no extra compensation to any public contractor, officer, agent or servant, after such contract shall have been made or such service rendered.*

No Title of Nobility shall be granted by the United States: And no Person holding any Office of Profit or Trust under them, shall, without the Consent of the Congress, accept of any present, Emolument, Office, or Title, of any kind whatever, from any King, Prince, or foreign State.

11. No title of nobility shall be granted by the *Confederate* States; and no person holding any office of profit or trust under them, shall, without the consent of the Congress, accept of any present, emolument, office or title of any kind whatever, from any king, prince, or foreign state.

12. Congress shall make no law respecting an establishment of religion, or prohibiting the free exercise thereof; or abridging the freedom of speech, or of the press; or the right of the people peaceably to assemble and petition the government for a redress of grievances.

13. A well-regulated militia being necessary to the security of a free state, the right of the people to keep and bear arms shall not be infringed.

14. No soldier shall, in time of peace, be quartered in any house without the consent of the owner; nor in time of war, but in a manner to be prescribed by law.

15. The right of the people to

be secure in their persons, houses, papers, and effects, against unreasonable searches and seizures, shall not be violated; and no warrants shall issue but upon probable cause, supported by oath or affirmation, and particularly describing the place to be searched, and the persons or things to be seized.

16. No person shall be held to answer for a capital or otherwise infamous crime, unless on a presentment or indictment of a grand jury, except in cases arising in the land or naval forces, or in the militia, when in actual service in time of war or public danger; nor shall any person be subject, for the same offence, to be twice put in jeopardy of life or limb; nor be compelled, in any criminal case, to be a witness against himself; nor be deprived of life, liberty, or property, without due process of law; nor shall private property be taken for public use without just compensation.

17. In all criminal prosecutions, the accused shall enjoy the right to a speedy and public trial, by an impartial jury of the State and district wherein the crime shall have been committed, which district shall have been previously ascertained by law, and to be informed of the nature and cause of the accusation; to be confronted with the witnesses against him; to have compulsory process for obtaining witnesses in his favor; and to have the assistance of counsel for his defence.

18. In suits at common law,

SECTION. 10. No State shall enter into any Treaty, Alliance, or Confederation; grant Letters of Marque and Reprisal; coin Money; emit Bills of Credit; make any Thing but gold and silver Coin a Tender in Payment of Debts; pass any Bill of Attainder, ex post facto Law, or Law impairing the Obligation of Contracts, or grant any Title of Nobility.

No State shall, without Consent of [the] Congress, lay any Imposts or Duties on Imports or Exports, except what may be absolutely necessary for executing its inspection Laws: and the net Produce of all Duties and Imposts, laid by any State on Imports or Exports, shall be for the Use of the Treasury of the United States; and all such Laws shall be subject to the Revision and Control of [the] Congress.

No State shall, without the Consent of Congress, lay any Duty of Tonnage, keep Troops, or Ships of

where the value in controversy shall exceed twenty dollars, the right of trial by jury shall be preserved; and no fact *so* tried by a jury shall be otherwise re-examined in any court of the *Confederacy,* than according to the rules of common law.

19. Excessive bail shall not be required, nor excessive fines imposed, nor cruel and unusual punishment inflicted.

20. *Every law, or resolution having the force of law, shall relate to but one subject, and that shall be expressed in the title.*

SECTION 10. 1. No State shall enter into any treaty, alliance, or confederation; grant letters of marque and reprisal; coin money; make anything but gold and silver coin a tender in payment of debts; pass any bill of attainder, or *ex post facto* law, or law impairing the obligation of contracts, or grant any title of nobility.

2. No State shall, without the consent of the Congress, lay any imposts or duties on imports or exports, except what may be absolutely necessary for executing its inspection laws; and the nett produce of all duties and imposts, laid by any State on imports or exports, shall be for the use of the Treasury of the *Confederate* States; and all such laws shall be subject to the revision and control of Congress.

3. No State shall, without the consent of Congress, lay any duty *on* tonnage, *except on sea-going*

War in time of Peace, enter into any Agreement or Compact with another State, or with a foreign Power, or engage in War, unless actually invaded, or in such imminent Danger as will not admit of delay.

vessels, for the improvement of its rivers and harbors navigated by the said vessels; but such duties shall not conflict with any treaties of the Confederate States with foreign nations; and any surplus revenue thus derived, shall, after making such improvement, be paid into the common treasury. Nor shall any State keep troops or ships-of-war in time of peace, enter into any agreement or compact with another State, or with a foreign power, or engage in war, unless actually invaded, or in such imminent danger as will not admit of delay. *But when any river divides or flows through two or more States, they may enter into compacts with each other to improve the navigation thereof.*

ARTICLE. II.

SECTION. 1. The executive Power shall be vested in a President of the United States of America. He shall hold his Office during the Term of four Years, and, together with the Vice President, chosen for the same Term, be elected, as follows

Each State shall appoint, in such Manner as the Legislature thereof may direct, a Number of Electors, equal to the whole Number of Senators and Representatives to which the State may be entitled in the Congress: but no Senator or Representative, or Person holding an Office of Trust or

ARTICLE II.

SECTION 1. 1. The executive power shall be vested in a President of the *Confederate* States of America. *He and the Vice President shall hold their offices for* the term of *six* years; *but the President shall not be re-eligible. The President and the Vice-President shall* be elected as follows:

2. Each State shall appoint, in such manner as the Legislature thereof may direct, a number of electors equal to the whole number of Senators and Representatives to which the State may be entitled in the Congress; but no Senator or Representative, or person holding an office of trust or

Profit under the United States, shall be appointed an Elector.

[3]The Electors shall meet in their respective States, and vote by Ballot for two Persons, of whom one at least shall not be an Inhabitant of the same State with themselves. And they shall make a List of all the Persons voted for, and of the Number of Votes for each; which List they shall sign and certify, and transmit sealed to the Seat of the Government of the United States, directed to the President of the Senate. The President of the Senate shall, in the Presence of the Senate and House of Representatives, open all the Certificates, and the Votes shall then be counted. The Person having the greatest Number of Votes shall be the President, if such Number be a Majority of the whole Number of Electors appointed; and if there be more than one who have such Majority and have an equal Number of Votes, then the House of Representatives shall immediately chuse by Ballot one of them for President; and if no Person have a Majority, then from the five highest on the List the said House shall in like Manner chuse the President. But in chusing the President, the Votes shall be taken by States, the Representation from each State having one Vote; a quorum for this Purpose shall consist of a Member or Members from two thirds of the States, and a Majority of all

profit under the *Confederate* States, shall be appointed an elector.

3. The electors shall meet in their respective States and vote by ballot for President and Vice President, one of whom, at least, shall not be an inhabitant of the same State with themselves; they shall name in their ballots the person voted for as President, and in distinct ballots the person voted for as Vice President, and they shall make distinct lists of all persons voted for as President, and of all persons voted for as Vice President, and of the number of votes for each, which lists they shall sign and certify, and transmit, sealed, to the seat of the government of the *Confederate* States, directed to the President of the Senate; the President of the Senate shall, in the presence of the Senate and House of Representatives, open all the certificates, and the votes shall then be counted, the person having the greatest number of votes for President shall be the President, if such number be a majority of the whole number of electors appointed; and if no person have such majority, then, from the persons having the highest numbers, not exceeding three, on the list of those voted for as President, the House of Representatives shall choose immediately, by ballot, the President. But in choosing the President, the votes shall be taken by States the representation from each State having one vote; a

3. Superseded by the twelfth amendment.

the States shall be necessary to a Choice. In every Case, after the Choice of the President, the Person having the greatest Number of Votes of the Electors shall be the Vice President. But if there should remain two or more who have equal Votes, the Senate shall chuse from them by Ballot the Vice President.

The Congress may determine the Time of chusing the Electors, and the Day on which they shall give their Votes; which Day shall be the same throughout the United States.

No Person except a natural born Citizen or a Citizen of the United States, at the time of the Adoption of this Constitution, shall be eligible to the Office of President;

quorum for this purpose shall consist of a member or members from two-thirds of the States, and a majority of all the States shall be necessary to a choice. And if the House of Representatives shall not choose a President, whenever the right of choice shall devolve upon them, before the fourth day of March next following, then the Vice-President shall act as President, as in the case of the death or other constitutional disability of the President.

4. The person having the greatest number of votes as Vice President, shall be the Vice President, if such number be a majority of the whole number of electors appointed; and if no person have a majority, then, from the two highest numbers on the list, the Senate shall choose the Vice President; a quorum for the purpose shall consist of two-thirds of the whole number of Senators, and a majority of the whole number shall be necessary to a choice.

5. But no person constitutionally ineligible to the office of President shall be eligible to that of Vice President of the *Confederate* States.

6. The Congress may determine the time of choosing the electors, and the day on which they shall give their votes; which day shall be the same through out the *Confederate* States.

7. No person except a natural born citizen of the *Confederate* States, or a citizen thereof at the time of the adoption of this Constitution, *or a citizen thereof born*

neither shall any person be eligible to that Office who shall not have attained to the Age of thirty five Years, and been fourteen Years a Resident within the United States.

In Case of the Removal of the President from Office, or of his Death, Resignation, or Inability to discharge the Powers and Duties of the said office, the Same shall devolve on the Vice President, and the Congress may by Law provide for the Case of Removal, Death, Resignation, or Inability, both of the President and Vice President, declaring what Officer shall then act as President, and such Officer shall act accordingly, until the Disability be removed, or a President shall be elected.

The President shall, at stated Times, receive for his Services, a Compensation, which shall neither be encreased nor diminished during the Period for which he shall have been elected, and he shall not receive within that Period any other Emolument from the United States, or any of them.

Before he enter on the Execution of his Office, he shall take the following Oath or Affirmation:—

"I do solemnly swear (or affirm) that I will faithfully execute the Office of President of the United States, and will to the best of my

in the United States prior to the 20th of December, 1860, shall be eligible to the office of President; neither shall any person be eligible to that office who shall not have attained the age of thirty-five years, and been fourteen years a resident within the *limits of the Confederate* States, *as they may exist at the time of his election.*

8. In case of the removal of the President from office, or of his death, resignation, or inability to discharge the powers and duties of the said office, the same shall devolve on the Vice President; and the Congress may, by law, provide for the case of removal, death, resignation, or inability, both of the President and Vice President, declaring what officer shall then act as President; and such officer shall act accordingly, until the disability be removed or a President shall be elected.

9. The President shall, at stated times, receive for his services a compensation, which shall neither be increased nor diminished during the period for which he shall have been elected; and he shall not receive within that period any other emolument from the *Confederate* States, or any of them.

10. Before he enters on the execution of his office, he shall take the following oath or affirmation:

"I do solemnly swear (or affirm) that I will faithfully execute the office of President of the *Confederate* States *of America,* and will, to the best of my ability, preserve,

Ability, preserve, protect and defend the Constitution of the United States."

SECTION. 2. The President shall be Commander in Chief of the Army and Navy of the United States, and of the Militia of the several States, when called into the actual Service of the United States; he may require the Opinion, in writing, of the principal Officer in each of the executive Departments, upon any Subject relating to the Duties of their respective Offices, and he shall have Power to grant Reprieves and Pardons for Offences against the United States, except in Cases of Impeachment.

He shall have Power, by and with the Advice and Consent of the Senate, to make Treaties, provided two thirds of the Senators present concur; and he shall nominate, and by and with the Advice and Consent of the Senate, shall appoint Ambassadors, other public Ministers and Consuls, Judges of the supreme Court, and all other Officers of the United States, whose Appointments are not herein otherwise provided for, and which shall be established by Law: but the Congress may by law vest the Appointment of such inferior Officers, as they think proper, in the President alone, in the Courts of Law, or in the Heads of Departments.

protect, and defend the Constitution *thereof.*"

SECTION 2. 1. The President shall be commander-in-chief of the Army and Navy of the *Confederate* States, and of the militia of the several States, when called into the actual service of the *Confederate* States; he may require the opinion, in writing, of the principal officer in each of the executive departments, upon any subject relating to the duties of their respective offices, and he shall have power to grant reprieves and pardons for offences against the *Confederate States,* except in cases of impeachment.

2. He shall have power, by and with the advice and consent of the Senate, to make treaties; provided two thirds of the Senators present concur; and he shall nominate, and by and with the advice and consent of the Senate, shall appoint ambassadors, other public ministers and consuls, judges of the Supreme Court and all other officers of the *Confederate* States, whose appointments are not herein otherwise provided for, and which shall be established by law; but the Congress may, by law, vest the appointment of such inferior officers, as they think proper, in the President alone, in the courts of law, or in the heads of departments.

3. *The principal officer in each of the executive departments, and all persons connected with the diplomatic service, may be removed from office at the pleasure*

of the President. All other civil officers of the executive departments may be removed at any time by the President, or other appointing power, when their services are unnecessary, or for dishonesty, incapacity, inefficiency, misconduct, or neglect of duty; and, when so removed, the removal shall be reported to the Senate, together with the reasons therefor.

The President shall have Power to fill up all Vacancies that may happen during the Recess of the Senate, by granting Commissions which shall expire at the End of their next Session.

4. The President shall have power to fill up all vacancies that may happen during the recess of the Senate, by granting commissions which shall expire at the end of their next session; *but no person rejected by the Senate shall be re-appointed to the same office during their ensuing recess.*

SECTION. 3. He shall from time to time give to the Congress Information of the State of the Union, and recommend to their consideration such Measures as he shall judge necessary and expedient; he may, on extraordinary Occasions, convene both Houses, or either of them, and in Case of Disagreement between them, with Respect to the time of Adjournment, he may adjourn them to such Time as he shall think proper; he shall receive Ambassadors and other public Ministers; he shall take Care that the Laws be faithfully executed, and shall Commission all the officers of the United States.

SECTION 3. 1. *The President* shall, from time to time, give to the Congress information of the state of the *Confederacy,* and recommend to their consideration such measures as he shall judge necessary and expedient: he may, on extraordinary occasions, convene both Houses, or either of them; and in case of disagreement between them, with respect to the time of adjournment, he may adjourn them to such time as he shall think proper; he shall receive ambassadors and other public ministers; he shall take care that the laws be faithfully executed, and shall commission all the officers of the *Confederate* States.

SECTION. 4. The President, Vice President and all civil Officers of the United States, shall be

SECTION 4. The President, Vice President, and all civil officers of the *Confederate* States, shall be removed from Office on Impeachment for, and conviction of, Treason, Bribery, or other high Crimes and Misdemeanors.

ARTICLE. III.

SECTION. 1. The judicial Power of the United States, shall be vested in one supreme Court, and in such inferior Courts as the Congress may from time to time ordain and establish. The Judges, both of the supreme and inferior Courts, shall hold their offices during good Behavior, and shall, at stated times, receive for their Services, a Compensation, which shall not be diminished during their Continuance in Office.

SECTION. 2. The judicial Power shall extend to all Cases, in Law and Equity, arising under this Constitution, the Laws of the United States, and Treaties made, or which shall be made, under their Authority;—to all Cases affecting Ambassadors, other public Ministers and Consuls;—to all Cases of admiralty and maritime Jurisdiction;—to Controversies to which the United States shall be a Party;—to Controversies between two or more States;—between a State and Citizens of another State;—between Citizens of different States;—between Citizens of the same State claiming Lands under Grants of different States, and between a State, or the Citizens thereof, and foreign States, Citizens or Subjects.

In all Cases affecting Ambassadors, other public Ministers and

removed from office on impeachment, for and conviction of, treason, bribery, or other high crimes and misdemeanors.

ARTICLE III.

SECTION 1. 1. The judicial power of the *Confederate* States shall be vested in one Supreme Court, and in such inferior Courts, as the Congress may, from time to time, ordain and establish. The judges, both of the Supreme and inferior Courts, shall hold their offices during good behavior, and shall, at stated times, receive for their services a compensation which shall not be diminished during their continuance in office.

SECTION 2. 1. The judicial power shall extend to all cases arising under this Constitution, the laws of the *Confederate* States, and treaties made, or which shall be made, under their authority; to all cases affecting ambassadors, other public ministers and consuls; to all cases of admiralty and maritime jurisdiction; to controversies to which the *Confederate* States shall be a party; to controversies between two or more States; between a State and citizens of another State, *where the State is plaintiff;* between citizens claiming lands under grants of different States; and between a State or the citizens thereof, and foreign states, citizens or subjects; *but no State shall be sued by a citizen or subject of any foreign state.*

2. In all cases affecting ambassadors, other public ministers and

Consuls, and those in which a State shall be Party, the supreme Court shall have original Jurisdiction. In all the other Cases before mentioned, the supreme Court shall have appellate Jurisdiction, both as to Law and Fact, with such Exceptions, and under such Regulations as the Congress shall make.

The trial of all Crimes, except in Cases of Impeachment, shall be by Jury; and such Trial shall be held in the State where the said Crimes shall have been committed; but when not committed within any State, the Trial shall be at such Place or Places as the Congress may by Law have directed.

SECTION. 3. Treason against the United States, shall consist only in levying War against them, or in adhering to their Enemies, giving them Aid and Comfort. No Person shall be convicted of Treason unless on the Testimony of two Witnesses to the same overt Act, or on Confession in open Court.

The Congress shall have Power to declare the Punishment of Treason, but no Attainder of Treason shall work Corruption of Blood, or Forfeiture except during the Life of the Person attainted.

ARTICLE. IV.

SECTION. 1. Full Faith and Credit shall be given in each State to the public Acts, Records, and judicial Proceedings of every other State. And the Congress may by general Laws prescribe

consuls, and those in which a State shall be a party, the Supreme Court shall have original jurisdiction. In all the other cases before mentioned, the Supreme Court shall have appellate jurisdiction both as to law and fact, with such exceptions and under such regulations as the Congress shall make.

3. The trial of all crimes, except in cases of impeachment, shall be by jury, and such trial shall be held in the State where the said crimes shall have been committed; but when not committed within any State, the trial shall be at such place or places as the Congress may by law have directed.

SECTION 3. 1. Treason against the *Confederate* States shall consist only in levying war against them, or in adhering to their enemies, giving them aid and comfort. No person shall be convicted of treason unless on the testimony of two witnesses to the same overt act, or on confession in open court.

2. The Congress shall have power to declare the punishment of treason; but no attainder of treason shall work corruption of blood, or forfeiture, except during the life of the person attainted.

ARTICLE IV.

SECTION 1. 1. Full faith and credit shall be given in each State to the public acts, records, and judicial proceedings of every other State. And the Congress may, by general laws, prescribe the

the Manner in which such Acts, Records and Proceedings shall be proved, and the Effect thereof.

manner in which such acts, records, and proceedings shall be proved, and the effect thereof.

SECTION. 2. The Citizens of each State shall be entitled to all Privileges and Immunities of Citizens in the several States.

SECTION 2. 1. The citizens of each State shall be entitled to all the privileges and immunities of citizens in the several States, *and shall have the right of transit and sojourn in any State of this Confederacy, with their slaves and other property; and the right of property in said slaves shall not be thereby impaired.*

A Person charged in any State with Treason, Felony, or other Crime, who shall flee from Justice, and be found in another State, shall on Demand of the executive Authority of the State from which he fled, be delivered up, to be removed to the State having Jurisdiction of the Crime.

2. A person charged in any State with treason, felony, or other crime *against the laws of such State,* who shall flee from justice, and be found in another State, shall, on demand of the Executive authority of the State from which he fled, be delivered up, to be removed to the State having jurisdiction of the crime.

No Person held to Service or Labour in one State, under the Laws thereof, escaping into another, shall, in Consequence of any Law or Regulation therein, be discharged from such Service or Labour, but shall be delivered up on Claim of the Party to whom such Service or Labour may be due.

3. *No slave or other* person held to service or labor *in any State or Territory of the Confederate States,* under the laws thereof, escaping *or lawfully carried* into another, shall, in consequence of any law or regulation therein, be discharged from such service or labor: but shall be delivered up on claim of the party *to whom such slave belongs, or* to whom such service or labor may be due.

SECTION. 3. New States may be admitted by the Congress into this Union; but no new State shall be formed or erected within the Jurisdiction of any other State; nor any State be formed by the Junction of two or more States, or Parts of States, without the Consent of the Legislatures of the

SECTION 3. 1. *Other States may be admitted into this Confederacy by a vote of two-thirds of the whole House of Representatives and two-thirds of the Senate, the Senate voting by States;* but no new State shall be formed or erected within the jurisdiction of any other State; nor any State

States concerned as well as of the Congress.

be formed by the junction of two or more States, or parts of States, without the consent of the legislatures of the States concerned, as well as of the Congress.

The Congress shall have power to dispose of and make all needful Rules and Regulations respecting the Territory or other Property belonging to the United States; and nothing in this Constitution shall be so construed as to Prejudice any Claims of the United States, or of any particular State.

2. The Congress shall have power to dispose of and make all needful rules and regulations *concerning* the *property of the Confederate* States, *including the lands thereof.*

3. *The Confederate States may acquire new territory; and Congress shall have power to legislate and provide governments for the inhabitants of all territory belonging to the Confederate States, lying without the limits of the several States; and may permit them, at such times, and in such manner as it may by law provide, to form States to be admitted into the Confederacy. In all such territory, the institution of negro slavery, as it now exists in the Confederate States, shall be recognized and protected by Congress and by the territorial government: and the inhabitants of the several Confederate States and Territories shall have the right to take to such Territory any slaves lawfully held by them in any of the States or Territories of the Confederate States.*

SECTION. 4. The United States shall guarantee to every State in this Union a Republican Form of Government, and shall protect each of them against Invasion; and on Application of the Legisla-

4. The *Confederate* States shall guarantee to every State *that now is, or hereafter may become, a member of this Confederacy,* a republican form of government; and shall protect each of them against

ture, or of the Executive (when the Legislature cannot be convened) against domestic Violence.

invasion; and on application of the legislature, (or of the executive when the legislature *is not in session,*) against domestic violence.

ARTICLE. V.

The Congress, whenever two thirds of both Houses shall deem it necessary, shall propose Amendments to this Constitution, or, on the Application of the Legislatures of two thirds of the several States, shall call a Convention for proposing Amendments, which, in either Case, shall be valid to all Intents and Purposes, as Part of this Constitution, when ratified by the Legislatures of three fourths of the several States, or by Conventions in three fourths thereof, as the one or the other Mode of Ratification may be proposed by the Congress; Provided that no Amendment which may be made prior to the Year One thousand eight hundred and eight shall in any Manner affect the first and fourth Clauses in the Ninth Section of the first Article; and that no State, without its Consent, shall be deprived of its equal Suffrage in the Senate.

ARTICLE V.

SECTION 1. 1. *Upon the demand of any three States, legally assembled in their several conventions, the Congress shall summon a Convention of all the States, to take into consideration such amendments to the Constitution as the said States shall concur in suggesting at the time when the said demand is made; and should any of the proposed amendments to the Constitution be agreed on by the said Convention—voting by States—and the same be ratified by the legislatures of two-thirds of the several States, or by conventions in two-thirds thereof*—as the one or the other mode of ratification may be proposed by the *general Convention—they shall thenceforward form a part of this Constitution. But* no State shall, without its consent, be deprived of its equal *representation* in the Senate.

ARTICLE. VI.

All Debts contracted and Engagements entered into, before the Adoption of this Constitution, shall be as valid against the United States under this Constitution, as under the Confederation.

ARTICLE VI.

1. *The Government established by this Constitution is the sucessor of the Provisional Government of the Confederate States of America, and all the laws passed by the latter shall continue in force until the same shall be repealed or modified; and all the officers appointed by the same shall remain in office until their*

successors are appointed and qualified, or the offices abolished.

2. All debts contracted and engagements entered into before the adoption of this Constitution shall be as valid against the *Confederate* States under this Constitution as under the *Provisional Government.*

This Constitution, and the Laws of the United States which shall be made in Pursuance thereof; and all Treaties made, or which shall be made, under the Authority of the United States, shall be the supreme Law of the Land; and the Judges in every State shall be bound thereby, any thing in the Constitution or laws of any State to the Contrary notwithstanding.

3. This Constitution, and the laws of the *Confederate* States made in pursuance thereof, and all treaties made, or which shall be made under the authority of the *Confederate* States, shall be the supreme law of the land; and the judges in every State shall be bound thereby, anything in the Constitution or laws of any State to the contrary notwithstanding.

The Senators and Representatives before mentioned, and the Members of the several State Legislatures, and all executives and judicial Officers, both of the United States and of the several States, shall be bound by Oath or Affirmation, to support this Constitution; but no religious Test shall ever be required as a Qualification to any Office or public Trust under the United States.

4. The Senators and Representatives before mentioned, and the members of the several State legislatures, and all executive and judicial officers, both of the *Confederate* States and of the several States, shall be bound by oath or affirmation to support this Constitution; but no religious test shall ever be required as a qualification to any office or public trust under the *Confederate* States.

5. The enumeration, in the Constitution, of certain rights, shall not be construed to deny or disparage others retained by the people *of the several States.*

6. The powers not delegated to the *Confederate* States by the Constitution, nor prohibited by it to the States, are reserved to the States, respectively, or to the people *thereof.*

ARTICLE. VII.

The Ratification of the Conventions of nine States, shall be sufficient for the Establishment of this Constitution between the States so ratifying the Same.

ARTICLE VII.

1. The ratification of the conventions of *five* States shall be sufficient for the establishment of this Constitution between the States so ratifying the same.

2. *When five States shall have ratified this Constitution, in the manner before specified, the Congress under the Provisional Constitution shall prescribe the time for holding the election of President and Vice President; and for the meeting of the Electoral College, and for counting the votes, and inaugurating the President. They shall, also, prescribe the time for holding the first election of members of Congress under this Constitution, and the time for assembling the same. Until the assembling of such Congress, the Congress under the Provisional Constitution shall continue to exercise the legislative powers granted them; not extending beyond the time limited by the Constitution of the Provisional Government.*

Done in convention by the Unanimous Consent of the States present the Seventeenth Day of September in the Year of our Lord one thousand seven hundred and eighty seven and of the Independence of the United States of America the Twelfth In Witness whereof We have hereunto subscribed our Names,

Go. Washington—
Presdt.
and deputy from
Virginia

Adopted unanimously by the Congress of the Confederate States of South Carolina, Georgia, Florida, Alabama, Mississippi, Louisiana and Texas, sitting in Convention at the capitol, in the city of Montgomery, Alabama, on the Eleventh day of March, in the year Eighteen Hundred and Sixty-One.

Howell Cobb,
President of the
Congress.

ARTICLES IN ADDITION TO, AND AMENDMENT OF, THE CONSTITUTION OF THE UNITED STATES OF AMERICA. PROPOSED BY CONGRESS, AND RATIFIED BY THE LEGISLATURES OF THE SEVERAL STATES, PURSUANT TO THE FIFTH ARTICLE OF THE ORIGINAL CONSTITUTION.

ARTICLE I.

Congress shall make no law respecting an establishment of religion, or prohibiting the free exercise thereof; or abridging the freedom of speech, or of the press; or the right of the people peacably to assemble, and to petition the Government for a redress of grievances.

ARTICLE II.

A well regulated Militia, being necessary to the security of a free State, the right of the people to keep and bear Arms, shall not be infringed.

ARTICLE III.

No Soldier shall, in time of peace be quartered in any house, without the consent of the Owner, nor in time of war, but in a manner to be prescribed by law.

ARTICLE IV.

The right of the people to be secure in their persons, houses, papers, and effects, against unreasonable searches and seizures, shall not be violated, and no Warrants shall issue, but upon probable cause, supported by Oath or affirmation, and particularly describing the place to be searched, and the persons or things to be seized.

ARTICLE V.

No person shall be held to answer for a capital, or otherwise infamous crime, unless on a presentment or indictment of a Grand Jury, except in cases arising in the land or naval forces, or in the Militia, when in actual service in time of War or public danger; nor shall any person be subject for the same offence to be twice put in jeopardy of life or limb; nor shall be compelled in any Criminal Case to be a witness against himself, nor be deprived of life, liberty, or property, without due process of law; nor shall private property be taken for public use, without just compensation.

ARTICLE VI.

In all criminal prosecutions, the accused shall enjoy the right to a speedy and public trial, by an impartial jury of the State and district wherein the crime shall have been committed, which district shall have been previously ascertained by law, and to be informed of the nature and cause of the accusation; to be confronted with the witnesses against him; to have Compulsory process for obtaining Witnesses in his favour, and to have the Assistance of Counsel for his defence.

Article VII.

In Suits at common law, where the value in controversy shall exceed twenty dollars, the right of trial by jury shall be preserved, and no fact tried by a jury shall be otherwise reëxamined in any Court of the United States, than according to the rules of the common law.

Article VIII.

Excessive bail shall not be required, nor excessive fines imposed, nor cruel and unusual punishments inflicted.

Article XII.

The Electors shall meet in their respective states, and vote by ballot for President and Vice President, one of whom, at least, shall not be an inhabitant of the same state with themselves; they shall name in their ballots the person voted for as President, and in distinct ballots the person voted for as Vice President, and they shall make distinct lists of all persons voted for as President, and of all persons voted for as Vice President, and of the number of votes for each, which lists they shall sign and certify, and transmit sealed to the seat of the government of the United States, directed to the President of the Senate;—The President of the Senate shall, in presence of the Senate and House of Representatives, open all the certificates and the votes shall then be counted;—The person having the greatest number of votes for President, shall be the President, if such number be a majority of the whole number of Electors appointed; and if no person have such majority, then from the persons having the highest numbers not exceeding three on the list of those voted for as President, the House of Representatives shall choose immediately, by ballot, the President. But in choosing the President, the votes shall be taken by states, the representation from each state having one vote; a quorum for this purpose shall consist of a member or members from two-thirds of the states, and a majority of all the states shall be necessary to a choice. And if the House of Representatives shall not choose a President whenever the right of choice shall devolve upon them, before the fourth day of March next following, then the Vice President shall act as President, as in the case of the death or other constitutional disability of the President.—The person having the greatest number of votes as Vice President, shall be the Vice President, if such number be a majority of the whole number of Electors appointed, and if no person have a majority, then from the two highest numbers on the list, the Senate shall choose the Vice President; a quorum for the purpose shall consist of two-thirds of the whole number of Senators, and a majority of the whole number shall be necessary to a choice. But no person constitutionally ineligible to the office of President shall be eligible to that of Vice President of the United States.

Bibliography

PRIMARY SOURCES

MANUSCRIPT COLLECTIONS

James Patton Anderson Papers. Southern Historical Collection, University of North Carolina.

David Crenshaw Barrow Papers. Southern Historical Collection, University of North Carolina.

John MacPherson Berrien Papers. Southern Historical Collection, University of North Carolina.

David Campbell Papers. Manuscript Department, Duke University.

Josiah A. Patterson Campbell Papers. Southern Historical Collection, University of North Carolina.

Claiborne Papers. Southern Historical Collection, University of North Carolina.

Thomas Reade Rootes Cobb Letters. Southern Historical Collection, University of North Carolina.

Thomas Reade Rootes Cobb Papers. Special Collections Division, University of Georgia.

Thomas Reade Rootes Cobb Original Draft of the Permanent Constitution of the Confederate States of America. Special Collections Division, University of Georgia.

Jabez Lamar Monroe Curry Papers. Southern Historical Collection, University of North Carolina.

Jabez Lamar Monroe Curry Papers. The Alabama State Department of Archives and History, Montgomery, Alabama.

Telamon Cuyler Collection. Special Collections Division, University of Georgia.

James Thomas Harrison Papers. Southern Historical Collection, University of North Carolina.

Hemphill Papers. Southern Historical Collection, University of North Carolina.

Hilary Abner Herbert Papers. Southern Historical Collection, University of North Carolina.

Charles Colcock Jones, collector, "Autograph Letters and Portraits of the Signers of the Constitution of the Confederate States." Augusta, Georgia, 1884. A Scrapbook. Manuscript Department, Duke University.

Francis Terry Leak Diary. Southern Historical Collection, University of North Carolina.

Josiah Kirby Lilly Collection. Rare Book Library, Indiana University.

Robert McKee Papers. The Alabama State Department of Archives and History, Montgomery, Alabama.

Colin John McRae Papers. The Alabama State Department of Archives and History, Montgomery, Alabama.

Christopher Gustavus Memminger Papers. Southern Historical Collection, University of North Carolina.

William Porcher Miles Papers. Southern Historical Collection, University of North Carolina.

William Henry Mitchell Papers. The Alabama State Department of Archives and History, Montgomery, Alabama.

James Lawrence Orr Papers. Southern Historical Collection, University of North Carolina.

John Perkins Papers. Southern Historical Collection, University of North Carolina.

Robert Barnwell Rhett Papers. Southern Historical Collection, University of North Carolina.

Robert Barnwell Rhett Papers. South Caroliniana Library, University of South Carolina.

Robert Hardy Smith Papers. Southern Historical Collection, University of North Carolina.

Alexander Hamilton Stephens Papers (microfilm). Southern Historical Collection, University of North Carolina.

Williams-Chesnut-Manning Papers. Southern Historical Collection, University of North Carolina.

Benjamin Cudworth Yancey Papers. Southern Historical Collection, University of North Carolina.

PUBLIC OR OFFICIAL DOCUMENTS

STATE

Chandler, Allen D., ed., *The Confederate Records of the State of Georgia,* 6 volumes. Atlanta: Charles P. Byrd, State Printer, 1909.

Documents of the 1st Session of the 5th Legislature of the State of Louisiana. Baton Rouge: J. M. Taylor, 1860.

Journal of the Acts and Proceedings of a General Convention of the State of Virginia Assembled at Richmond on Wednesday, the Thirteenth Day of February, Eighteen Hundred and Sixty-one. Richmond: Wyatt M. Elliott, Printer, 1861.

Journal of the Convention of the People of North Carolina Held on the 20th Day of May, A.D. 1861. Raleigh: J. W. Syme, Printer to the Convention, 1862.

Journal of the Convention of the People of South Carolina, Held in 1860, 1861 and 1862. Columbia: R. W. Gibbes, 1862.

Journal of the Convention of the People of South Carolina, Held in 1860-'61. Charleston: Evans and Cogswell, Printers to the Convention, 1861.

Journal of the Convention of the State of Arkansas, Which Were Begun and Held in the Capitol, in the City of Little Rock. Little Rock: Johnson and Yerkes, State Printers, 1861.

Journal of the House of Representatives for the Called Session of November, 1860. Columbia: R. W. Gibbes, 1860.

Journal of the House of Representatives of the State of Georgia at the Annual Session of the General Assembly, Commenced at Milledgeville, Nov. 7th, 1860. Milledgeville: Boughton, Nisbet and Barnes, 1860.

Journal of the Proceedings of the Convention of the People of Florida, Begun and Held at the Capital in the City of Tallahassee, on Thursday, January 3, A.D. 1861. Tallahassee: Dyke and Carlisle, 1861.

Official Journal of the Proceedings of the Convention of the State of Louisiana. New Orleans: J. O. Nixon, 1861.

A Journal of the Proceedings of the House of Representatives of the General Assembly of the State of Florida, at its 10th Session, begun and held at the Capital, in the city of Tallahassee, on Monday, November 26, 1860. Tallahassee: Dyke and Carlisle, 1860.

Journal of the Public and Secret Proceedings of the Convention of the People of Georgia, Held in Milledgeville and Savannah in 1861. Together with the Ordinances Adopted. Milledgeville: Boughton, Nisbet and Barnes, 1861.

Journal of the Secession Convention of Texas 1861. Edited from the Original by Ernest William Winkler. Austin: Austin Printing Company, 1912.

*Journal of the Senate, Extra Session of the Rebel Legislature, called together by a Proclamation of C. F. Jackson, begun and held at the Town of Neosho, Newton County, Missouri, on the Twenty-First

Day of October, Eighteen Hundred and Sixty-One. Jefferson City: Emory S. Foster, 1865.

Journal of the Senate of South Carolina: Being the Sessions of 1860. Columbia: R. W. Gibbes, 1860.

Journal of the State Convention, Held in Milledgeville, in December 1850. Milledgeville: R. M. Orme, State Printer, 1850.

Journal of the State Convention and Ordinances and Resolutions Adopted on January, 1851, With an Appendix. Jackson: E. Barksdale, 1861.

Journal of the State Convention and Ordinances and Resolutions Adopted in March, 1851. Jackson: E. Barksdale, 1861.

Ordinances Adopted by the People of the State of Alabama, In Convention, At Montgomery, Commencing on the Seventh Day of January, 1851. Montgomery: Shorter and Reid, State Printers, 1861.

Proceedings of the Convention of the People of Florida, at Called Sessions, Begun and Held at the Capital in Tallahassee, on Tuesday, Feb. 26th and Thursday, April 18, 1861. Tallahassee: Dyke and Carlisle, 1861.

Proceedings of the Convention Establishing Provisional Government of Kentucky. Augusta: Steam Press of Chronicle and Sentinel, 1863.

Proceedings of the Mississippi State Convention, Held January 7th to 26th A.D. 1861. Jackson, Mississippi: Power and Cadwallader, Book and Job Printers, 1861.

Public Acts of the State of Tennessee Passed at the Extra Session of the Thirty-Third General Assembly, April 1861. Nashville: J. O. Griffith and Company, Public Printers, 1861.

Smith, William Russell, *The History and Debates of the Convention of the People of Alabama, Begun and Held in the City of Montgomery, on the Seventh Day of January, 1861.* Montgomery: White, Pfister, and Company, 1861.

CONFEDERATE STATES OF AMERICA

Executive and Congressional Directory of the Confederate States 1861-1865. Compiled from official records. Record and Pension Office, 1899.

Journal of the Congress of the Confederate States of America, 1861-1865, 7 volumes. Washington: Government Printing Office, 1904-1905.

Matthews, James Muscoe, ed., *The Statutes at Large of the Provisional Government of the Confederate States of America, From the Institution of the Government, February 8, 1861, to its Termination, February 18, 1862, Inclusive.* Richmond: R. M. Smith, 1864.

Permanent Constitution of the Confederate States of America, Vellum Copy. Special Collections Division, University of Georgia.

Provisional Constitution of the Confederate States of America, Vellum Copy. Confederate Museum, Richmond, Virginia.

Proceedings of the Congress of the Announcement of the Death of Col. Francis S. Bartow, of the Army of the Confederate States, and Late a Delegate in the Congress, from the State of Georgia. Published By Order of the Congress, By J. J. Hooper, Secretary. Richmond: Enquirer Book and Job Press, 1861.

Richardson, James Daniel, ed., *A Compilation of Messages and Papers of the Confederacy, Including the Diplomatic Correspondence, 1861-1865,* 2 volumes. Nashville: United States Publishing Company, 1906.

UNITED STATES OF AMERICA

Biographical Directory of the American Congress 1774-1949. Washington: Government Printing Office, 1950.

Congressional Globe, 35 Congress. Washington: John C. Rives, 1859.

Eighth Census of the United States, 1860, Manuscript Returns of Schedule No. 1, Free Inhabitants, and Schedule No. 2, Slave Inhabitants, for the states of South Carolina, Georgia, Florida, Alabama, Louisiana, Mississippi, and Texas. National Archives, Washington, D. C.

Farrand, Max, ed., *The Records of the Federal Convention,* 3 volumes. New Haven: Yale University Press, 1911.

Official Records of the Union and Confederate Navies in the War of the Rebellion, 30 volumes. Washington: Government Printing Office, 1894-1927.

Presidential Inability. Washington: Government Printing Office, 1956.

Richardson, James Daniel, ed., *Compilation of the Messages and Papers of the Presidents, 1789-1897,* 10 volumes. Washington: Government Printing Office, 1907.

Thorpe, Francis Newton, ed., *The Federal and State Constitutions, Colonial Charters, and Other Organic Laws of the States, Territories, and Colonies Now or Heretofore Forming the United States,* 7 volumes. Washington: Government Printing Office, 1909.

United States, Bureau of Census, *Eighth Census of the United States: 1860.* Population, I. Washington: Government Printing Office, 1864.

War of the Rebellion: A Compilation of the Official Records of the the Union and Confederate Armies, 70 volumes. Washington: Government Printing Office, 1880-1901.

NEWSPAPERS AND PERIODICALS

The Alabama *Sentinel,* 1860-1861.
The Atlanta *Constitution,* 1879 and 1937.
The Atlanta *Journal,* 1951.
Charleston *Mercury,* 1861.
Daily Confederation, 1861, Montgomery.
De Bow's Review, 43 volumes. New Orleans, 1846-1880.
Frank Leslie's Illustrated Newspaper, 1861.
Harper's Weekly, 1861.
The Illustrated London News, 1861.
Mobile *Daily Advertiser and Register,* 1867.
Mobile *Evening News,* 1860.
The Mobile *Weekly Register,* 1861.
Montgomery *Daily Advertiser,* 1861.
Montgomery *Daily Mail,* 1860-1861.
Montgomery *Daily Post,* 1860-1861.
Montgomery *Weekly Advertiser,* 1861.
Montgomery *Weekly Mail,* 1860-1861.
Montgomery *Weekly Post,* 1860-1861.
Nashville *Union and American,* 1861.
The New Orleans *Bee,* 1861.
The New York *Tribune,* 1861.
Norfolk-Virginian-*Pilot,* 1951.
Ocala *Star-Banner,* 1958.
Richmond *Enquirer,* 1861-1862.
The Tallahassee *Weekly Floridian,* 1872.
Marion, *The Weekly Commonwealth,* 1860.
Selma, *The Weekly Issue,* 1861.

CONTEMPORARY PAMPHLETS AND BOOKS

The American Annual Cyclopedia and Register of Important Events, 15 volumes. New York: D. Appleton and Company, 1869-1875.

Baldwin, Joseph Glover, *The Flush Times of Alabama and Mississippi.* New York: D. Appleton and Company, 1853.

Bryan, Edward B., *A Scrapbook of Pamphlets, 1850-1852,* 10 volumes. University of North Carolina Library.

Champomier, P. A., *Statement of the Sugar Crop in Louisiana, 1844-1861.* New Orleans: Cook, Young and Company, 1845-1862.

Cobb, Howell, *A Scriptual Examination of the Institution of Slavery in the United States; with its Objects and Purposes.* Georgia: Printed for the Author, 1856.

Cobb, Thomas Reade Rootes, *An Historical Sketch of Slavery, From the Earliest Periods.* Philadelphia: T. and J. W. Johnson and Company, 1858.

Cobb, Thomas Reade Rootes, *An Inquiry into the Law of Negro Slavery in the United States of America*. Philadelphia: T. and J. W. Johnson and Company, 1858.

The Confederate States Almanac and Repository of Useful Knowledge for 1862. Compiled and Published by H. C. Clarke, Vicksburg, Mississippi. Southern Historical Collection, University of North Carolina.

Curry, Jabez Lamar Monroe, *Civil History of the Government of the Confederate States of America with Some Personal Reminiscences.* Richmond: B. F. Johnson Publishing Company, 1901.

Curry, Jabez Lamar Monroe, *The Southern States of the American Union Considered in their Relations to the Constitution of the United States and to the Resulting Union.* Richmond: B. F. Johnson Publishing Company, 1895.

Davis, Jefferson, *The Rise and Fall of the Confederate Government,* 2 volumes. New York: Thomas Yoseloff, 1958.

DeRenne, Wymberly Jones, *A Short History of the Constitutions of the Confederate States of America, 1861-1899.* Savannah: Morning News Press, 1909. Special Collections Division, University of Georgia.

Jones, Charles Colcock, *An Address Delivered before the Confederate Survivors' Association, in Augusta, Georgia, on the Occasion of its Eleventh Annual Reunion on Memorial Day, April 26, 1889.* Augusta: Chronicle Publishing Company, 1889. The Treasure Room, Duke University.

Plan of a Provisional Government For the Southern Confederacy. Charleston: Evans and Cogswell, 1861. Special Collections Division, University of Georgia.

Smith, Robert Hardy, *An Address to the Citizens of Alabama on the Constitution and Laws of the Confederate States of America.* Mobile: Mobile Daily Register Print, 1861. The Treasure Room, Duke University.

Snowden, Yates, *Wartime Publications (1861-1865) From the Press of Walker, Evans and Cogswell Company.* Charleston: Walker, Evans and Cogswell Company, 1922.

Stephens, Alexander Hamilton, *A Constitutional View of the Late War Between the States,* 2 volumes. Philadelphia: National Publishing Company, 1868 and 1870.

Tariff of the Confederate States of America; or, Rates of Duties, Payable on Goods, Wares and Merchandise Imported into the Confederate States, on and after August 31, 1861. Also, United States Tariff of 1861, in Parallel Columns. Augusta: D. H. Van Buren and Company, 1861. The Treasure Room, Duke University.

Wood, Robert Crooke, *Confederate Hand-Book; A Compilation of Im-*

portant Data and Other Interesting and Valuable Matter Relating to the War Between the States, 1861-1865. Washington, 1900.

MEMOIRS, DIARIES, AND AUTOBIOGRAPHIES

Bell, Hiram Parks, *Men and Things.* Atlanta: Foote and Davies Company, 1907.

Chesnut, Mary Boykin, *A Diary from Dixie.* Edited by Ben Ames Williams. Boston: Houghton Mifflin Company, 1949.

Clay-Clopton, Mrs. Virginia, *A Belle of the Fifties, Memoirs of Mrs. Clay, of Alabama, Covering Social and Political Life in Washington and the South, 1853-66. Put into Narrative Form by Ada Sterling.* New York: Doubleday, Page and Company, 1905.

Davis, Reuben, *Recollections of Mississippi and Mississippians.* Boston: Houghton, Mifflin and Company, 1889.

Davis, Varina Howell, *Jefferson Davis, A Memoir by His Wife,* 2 volumes. New York: Belford Company, 1890.

De Leon, Thomas Cooper, *Belles Beaux and Brains of the 60's.* New York: G. W. Dillingham Company, 1907.

De Leon, Thomas Cooper, *Four Years in Rebel Capitals.* Mobile: The Gossip Printing Company, 1892.

Garrett, William, *Reminiscences of Public Men in Alabama, for Thirty Years.* Atlanta: Plantation Publishing Company, 1872.

Gilmer, Francis Meriwether, "Memoir Concerning the Organization of the Confederate Government," *Jefferson Davis Constitutionalist: His Letters, Papers and Speeches,* 10 volumes. Edited by Dunbar Rowland. Jackson: Mississippi Department of Archives and History, 1923. VIII, 462-463.

Gordon, John Brown, *Reminiscences of the Civil War.* New York: Charles Scribner's Sons, 1904.

Jones, John Beauchamp, *A Rebel War Clerk's Diary at the Confederate States Capital,* 2 volumes. Edited by Howard Swiggett. New York: Old Hickory Bookshop, 1935.

Perry, Benjamin Franklin, *Reminiscences of Public Men.* Philadelphia: John D. Avil and Company, 1883.

Reagan, John Henninger, *Memoirs, with Special Reference to Secession and the Civil War.* Edited by Walter Flavius McCaleb. New York: The Neale Publishing Company, 1906.

Russell, William Howard, *My Diary North and South.* Boston: T. O. H. P. Burnham, 1863.

Taylor, Richard, *Destruction and Reconstruction: Personal Experiences of the Late War.* New York: D. Appleton and Company, 1879.

Wright, Louise Wigfall, *A Southern Girl in '61, The War-Time Memoirs of a Confederate Senator's Daughter.* New York: Doubleday, Page and Company, 1905.

MISCELLANEOUS SOURCES

"From the Autobiography of Herschel V. Johnson, 1856-1867," *The American Historical Review*, XXX (October, 1924), 311-36.

Calhoun, John Caldwell, *The Works of John C. Calhoun,* 6 volumes. Edited by Richard Kenner Cralle. New York: D. Appleton and Company, 1853-1855.

Alexander Birch Clitherall Scratcher Copy of Permanent Constitution of the Confederate States of America, 1861. This printed document with Clitherall's annotations constitutes the final draft of the Permanent Constitution. The Alabama State Department of Archives and History, Montgomery, Alabama.

Alexander Clitherall Birch Speech. 1940. 1 item. "The Constitution of the Confederate States of America," a speech delivered before the Alabama State Bar Association; copy prepared and presented to the University of Georgia Library by Herbert U. Febelman of Miami, Florida, January 25, 1940. Special Collections Division, University of Georgia.

Commager, Henry Steele, *Documents of American History,* Sixth Edition. New York: Appleton-Century-Crofts, Inc., 1958.

Dumond, Dwight Lowell, ed., *Southern Editorials on Secession.* New York: The Century Company, 1931.

Hoole, William Stanley, "The Diary of Dr. Basil Manly, 1858-1867," *The Alabama Review,* IV (April, 1951), 127-49.

Hough, Franklin Benjamin, *American Constitutions: Comprising the Constitution of Each State in the Union and of the United States,* 2 volumes. Albany: Weed, Parsons and Company, 1872.

Hull, Augustus Longstreet, ed., "Correspondence of Thomas Reade Rootes Cobb, 1860-1862," *Publications of the Southern History Association,* XI (1907), 147-85, 233-60, 312-28.

Hull, Augustus Longstreet, ed., "Thomas R. R. Cobb: Extracts from Letters to his Wife, February 3, 1861-December 10, 1862," *Southern Historical Society Papers,* XXVIII (1900), 280-301.

Johnson, Robert Underwood and Clarence Clough Buel, eds., *Battles and Leaders of the Civil War,* 4 volumes. New York: The Century Company, 1884-1887.

"Letter of Stephen R. Mallory, 1861," *The American Historical Review,* XII (October, 1906), 103-8.

McPherson, Edward, *The Political History of the United States of America During the Great Rebellion,* Second Edition. Washington: Philip and Solomons, 1865.

Moore, Frank, compiler, *The Rebellion Record: A Diary of American Events, with Documents, Narratives, Illustrative Incidents, Poetry, etc.,* 11 volumes. New York: G. P. Putnam, 1861-1863.

Perkins, Howard Cecil, ed., *Northern Editorials on Secession.* New York: D. Appleton-Century Company, 1942.

Phillips, Ulrich Bonnell, ed., *The Correspondence of Robert Toombs, Alexander H. Stephens and Howell Cobb,* American Historical Association, *Annual Report, 1911,* II. Washington: Government Printing Office, 1913.

Rowland, Dunbar, ed., *Jefferson Davis, Constitutionalist: His Letters, Papers and Speeches,* 10 volumes. Jackson: Mississippi Department of Archives and History, 1923.

Tilley, Nannie May, ed., "Letters of Judge Alexander M. Clayton Relative to Confederate Courts in Mississippi," *The Journal of Southern History,* VI (August, 1940), 393-401.

SECONDARY WORKS

GENERAL WORKS

Beard, Charles Austin and Mary Ritter Beard, *The Rise of American Civilization,* 2 volumes. New York: The Macmillan Company, 1928.

Bryce, James, *The American Commonwealth,* New Edition, 2 volumes. New York: The Macmillan Company, 1915 and 1916.

Bryce, James, *Studies in History and Jurisprudence,* 2 volumes. New York: Oxford University Press, 1901.

Coulter, Ellis Merton, *The Confederate States of America 1861-1865.* Baton Rouge: Louisiana State University Press, 1950.

Craven, Avery, *The Coming of the Civil War.* New York: Charles Scribner's Sons, 1950.

Dowdey, Clifford, *The Land they Fought For: The Story of the South as the Confederacy 1832-1865.* Garden City, New York: Doubleday and Company, Inc., 1955.

Eaton, Clement, *A History of the Southern Confederacy.* New York: The Macmillan Company, 1954.

Farrand, Max, *The Framing of the Constitution of the United States.* New Haven: Yale University Press, 1946.

Gray, Lewis Cecil and Esther Katherine Thompson, *History of Agriculture in the Southern United States to 1860,* 2 volumes. Washington: The Carnegie Institution of Washington, 1933.

Hamilton, William Baskerville, "Holly Springs, Mississippi, to the Year 1878." Unpublished master's thesis, University of Mississippi.

Hesseltine, William Best, *Confederate Leaders in the New South.* Baton Rouge: Louisiana State University Press, 1950.

Kelly, Alfred H. and Winfred Audif Harbison, *The American Constitution, Its Origins and Development,* Revised Edition. New York: W. W. Norton and Company, Inc., 1955.

Nichols, Roy Franklin, *The Disruption of American Democracy.* New York: Macmillan Company, 1948.

Phillips, Ulrich Bonnell, *Life and Labor in the Old South.* Boston: Little, Brown, and Company, 1929.

Randall, John Garfield, *The Civil War and Reconstruction.* Boston: D. C. Heath and Company, 1937.

Rhodes, James Ford, *History of the United States from the Compromise of 1850,* 7 volumes. New York: The Macmillan Company, 1904-1906.

Rowland, Dunbar, ed., *Encyclopedia of Mississippi History,* 2 volumes. Madison, Wisconsin: Selwyn A. Brant, 1907.

Schwab, John Christopher, *The Confederate States of America 1861-1865.* New York: Charles Scribner's Sons, 1901.

MONOGRAPHS AND SPECIAL STUDIES

Bagehot, Walter, *The English Constitution, and other Political Essays.* New York: D. Appleton and Company, 1877.

Beale, J. D. and Phelan, Assisted by M. P. Blue, *City Directory and and History of Montgomery, Alabama, with a Summary of Events in that History, Calendarically Arranged Besides other valuable and Useful Information.* Montgomery, Alabama: T. C. Bingham and Company, 1878.

Bragg, Jefferson Davis, *Louisiana in the Confederacy.* Baton Rouge: Louisiana State University Press, 1941.

Bryan, Thomas Conn, *Confederate Georgia.* Athens: The University of Georgia Press, 1953.

Bummer, Sidney D., "The Judicial Interpretation of the Confederate Constitution," *Studies in Southern History and Politics.* New York: Columbia University Press, 1941. Pp. 107-33.

Buttersworth, John Knox, *Confederate Mississippi.* Baton Rouge: Louisiana State University Press, 1943.

Carpenter, Jesse Thomas, *The South as a Conscious Minority.* New York: The New York University Press, 1930.

Cash, William Thomas, *History of the Democratic Party in Florida.* Tallahassee: Florida Democratic Historical Foundation, 1936.

Cauthen, Charles Edward, *South Carolina Goes to War 1860-1865.* Chapel Hill: The University of North Carolina Press, 1950.

Crandall, Marjorie Lyle, *Confederate Imprints,* 2 volumes. The Boston Athenaeum, 1955.

Craven, Avery Odelle, *The Growth of Southern Nationalism, 1848-1861.* Baton Rouge: Louisiana State University Press, 1945.

Crenshaw, Ollinger, *The Slave States in the Presidential Election of 1860.* Baltimore: Johns Hopkins Press, 1945.

Davis, William Watson, *The Civil War and Reconstruction in Florida.* New York: Columbia University, 1913.

Denman, Clarence Phillips, *The Secession Movement in Alabama.* Montgomery: Alabama State Department of Archives and History, 1933.

Diggs, Ellen-Fairbanks Dingledine, "The Role of the Interstate Commissioners in the Secession Conventions, 1860-1861." Unpublished master's thesis, University of North Carolina.

Doherty, Herbert Joseph, Jr., "The Florida Whigs." Unpublished master's thesis, University of Florida.

Dorman, Lewy, *Party Politics in Alabama from 1850 through 1860.* Wetumpka: Alabama State Department of Archives and History, 1935.

Dumond, Dwight Lowell, *The Secession Movement, 1860-1861.* New York: The Macmillan Company, 1931.

Fleming, Walter Lynwood, *Civil War and Reconstruction in Alabama.* New York: The Columbia University Press, 1905.

Green, Fletcher Melvin, *Constitutional Development in the South Atlantic States, 1776-1860.* Chapel Hill: The University of North Carolina Press, 1930.

Handy, Joseph Breckinridge, *A Genealogical Compilation of the Wilson Family.* New York: Schoharie, 1897.

Hendricks, Burton Jesse, *Statesmen of the Lost Cause.* New York: The Literary Guild of America, Inc., 1939.

Hodgson, Joseph, *The Cradle of the Confederacy.* Mobile: Register Publishing Office, 1876.

Hollis, Daniel Walker, *University of South Carolina,* 2 volumes. Columbia: University of South Carolina Press, 1951 and 1956.

Irons, George Vernon, "The Secession Movement in Georgia 1850-61." Unpublished doctoral dissertation, Duke University, 1936.

Jenkins, William Sumner, *Pro Slavery Thought in the Old South.* Chapel Hill: University of North Carolina Press, 1935.

Johnson, Zachary Taylor, *The Political Policies of Howell Cobb.* Nashville: George Peabody College for Teachers, 1929.

La Bree, Ben, ed., *The Confederate Soldier in the Civil War, 1861-1865.* Louisville: The Courier-Journal Job Printing Company, 1895.

Long, Melvin Durwood, Jr., "Alabama in the Making of the Confederacy." Unpublished doctoral dissertation, University of Florida, 1959.

McDonald, Forrest, *We the People, The Economic Origins of the Constitution.* Chicago: University of Chicago Press, 1958.

McMillan, Malcolm Cook, *Constitutional Development in Alabama,*

1798-1901: A Study in Politics, the Negro, and Sectionalism. Chapel Hill: The University of North Carolina Press, 1955.

Moore, Albert Burton, *History of Alabama.* Tuscaloosa: University Book Store, 1935.

Nevins, Allan, *The Statesmanship of the Civil War.* New York: The MacMillan Company, 1953.

Owsley, Frank Lawrence, *State Rights in the Confederacy.* Chicago: The University of Chicago Press, 1925.

Patrick, Rembert Wallace, *Jefferson Davis and His Cabinet.* Baton Rouge: Louisiana State University Press, 1944.

Phillips, Ulrich Bonnell, *American Negro Slavery.* New York: D. Appleton and Company, 1918.

Phillips, Ulrich Bonnell, *The Course of the South to Secession.* New York: D. Appleton-Century Company, Inc., 1939.

Potter, David Morris, *Lincoln and His Party in the Secession Crisis.* New Haven: Yale University Press, 1942.

Rainwater, Percy Lee, *Mississippi, Storm Center of Secession, 1856-1861.* Baton Rouge: Otto Claitor, 1938.

Ramsdell, Charles William, *Civil War and Reconstruction in Texas.* New York: Longmans, Green, and Company, 1910.

Robinson, William Morrison, Jr., *Justice in Grey.* Cambridge: Harvard University Press, 1941.

Russel, Robert Royal, *Economic Aspects of Southern Sectionalism, 1840-1861.* Urbana, Illinois: University of Illinois, 1924.

Saye, Albert Berry, *A Constitutional History of Georgia 1732-1945.* Athens: The University of Georgia Press, 1948.

Schultz, Harold Seessel, "Movement to Revive the Foreign Slave Trade 1853-1861." Unpublished master's thesis, Duke University, 1940.

Schultz, Harold Seessel, *Nationalism and Sectionalism in South Carolina 1852-1860.* Durham: Duke University Press, 1950.

Silva, Ruth Caridad, *Presidential Succession.* Ann Arbor: University of Michigan Press, 1951.

Sitterson, Joseph Carlyle, *The Secession Movement in North Carolina.* Chapel Hill: The University of North Carolina Press, 1939.

Stanwood, Edward, *American Tariff Controversies in the Nineteenth Century,* 2 volumes. Boston: Houghton, Mifflin and Company, 1904.

Sydnor, Charles Sackett, *The Development of Southern Sectionalism, 1819-1848.* Baton Rouge: Louisiana State University Press, 1948.

Taussig, Frank William, *The Tariff History of the United States.* New York: G. P. Putnam's Sons, 1928.

Van Deusen, John George, *Economic Bases of Disunion in South Carolina.* New York: Columbia University Press, 1928.

Venable, Austin Louis, *The Role of William L. Yancey in the Secession Movement.* Nashville: The Joint University Libraries, 1945.

Ware, Ethel Kime, *A Constitutional History of Georgia.* New York: Columbia University Press, 1947.

Williams, Edwin Lacy, Jr., "Florida in the Union, 1845-1861." Unpublished doctoral dissertation, University of North Carolina, 1951.

Wilson, Woodrow, *Congressional Government, A Study in American Politics,* Fifteenth Edition. Boston: Houghton, Mifflin and Company, 1900.

Wilson, Woodrow, *Division and Reunion, 1829-1889,* New Edition. New York: Longmans, Green and Company, 1926.

Wooster, Ralph Ancil, "The Secession Conventions of the Lower South: A Study of their Membership." Unpublished doctoral dissertation, University of Texas, 1954.

Yearns, Wilfred Buck, Jr., *The Confederate Congress.* Athens: The University of Georgia Press, 1960.

BIOGRAPHIES

Abele, Rudolph Von, *Alexander H. Stephens, A Biography.* New York: Alfred A. Knopf, 1946.

Alderman, Edwin Anderson and Armistad Churchill Gordon, *J. L. M. Curry.* New York: Macmillan Company, 1911.

Avery, Isaac Wheeler, *In Memory of Alexander Hamilton Stephens.* Atlanta: V. P. Sission, 1883.

Biographical and Historical Memoirs of Louisiana, 2 volumes. Chicago: The Goodspeed Publishing Company, 1891.

Biographical and Historical Memoirs of Mississippi, 2 volumes. Chicago: The Goodspeed Publishing Company, 1891.

Boykin, Samuel, *A Memorial Volume of the Hon. Howell Cobb of Georgia.* Philadelphia: J. B. Lippincott and Company, 1870.

Bradford, Gamaliel, *Confederate Portraits.* New York: Houghton, Mifflin Company, 1914.

Brooks, Ulysses Robert, *South Carolina Bench and Bar.* Columbia: The State Company, 1908.

Brown, John Howard, *The Cyclopedia of American Biographies,* 7 volumes. Boston: The Cyclopedia Publishing Company, 1897-1903.

Brown, John Howard, ed., *Lamb's Biographical Dictionary of the United States,* 7 volumes. Boston: Federal Book Company of Boston, 1900-1903.

Capers, Gerald Mortimer, *Stephen A. Douglas: Defender of the Union.* Boston: Little Brown and Company, 1959.

Capers, Henry Dickson, *The Life and Times of C. G. Memminger.* Richmond: Everett Waddey Company, 1893.

Cleveland, Henry, *Alexander H. Stephens, In Public and Private. With Letters and Speeches, Before, During, and Since the War.* Philadelphia: National Publishing Company, 1866.

Craven, Avery Odelle, *Edmund Ruffin Southerner, A Study in Secession.* New York: D. Appleton and Company, 1932.

Du Bose, John Witherspoon, *The Life and Times of William Lowndes Yancey,* 2 volumes. New York: Peter Smith, 1942.

Flippin, Percy Scott, *Herschel V. Johnson of Georgia: State Rights Unionist.* Richmond: The Dietz Printing Company, 1931.

Hill, Benjamin Harvey, Jr., *Senator Benjamin H. Hill of Georgia: His Life, Speeches and Writings.* Atlanta: H. C. Hudgins and Company, 1891.

Hoole, William Stanley, *Alias Simon Suggs, The Life and Times of Johnson Jones Hooper.* University, Alabama: University of Alabama Press, 1952.

Johnson, Allen and Dumas Malone, eds., *Dictionary of American Biography,* 21 volumes. New York: Charles Scribner's Sons, 1928-1937.

Johnston, Richard Malcolm and William Hand Browne, *Life of Alexander H. Stephens.* Philadelphia: J. B. Lippincott and Company, 1878.

Lynch, James Daniel, *The Bench and Bar of Mississippi.* New York: E. J. Hale and Son, 1881.

Lynch, James Daniel, *The Bench and Bar of Texas.* St. Louis: Nixon-Jones Printing Company, 1885.

Montgomery, Horace, *Howell Cobb's Confederate Career.* Tuscaloosa: Confederate Publishing Company, Inc., 1959.

The National Cyclopedia of American Biography, 13 volumes. New York: James T. White and Company, 1892 and 1906.

Nicholay, John George and John Hay, eds., *Abraham Lincoln: A History,* 10 volumes. New York: The Century Company, 1890.

Northen, William J., ed., *Men of Mark in Georgia,* 6 volumes. Atlanta: A. B. Caldwell, 1907-1912.

Norton, Frank Henry, *The Life of Alexander H. Stephens.* New York: John B. Alden, 1883.

Owen, Thomas McAdory, *History of Alabama and Dictionary of Alabama Biography,* 4 volumes. Chicago: The S. J. Clarke Publishing Company, 1921.

Pearce, Haywood Jefferson, *Benjamin H. Hill, Secession and Reconstruction.* Chicago: The University of Chicago Press, 1928.

Phillips, Ulrich Bonnell, *The Life of Robert Toombs.* New York: The Macmillan Company, 1913.

Pollard, Edward Alfred, *Life of Jefferson Davis with a Secret History of the Confederacy, gathered "Behind the Scenes in Richmond."* Philadelphia: National Publishing Company, 1869.

Rice, Jessie Pearl, *J. L. M. Curry, Southerner, Statesman and Educator.* New York: King's Crown Press, 1949.

Richardson, Eudora Ramsay, *Little Aleck, A Life of Alexander H. Stephens, the Fighting Vice-President of the Confederacy.* Indianapolis: The Bobbs-Merrill Company, 1932.

Rowland, Dunbar, *Courts, Judges, and Lawyers of Mississippi, 1798-1935.* Jackson: State Department of Archives and History, 1935.

Rowland, Eron Opha, *Varina Howell, Wife of Jefferson Davis,* 2 volumes. New York: The Macmillan Company, 1927-1931.

Stovall, Pleasant Alexander, *Robert Toombs, Statesman, Speaker, Soldier, Sage.* New York: Cassell Publishing Company, 1892.

Strode, Hudson, *Jefferson Davis: American Patriot.* New York: Harcourt Brace and Company, 1955.

Strode, Hudson, *Jefferson Davis: Confederate President.* New York: Harcourt Brace and Company, 1959.

White, Laura Amanda, *Robert Barnwell Rhett: Father of Secession.* New York: The Century Company, 1931.

PERIODICAL ARTICLES

Boucher, Chauncey Samuel, "Sectionalism, Representation, and the Electoral Question in Ante-Bellum South Carolina," *Washington University Studies,* IV (October, 1916), 3-62.

Boucher, Chauncey Samuel, "South Carolina and the South on the Eve of Secession, 1852 to 1860," *Washington University Studies,* XXIV (April, 1919), 79-144.

Brooks, Robert Preston, "Howell Cobb and the Crisis of 1850," *The Mississippi Valley Historical Review,* IV (December, 1917), 279-98.

Brooks, Robert Preston, "Howell Cobb Papers," *The Georgia Historical Quarterly,* V (June, 1921), 29-53.

Brown, George William, "Trends Toward the Formation of a Southern Confederacy," *The Journal of Negro History,* XVIII (July, 1933), 256-82.

Bryan, Thomas Conn, "The Secession of Georgia," *The Georgia Historical Quarterly,* XXXI (June, 1947), 89-112.

Calhoun, Robert Dabney, "A History of Concordia Parish," *Louisiana Historical Quarterly,* XV (July, 1932), 428-48.

Calhoun, Robert Dabney, "The John Perkins Family of Northeast Louisiana," *The Louisiana Historical Quarterly,* XIX (January, 1936), 70-88.

Cauthen, Charles Edward, "South Carolina's Decision to Lead the Secession Movement," *North Carolina Historical Review,* XVIII (October, 1941), 360-72.

Cobb, Andrew J., "The Constitution of the Confederate States; Its Influences on the Union it Sought to Dissolve," *The Georgia Historical Quarterly,* V (June, 1921), 7-16.

Cole, Arthur Charles, "Lincoln's Election an Immediate Menace to Slavery in the States?" *The American Historical Review,* XXXVI (July, 1931), 740-67.

Collins, William B., "Herschel V. Johnson in the Georgia Secession Convention," *The Georgia Historical Quarterly,* XI (December, 1927), 330-34.

Craven, Avery Odelle, "Coming of the War Between the States: An Interpretation," *Journal of Southern History,* II (August, 1936), 303-22.

Crenshaw, Ollinger, "Christopher G. Memminger's Mission to Virginia, 1860," *The Journal of Southern History,* VIII (August, 1942), 334-49.

Curry, Jabez Lamar Monroe, "Reminiscences of Talledega," *The Alabama Historical Quarterly,* VIII (Winter Issue, 1946), 348-68.

Curtis, M. E., "Alabama's Representatives in the Confederate Congress," *Confederate Veteran,* XXXV (April, 1927), 146-47.

Darden, David L., "Alabama Secession Convention," *Alabama Historical Quarterly,* III (Fall and Winter, 1941), 287-356.

Darden, David L., "Delegates to the Alabama Secession Convention," *Alabama Historical Quarterly,* III (Fall and Winter, 1941), 368-426.

Darden, David L., "Events Preceding Secession," *Alabama Historical Quarterly,* III (Fall and Winter, 1941), 277-86.

Darden, David L., "Withdrawal of the Alabama Delegation from the Congress of the United States," *Alabama Historical Quarterly,* III (Fall and Winter, 1941), 427-46.

Dodd, Dorothy, ed., "Edmund Ruffin's Account of the Florida Secession Convention, 1861," *The Florida Historical Quarterly,* XII (October, 1933), 67-76.

Dodd, Dorothy, "The Secession Movement in Florida, 1850-1861, Part I," *The Florida Historical Quarterly,* XII (July, 1933), 3-24.

Dodd, Dorothy, "The Secession Movement in Florida, 1850-1861, Part II," *The Florida Historical Quarterly,* XII (October, 1933), 45-66.

Fitts, Albert N., "The Confederate Convention: The Constitutional Debate," *The Alabama Review,* II (July, 1949), 189-210.

Fitts, Albert N., "The Confederate Convention: The Provisional Constitution," *The Alabama Review,* II (April, 1949), 83-101.

Gerson, Armand J., "The Inception of the Montgomery Convention," *American Historical Association, Annual Report, 1910.* Washington: Government Printing Office, 1912.

Gunderson, Robert Gray, "The Washington Peace Conference of 1861:

Selection of Delegates," *The Journal of Southern History,* XXIV (April, 1958), 347-59.

Hamilton, Joseph Gregoire deRoulhac, "Lincoln's Election an Immediate Menace to Slavery in the States?" *The American Historical Review,* XXXVIII (July, 1932), 700-11.

Hamilton, Joseph Gregoire deRoulhac, "The State Courts and the Confederate Constitution," *The Journal of Southern History,* IV (November, 1938), 425-49.

Henry, C. S., "Kenner's Mission to Europe," *William and Mary Quarterly,* XXV (1917), 9-12.

Hull, Augustus Longstreet, ed., "The Making of the Confederate Constitution," *Publications of the Southern History Association,* IX (1905), 272-92.

Inzer, John W., "Alabama's Secession Convention," *Confederate Veteran,* XXXI (January, 1923), 7-9.

Irvine, Dallas Dee, "The Fate of the Confederate Archives," *The American Historical Review,* XLIV (July, 1939), 823-41.

Johnson, Bradley Tyler, John V. Wright, Jehu A. Orr, and L. Quinton Washington, "Why the Confederate States of America Had No Supreme Court," *Southern History Association,* IV (March, 1900), 81-101.

Kendall, Lane Carter, "The Interregnum in Louisiana in 1861," *The Louisiana Historical Quarterly,* XVII (July, 1934), 524-37.

King, Alma Dexta, "The Political Career of William Simpson Oldham," *The Southwestern Historical Quarterly,* XXXIII (October, 1929), 112-34.

"Louisiana in Confederate Congresses," *Confederate Veteran,* XXXV (June, 1927), 220-21.

Martin, Lillie, "Georgians in the Confederate Congress," *Confederate Veteran,* XXXVI (October, 1928), 369-70.

McCabe, W. Gordon, "The Original Confederate Constitution," *Southern Historical Society Papers,* XLI (September, 1916), 34-36.

McLure, Mary Lilla, "The Elections of 1860 in Louisiana," *The Louisiana Historical Quarterly,* IX (October, 1926), 601-703.

Nixon, Herman Clarence and John T. Nixon, "The Confederate Constitution Today," *The Georgia Review,* IX (Winter 1955), 369-77.

Odom, Van D., "The Political Career of Thomas Overton Moore, Secession Governor of Louisiana," *The Louisiana Historical Quarterly,* XXVI (January-October, 1943), 975-1054.

Orr, Jehu Amaziah, "Life of Hon. James T. Harrison," *Publications of the Mississippi Historical Society,* VIII (1904), 187-200.

Owsley, Frank Lawrence, "The Fundamental Cause of the Civil War: Egocentric Sectionalism," *Journal of Southern History,* VII (February, 1941), 3-18.

Prescott, Frank Williams, "A Footnote on Georgia's Constitutional History: The Item Veto of the Governors," *The Georgia Historical Quarterly,* XLII (March, 1958), 1-25.

Prescott, Frank Williams, "The Executive Veto in American States," *The Western Political Quarterly,* III (March, 1950), 98-113.

Prescott, Frank Williams, "The Executive Veto in Southern States," *The Journal of Politics,* X (November, 1948), 659-76.

Rabun, James Zachary, "Alexander H. Stephens and Jefferson Davis," *The American Historical Review,* LVIII (January, 1953), 290-321.

Rainwater, Percy Lee, "An Analysis of the Secession Controversy in Mississippi," *The Mississippi Valley Historical Review,* XXIV (June, 1937), 35-42.

Ramsdell, Charles William, "The Natural Limits of Slavery Expansion," *Mississippi Valley Historical Review,* XVI (September, 1929), 151-71.

Reed, John Calvin, "Reminiscences of Ben Hill," *The South Atlantic Quarterly,* V (April, 1906), 134-50.

Robinson, William Morrison, Jr., "A New Deal in Constitutions," *The Journal of Southern History,* IV (November, 1938), 449-61.

Robinson, William Morrison, Jr., "Legal System of the Confederate States," *The Journal of Southern History,* II (November, 1936), 453-68.

Sandbo, Anna Irene, "First Session of the Secession Convention in Texas," *The Southwestern Historical Quarterly,* XVIII (October, 1914), 162-95.

Sellers, Charles Grier, Jr., "Who Were the Southern Whigs?" *American Historical Review,* LIX (January, 1954), 341-46.

Smith, Clarence McKittrick, Jr., "William Porcher Miles, Progressive Mayor of Charleston, 1855-1857," *The Proceedings of the South Carolina Historical Association,* XII (1942), 30-40.

Stephenson, Nathaniel Wright, "Southern Nationalism in South Carolina in 1851," *The American Historical Review,* XXXVI (October, 1930), 314-35.

Sumner, John Osborne, "Materials for the History of the Government of the Southern Confederacy," *American Historical Association,* Papers, IV (1890), 5-19.

Thompson, William Young, "The Toombs Legend," *The Georgia Historical Quarterly,* XLI (December, 1957), 337-48.

Venable, Austin Louis, "William L. Yancey and the League of United Southerners," *The Proceedings of the South Carolina Historical Association* (1946), 3-13.

Wells, Robert H., "The Item Veto and State Budget Reform," *The American Political Science Review,* XVIII (November, 1924), 782-91.

White, Laura Amanda, "The Fate of Calhoun's Sovereign Convention in South Carolina," *The American Historical Review*, XXXIV (July, 1929), 757-71.

Woods, Thomas H., "A Sketch of the Mississippi Secession Convention of 1861,—Its Membership and Work," *Publications of the Mississippi Historical Society*, IV (1902), 92-104.

Woodson, A. A. (Mrs.), "South Carolina's Representatives in the Confederate Congress," *Confederate Veteran*, XXXV (January, 1927), 16-19.

Wooster, Ralph Ancil, "An Analysis of the Membership of Secession Conventions in the Lower South," *The Journal of Southern History*, XXIV (August, 1958), 360-68.

Wooster, Ralph Ancil, "The Florida Secession Convention," *Florida Historical Quarterly*, XXXVI (April, 1958), 373-85.

Wooster, Ralph Ancil, "The Georgia Secession Convention," *Georgia Historical Quarterly*, XL (March, 1956), 21-56.

Index